CookSmart

Books by Pam Anderson

How to Cook Without a Book

The Perfect Recipe

CookSmart

Houghton Mifflin Company
Boston   New York

CookSmart
Perfect Recipes *for* Every Day

Pam Anderson

Food columnist of *USA WEEKEND magazine*
and author of the best-selling *PERFECT RECIPE*

Library of Congress Cataloging-in-Publication Data

Anderson, Pam, date.
CookSmart : perfect recipes for every day / Pam Anderson.
p.   cm.
Includes index.
ISBN 0-618-09151-3
1. Cookery, American. I. Title.

TX715 .A566653 2002
641.5973—dc21   2001051881

The *CookSmart* and *USA WEEKEND* trademarks have been
licensed by *USA WEEKEND* for use for certain purposes by
Houghton Mifflin Company. All trademarks used in the text
are the property of their respective owners.

Book design by Anne Chalmers
Photographs by Melanie Acevedo
Food styling by Melissa DeMayo
Illustrations by Laura Hartman Maestro

Printed in the United States of America

QWT 10 9 8 7 6 5 4 3 2

To my daughters,
MAGGY AND SHARON,
who made me learn to cook smart

And to the memory of
KATE HANNAN

If I hadn't grown up eating authentic food, I wouldn't have had the culinary insight to produce a book like this, so thanks, Mom and Dad, for making eating well a top priority.

Of course, I didn't bake all those pecan and pumpkin pies, roast all those hams and legs of lamb, and make all those chocolate cakes and crab cakes by myself. Friend and colleague Maryellen Driscoll generously gave her mind, soul, and body to this project. Her keen insight and good taste are evident on every page.

Thanks also to:

Rux Martin, who edited this book with clear-eyed vision, ensuring that *CookSmart* also read smart.

Agent Sarah Jane Freymann, for her wisdom and savvy in dealing with today's complex and changing publishing world.

Lori Galvin-Frost, Deborah DeLosa, and Maire Gorman at Houghton Mifflin, for friendship and support that just keeps on giving.

All those at *USA WEEKEND* magazine — especially Jack Curry, Brenda Turner, and Connie Kurz — for giving me a monthly voice and for allowing me to use the name of my *CookSmart* column as the title for this book.

Cook's Illustrated magazine, for publishing the following chapters in a slightly different form: oven-fried chicken, iced tea, chicken Parmesan, ham and split pea soup, chicken and dumplings, beef tenderloin.

Gabrielle Hamilton, for her inspired work on split pea soup and oven-fried chicken.

Melissa Hamilton, for her excellent insight on beef tenderloin, chicken and dumplings, and chicken Parmesan.

Dan Macey, for his energetic research and assistance on iced tea.

Robin Kline, for her generous help on the ham, pork tenderloin, and split pea soup chapters.

Jane and Jim Faraco, for developing the best onion rings, so I didn't have to.

Jeffrey Steingarten, for doing my french-fry homework for me in *The Man Who Ate Everything* (Knopf, 1997).

Friend and neighbor Jane McNeill, for allowing me to use her oven on the days when mine refused to be pushed any further.

The Trinity Church community in Solebury, Pennsylvania, for its constant love and support and for blessing my absence as I finished *CookSmart*.

Those who help me eat and drink well every day: Brian McCabe at Coté and Co., Dick Phillips and George Garrison at Phillips Fine Wines, and Greg Heller and Scott Espenshade at Heller's Seafood.

And to my husband, David, for his steadfast support as a spouse and fellow writer.

Pot roasts were a regular item on my mother's menu. Sometimes she'd simmer the roasts on top of the stove. Other times she'd pull out her crock pot. Regardless of how she cooked them, her roasts were always rich, beefy, and so meltingly tender that she barely needed a knife to slice them. Following my mother's example, I cooked pot roast regularly during my early married years, but over time I made the dish less frequently. At first I thought that it had become a victim of my busy schedule, but I gradually realized that good pot roast had become a mere food memory. Had I forgotten the proper cooking temperature, a recipe step, or an ingredient? Whatever the cause, the meat was tough and dry.

Many of my beloved dishes were like my pot roast — better in the imagination than they were in real life. Often, they had quirks that frustrated me when I made them or prevented me from enjoying them completely. But like most people, I had little time for less-than-perfect results. When I cooked, I wanted to make my favorites right, and I wanted them to be perfectly convenient, too.

That's where *CookSmart* begins. In this book, I perfect many of the everyday dishes I love, like oven-fried chicken, fajitas, and Caesar salad, as well as dishes for special occasions, such as crab cakes and chocolate cake.

For me, no-nonsense perfection often means reducing the time and effort that go into a dish. I knew I could make gutsy, memorable ribs by cooking them for hours over a slow charcoal-and-wood-chunk fire, but it took so long that I rarely attempted them. My recipe for cinnamon buns was exceptional, but they needed the better part of twenty-four hours. No wonder I usually opted to buy mediocre ones at the bakery! My french fries required a gallon of oil and two separate fryings, so I left that messy dish to restaurants.

Sometimes no-nonsense perfection means cutting the fat and calories. Did the frosting on my chocolate cake really need three sticks of butter? Did the cream of mushroom soup have to be so rich that guests called it quits after the first course? Perfection also has to ensure safety. With favorites like Caesar salad and Key lime pie, I wanted great taste without raw or undercooked eggs.

Most important, perfection means making a dish the best it can be. A superior shrimp cocktail demands shrimp that are shapely, moist, and firm rather than tight, chewy, and dry. A gazpacho shouldn't taste like cardboard winter tomatoes: it needs a big, sunny, summer-ripe flavor. Pasta salad not only must stand up during parties and potlucks but taste as impressive as it looks. Perfect waffles should stay crisp long after they're pulled from the iron. Pie isn't perfect unless it's juicy but firm enough for you to get a clean cut.

Before setting out, I analyzed fifty, seventy-five, and sometimes even more recipes to see what made the dish tick. From there, I moved to the kitchen, testing each technique and ingredient and eliminating any unnecessary steps.

In the short essays that precede each recipe, I show you my work, so that you, too, can understand the dish. By seeing what was successful and what wasn't, you'll know why the recipe is designed the way it is and how to avoid pitfalls. You'll even learn principles that you can apply to other dishes.

I've developed these recipes so they work perfectly in real cooking and entertaining. What good is the ultimate onion ring if it requires forty-five minutes of constant attention during the first quarter of your Super Bowl party? For me, the all-time best onion rings are those I can prepare a day ahead and fry thirty minutes before guests ever show up.

Though I occasionally mail-order unusual ingredients, I don't like to rely on recipes that require this sort of advance planning. For that reason, *CookSmart* recipes call for common supermarket ingredients. My recipes also don't demand special gizmos and gadgets; they've been developed using ordinary kitchen equipment.

My family can now enjoy pot roast whenever we're in the mood for a warm, homey supper that, with all due respect, is as good as my mother's. That's the spirit of *CookSmart*: sensible perfection. Enjoy the recipes that follow, and try some of my techniques to improve your favorite dishes. Cooking is usually satisfying. Cooking smart is downright fun.

Super
Bowls

One late summer when I was making gazpacho, my mother volunteered to help. Since this cold summer soup of Spanish descent calls for chopping lots of tomatoes, peppers, cucumbers, and onions, I accepted her offer. Afterward, Mother let me know that she didn't mind the work but didn't much care for the job. As someone who had lived through the Depression, she thought that seeding tomatoes was wasteful. She held up a big container of the seeds, pulp, and juice and asked if there wasn't something we could do with this incredibly flavorful substance.

I remember telling her I didn't have time to salvage tomato pulp and poured it down the disposal.

Nearly every time I seed a tomato, I think about that moment, and after preparing forty-eight pounds of tomatoes for my gazpacho tests, I've come to realize that Mother was right. As you'll see, you shouldn't toss perfectly good tomato juice.

Although there are many styles of authentic gazpacho — green, white, and even some with meat — I decided to focus on the kind I make most often and that we in America know best.

CHUNKY OR SMOOTH? ROOM TEMPERATURE OR COLD?

The gazpachos I'd made in the past were usually chock-full of chopped vegetables — tomatoes, cucumbers, peppers, and onions — but my research led me to a version as simple as pureed tomatoes drizzled with olive oil and served with diced fresh vegetables passed separately at the table. Between the two extremes, there was every possible vegetable combination.

There were also dramatic differences in technique. Some recipes demanded hand-diced vegetables. More lenient ones allowed the vegetables to be chopped in a food processor or blender. Some recipes pureed the vegetables, then strained them, while others called for some of the vegetables to be chopped and the other portion pureed.

Many recipes included soaked bread that was either left in bits or included in the puree. Was this simply a way to use up the daily baguette or did a good gazpacho demand it?

Since I had thought that gazpacho was a relative newcomer to the United States (one of my sources said it had been introduced to this country at the 1964 World's Fair), I was surprised to find a recipe in *The Virginia House-wife*, first published in 1824. For author Mary Randolph, "gaspacha" was made as follows:

> Put some soft biscuit or toasted bread in the bottom of a sallat bowl, put in a layer of sliced tomatas with the skin taken off, and one of sliced cucumbers, sprinkled with pepper, salt, and chopped onion; do this until the bowl is full, stew some tomatas quite soft, strain the juice, mix in some mustard and oil, and pour it over; make it two hours before it is eaten.

My mother would have liked that recipe. The tomatoes were peeled, sliced, layered, salted, and allowed to sit for a couple of hours so that their flavorful juices could drain and make soup. Unlike recent gazpacho recipes that insist the soup be served ice-cold (some even call for ice cubes on the surface), this soup seemed to be served at room temperature.

To get my bearings, I began by testing two very different styles of gazpacho. The first recipe, from the new *Joy of Cooking* (Simon & Schuster, 1998), was chunky and simple to prepare: peeled, seeded, and coarsely chopped tomatoes, cucumbers, and green peppers were further chopped in batches in a food processor, along with onion and parsley. Minced garlic, oil, vinegar, and bottled tomato juice were then stirred into the vegetable mixture and refrigerated for 2 hours.

Although the soup was simple to prepare and tasted fresh and full-flavored, the vegetables looked jagged and unevenly chopped, the tomatoes tasted spongy, and the olive oil, which had solidified under refrigeration, left a greasy film on the lips and spoon.

The second soup, featured in Spanish culinary expert Penelope Casas's *Delicioso!* (Knopf, 1996), came from restaurant owner Salvador Lucero, owner of Bar Bahia in Cádiz, Spain. Described as the gazpacho by which all others are judged, this soup was smooth and refined. All the soup ingredients — tomatoes, onions, Kirby cucumbers, frying peppers, water-soaked bread, lots of garlic and vinegar, as well as olive oil — were placed in a food processor and pureed to a liquid, then passed through a food mill. Two cups of cold water were added to the strained vegetable liquid. The well-chilled soup was served with little cups of diced vegetables passed separately.

Although I might enjoy this style of soup if it were served to me, it wasn't what I was looking for. With its 7 garlic cloves, $1/2$ cup of vinegar, and 2 cups of water, the soup was more like a zippy V8 juice than soup.

From my research and initial testing, I knew now what I didn't want. I didn't want a pureed and strained gazpacho, nor did I want one filled with jagged vegetables. And although gazpacho is meant to be eaten cold, I didn't want one that tasted like salad that had been in the refrigerator for a day or so.

VEGETABLE BY VEGETABLE

Tomatoes were a given in my gazpacho, but what other vegetables did I want? My strategy was to start with only tomatoes, then to test each vegetable in combination with tomatoes to see what I liked. I started with a base of peeled, seeded, and chopped tomatoes flavored with salt, garlic, olive oil, and vinegar. Not surprisingly, this gazpacho, served with the remaining vegetables passed separately, tasted like . . . chopped tomatoes with vegetables passed separately. Like vegetable soup that needs heat for flavors to marry, gazpacho needs refrigerator time. I began to build my gazpacho.

For me, cucumbers in gazpacho are a must. Unlike the more assertive peppers and onions, they give the soup a cool freshness. After trying gazpacho with small Kirby cucumbers used for pickling, a hothouse (seedless) variety that usually comes wrapped in cellophane, and regular cucumbers, I preferred the seedless hothouse. The pale green flesh of the seedless cucumber was the most crisp, flavorful, and colorful of the three.

To see whether peppers belonged in my gazpacho, I made batches with green, red, and yellow bell peppers, as well as jarred red peppers and canned green chiles. Upon the recommendation of one recipe, I also made a batch with the pale green frying peppers. Lacking crunch and freshness, the jarred and canned peppers did not appeal. The green frying peppers started out mild but finished a bit bitter. Although I liked the sweet crunch of the red bell pepper, it didn't provide any color contrast with the tomatoes.

I nearly opted for assertive, crisp green bell peppers until I tasted the gazpacho made with the yellow variety. Offering both sweet flavor and visual contrast, yellow bell peppers were my choice. (Green peppers, however, are certainly an option if yellow ones are unavailable or too pricey.)

I had found recipes calling for nearly every major variety of onions — utility yellow onions, and sweet, mild varieties such as Vidalias, Spanish, and whites. Red onions were also common, as were scallions.

Surprisingly, the standard yellow and white onions tasted the least harsh. Because of their wimpy crunch, the scallions were the first to be eliminated. Even after refrigerator time, the other onions had a noticeably harsh onion flavor.

Vinegar is a key ingredient in gazpacho, and I knew from experience that soaking onions in vinegar removes their bite. Even just a few minutes of soaking, however, made the onions taste distinctly pickled. If I had to, I knew I could soak the onions in ice water, but I wanted to avoid that step. I put that decision on hold and proceeded to test the tomato base with the following combinations:

Cucumbers and yellow peppers
Cucumbers and onions
Yellow peppers and onions
Cucumbers, peppers, and onions

Providing the onions lost their bite and the vegetable proportions were right, I liked them all. Too much cucumber wasn't a problem, but too much bell pepper or onion put the soup out of whack.

It was time to determine the right technique. Should the vegetables be hand-diced, or would peeling, seeding, and pureeing give the proper texture? Or would pureeing half of them and leaving the other half chunky be the smart solution?

STRAIN THE SEEDS, SQUEEZE THE SKINS

After testing all the different preparation techniques, I favored the ones made with hand-chopped vegetables, but this style of soup needed added liquid. Bottled tomato juice tasted too distinct, and V8 was even more obvious. Water enhanced the soup's freshness but diluted its flavor.

The tomatoes in the soup presented an even bigger problem. Refrigerating the tomato chunks even for a short time made them cottony, compromising the soup's quality. (Most cooks know the quickest way to ruin a tomato's texture and flavor is to store it in the refrigerator.)

To solve this problem, I started by peeling and seeding the tomatoes. Rather than tossing out the juice and seeds, however, I strained the seeds through a fine-mesh strainer, pressing down with a rubber spatula to release all of the juice. I also used both hands to squeeze all the excess juice from the tomato skins. From the seeds and skins of 2½ pounds of tomatoes, I got nearly a cup of fresh tomato juice.

Next, I chopped the tomatoes coarsely, sprinkled them with salt and drained them in a colander set over a bowl. Within 45 minutes, I had nearly another cup of juice. There was no need to add any other kind of liquid. While the tomatoes drained, I prepared the cucumbers, bell peppers, onions, and garlic, then mixed the vegetables and vinegar into the tomato liquid and refrigerated the mixture — without the tomatoes.

While the soup chilled (about 30 minutes in a 13-by-9-inch Pyrex dish), I added the accumulated juices as the tomatoes continued to drain. Then I processed the tomatoes to a chunky puree in the food processor and stirred them, along with the oil, into the soup.

Not only were the tomatoes soft, sweet, and intensely flavorful, but the onions had lost their nasty bite. Although I had worried that adding room-temperature tomatoes might warm up the soup too much, it was decidedly cold.

My ideal gazpacho was just a taste or two away, but two things still bothered me. Since the olive oil wasn't refrigerated in this version, it hadn't coagulated. Adding it at the end, however, resulted in a very noticeable oil slick. And the tomato puree was nice, but I wanted some tomato chunks, too.

These problems were easily solved. I pureed only half the tomatoes and hand-chopped the rest into chunks. Thinking the soup might not need oil, I left it out of one batch but quickly realized it was essential for both underlying flavor and body. I decided to process the oil along with the tomatoes, thereby creating an emulsion that eliminated the slick.

Although some gazpachos may need water-soaked bread for body and texture, mine did not. In fact, it messed up the beautiful soup I had worked so hard to achieve.

DEATH OF A TOMATO

Refrigeration kills the flavor and texture of a tomato. According to Eric Resnick, coordinator of education and promotion for the Florida Tomato Committee, tomatoes are made up mostly of water housed in their cell walls. Much like heat, cold causes water to expand (think of an exploded frozen soda can). Under refrigeration, the water in tomatoes expands and breaks down the cell walls, resulting in the mealy texture we all know and hate.

"Picture a cluster of water-filled balloons," Resnick suggests. "Bring in cold temperatures and the water expands, causing the balloons to pop. It's the same with tomatoes."

Refrigeration destroys a tomato's flavor as well. Exposed to temperatures below 55 degrees, the tomato will not develop any further flavor. In fact, Resnick says, "The longer the tomato is refrigerated, the more flavor it loses." Once the flavor is gone, it can never be recaptured — even by returning the tomato to room temperature.

Garlic croutons (see page 178) are another matter. If you have time to make them — and they take only about 15 minutes — do.

Since vinegar or some other acid plays an important role in gazpacho, I had one more test to go. After tasting soups made with red wine vinegar, sherry vinegar, rice wine vinegar, white wine vinegar, balsamic vinegar, lemon juice, and lime juice, sherry vinegar got my vote, hitting the right notes of sweet, potent, and piquant and pulling the dish together.

Mom might not have taught me how to make gazpacho, but her lesson about tomato flavor helped me make the best one I've ever tasted.

Great Gazpacho

Although I've made the garlic croutons optional, they add such flavor and textural contrast to the soup that they should be mandatory. You can use the leftover minced garlic from the croutons to make the soup.

2½ pounds ripe tomatoes (about 5 medium)

1½ teaspoons salt

1 small hothouse seedless cucumber, peeled and cut into ¼-inch dice, or enough to yield 2 cups

1 small yellow bell pepper, stemmed, seeded, and cut into ¼-inch dice, or enough to yield ¾ cup (green bell peppers can be substituted as well)

1 small yellow or white onion, cut into small dice, or enough to yield ½ cup

1 small jalapeño, stemmed, seeded, and minced (optional, but nice)

2 medium garlic cloves, minced

2 tablespoons sherry vinegar

2 tablespoons extra-virgin olive oil

2 tablespoons minced fresh parsley or cilantro

Garlic Croutons, page 178 (optional, but nice)

Peel tomatoes following illustrations below.

To peel in-season, ripe tomatoes, lightly scrape the edge of the spoon over the entire tomato to loosen the skin. Peel the skin off the tomato and reserve.

If the tomatoes do not peel easily, score an X on the blossom end of each one, then drop into boiling water for 15 seconds, and peel.

Halve the tomatoes crosswise, then seed them over a small strainer set over a Pyrex measuring cup. With a rubber spatula, press on the seeds to release their juices.

2 Halve tomatoes and seed as shown. Squeeze juice from tomato skins into measuring cup; reserve juice and discard skins. (If tomatoes are juicy and ripe, you should have $3/4$ to 1 scant cup accumulated juices.)

Coarsely chop tomatoes, sprinkle with salt, and place in a colander set over a medium bowl. Allow them to drain, occasionally stirring and pressing on them lightly, until they release another $3/4$ to 1 cup juice, 30 to 45 minutes.

4 Mix cucumber, bell pepper, onion, jalapeño (if using), garlic, vinegar, and reserved tomato juice in a 13-by-9-inch Pyrex dish or other shallow, nonreactive pan. Refrigerate until well chilled, about 45 minutes. (The mixture can be refrigerated up to 3 hours.)

While gazpacho chills, transfer half of drained tomatoes to a food processor. Add oil and pulse until reduced to a chunky puree, about four 1-second pulses. Transfer to a medium bowl. Cut remaining tomatoes into medium dice and add to bowl; set aside at room temperature.

6 When ready to serve, stir tomatoes and parsley or cilantro into refrigerated soup and serve immediately, garnished with optional croutons, if desired.

Cream of
Mushroom
Soup Without the
Cream

Until I was well into adulthood, my encounters with cream of mushroom soup were limited to the brown-speckled, pasty white kind from a can. In the casserole world, this soup has its place, but it's not the kind of thing you're proud of serving.

In developing a cream of mushroom soup, I wanted one that tasted full-flavored but not heavy, hearty enough to serve as a main course, but refined enough to commence the most elegant of dinners.

A SURPRISING THICKENER

After reviewing nearly two hundred vegetable-soup recipes, I identified twenty very different ways to thicken them and began testing them one by one.

Whisking flour into the sautéed onion before adding the liquid was probably the most common thickening method, and for good reason. This roux-thickened soup was simple, and cooking the flour and butter together added a pleasantly rich, nutty flavor to the soup. If I hadn't found a better way, this might have been it.

In addition, I tried thickening the soup with water/starch mixtures, or "slurries," toward the end of cooking. I made four different ones — flour, cornstarch, potato starch, and arrowroot — none of which was exceptional. Although it was a very effective thickener, instant flour didn't taste very good.

A soup can be thickened with potatoes as well, and I made four attempts. In addition to using waxy and starchy potatoes, I also tried stirring in already mashed potatoes as well as sprinkling in dehydrated potato flakes. Starchy potatoes like the Idaho thickened the soup quite well but masked flavors, while waxy reds offered clean unobtrusive flavor but flopped as a thickener. Canned mashed white beans were no better. Pureed with the soup base, crackers and breads melted beautifully into the soup, offering a smooth, creamy texture, but their flavor was too distinct.

Sour cream proved to be a better enricher than a thickener, and egg yolks tasted . . . well, eggy.

In addition, I experimented with oddball possibilities, for I'd seen recipes for soups thickened with tapioca, cornmeal, cream of wheat, oatmeal, and ground almonds. I didn't want to judge them without a trial, although I didn't think they'd work. My instincts were right; they didn't.

The winner was rice. When pureed, it gave the soup silky, smooth body. It enriched the soup without masking its flavor. It contributed rich, creamy color without adding calories and was substantial and thick, yet heat-stable.

Since the rice needed a full 20 minutes to cook, I noticed that a significant amount of broth had evaporated by the time it was done. I wasn't a fan of Minute Rice's soft, mushy texture, but since it was to be pureed, I wondered if I could get away with using it. If so, it would eliminate broth evaporation and shave a little time off the recipe, too.

Minute Rice was a great discovery. Following the package instructions, I brought the rice to a boil, covered it, turned off the heat, and let it stand for 5 minutes. After pureeing it in the blender with broth, I'd have never guessed I was eating rice, much less the minute version.

MUSHROOMS MAKE THE BROTH

During the first round of tests, I had used canned chicken broth as the soup base, enriching it with a drizzle of cream. With the thickener settled, I was ready to compare soups made with chicken broth to those made with vegetable broth, water, milk, and a mix of milk and broth.

Even good-quality vegetable broth lacked depth and tasted too distinct. Besides boiling over, sticking to the pan, and creating a general mess, the vegetable soup made with all milk was sweet and the overwhelming dairy masked the bright vegetable flavor. A mix of chicken broth and milk was also bland. Experiments demonstrated that it was better to enrich the soup with a little cream or sour cream at the end rather than try to make it part of the base. Chicken broth was the best of the liquids, but unless I figured out how to infuse it with mushroom flavor, the soup was never going to taste like much more than sliced mushrooms floating in thickened chicken broth.

To determine how to make a broth that tasted distinctly of mushrooms, I tested three different approaches. For broths one and two, I simmered the stems from $1/2$ pound of mushrooms in 2 cups of chicken broth. To see if aromatics might further enhance flavor, I simmered a little carrot, celery, and garlic along with the stems in broth two. In broth three, I simmered $1/4$ ounce of dried mushrooms plus the stems from $1/2$ pound of mushrooms in 2 cups of broth.

The fresh mushroom stems dramatically improved the broth's flavor. Although pleasant, the aromatics muddied the pure mushroom flavor I wanted. Broth three, however, was superior. The combination of fresh mushroom stems and dehydrated mushrooms created an incredibly rich and potent mushroom base for the soup. In just ten minutes, the dried mushrooms and fresh stems seemed to have completely given up their flavor to the broth.

The broth still needed something — an herb, I thought, or maybe a little fortified wine. After testing seven different flavorings — lemon juice, sweet and dry sherry, sweet and dry vermouth, Madeira and white wine — I initially chose Madeira for its subtly sweet brooding effect on the soup. But in subsequent tests, Madeira's sweetness predominated, rather than its flavor, so I left it out. As it turned out, one small rosemary branch simmered in the broth was all the help it needed.

I still needed to figure out how to cook and when to add the mushrooms. It appeared I had three choices.

I could cook the sliced mushrooms in the broth and then add them to the finished soup. This would mean having to sort through the mushrooms and separate the slices from stems and dried pieces. And since the mushrooms seemed to lose nearly all their flavor to the broth, the slices I'd be adding would be as tasteless as those from a can. I could add raw mushroom slices to the thickened soup base and cook them until tender. Trying this, I found that if the base simmered for any length of time, it tended to stick, and the mushrooms weren't very flavorful. Finally, I could sauté the mushrooms with the onions and add them to the rice-thickened soup base. Not only did this soup require using three pans, it tasted as though the three components had been cooked separately and thrown together at the last minute.

But the soup was incredibly rich, flavorful, and attractive with the sautéed mushrooms, and I was closer than I thought to unifying this soup. Here's how. Using fresh-mushroom stems and dried mushrooms, I made a broth and strained it. While the broth simmered, I browned sliced mushrooms in a separate skillet, adding some of the broth, which helped release their flavor.

I used the pot in which I'd made the broth to sauté the onions and cook the rice. Then I pureed the two and returned the mixture to the pot with the sautéed mushrooms and broth. After just a few minutes of simmering, the soup was thickened and ready.

To freshen and enrich it, I stirred in a little parsley and scallion and topped each bowl with a dollop of sour cream. Unlike the canned variety, this cream of mushroom soup doesn't have to be relegated to casseroles. From its rich appearance and flavor, you'd never guess that the only cream is the dollop on top.

Creamless Cream of Mushroom Soup

The only cream in this soup is the optional sour cream garnish. If you don't have a blender, the soup can be pureed in a food processor, but it will not be quite as smooth. If you don't have a 12-inch skillet, you may want to cook the mushrooms in batches. If cooked in a crowded pan, the mushrooms will stew rather than brown.

6 **cups chicken broth, in a carton, canned, or homemade**

1 **pound domestic white mushrooms, rinsed quickly, stems removed, caps sliced thin**

3/4 **ounce dried mushrooms**

1 **rosemary sprig (about 3 inches long)**

3 **tablespoons butter**

 Salt and freshly ground black pepper

1 **medium onion, cut into medium dice**

2/3 **cup Minute Rice**

2 **scallions, green part only, minced (about 2 tablespoons)**

2 **tablespoons chopped fresh parsley leaves**

6 **tablespoons sour cream (optional)**

Bring chicken broth, mushroom stems, dried mushrooms, and rosemary sprig to a boil in a Dutch oven or large pot. Reduce heat to low and simmer, partially covered, until mushrooms have given up their flavor to broth, about 10 minutes. Strain broth into a 2-quart Pyrex measuring cup or large bowl; set aside.

2 Meanwhile, heat 2 tablespoons butter in a large (12-inch) skillet over medium-high heat until butter solids turn nutty brown. Increase heat to high and immediately add sliced mushrooms, sprinkling them generously with salt and pepper. Let mushrooms cook, without stirring, until browned on the bottom, about 4 minutes. Continue to cook, stirring occasionally, until well browned and liquid has evaporated, 4 to 5 minutes longer. Add all but 2 cups reserved mushroom broth to pan; simmer to blend flavors, 2 to 3 minutes. Turn off heat and set aside.

Heat remaining 1 tablespoon butter in the pot you cooked the broth in. Add onion and sauté until softened, 4 to 5 minutes.

Add rice and remaining 2 cups broth; bring to a boil. Cover, remove from heat, and let stand until rice has cooked, about 5 minutes.

4 Transfer rice mixture and liquid to a blender. Puree until completely smooth and creamy, about 1 minute.

5 Return puree to Dutch oven. Add cooked mushroom mixture and simmer until it thickens slightly and flavors blend, 3 to 5 minutes. Stir in scallions and parsley and season to taste with salt and pepper. Ladle into bowls, garnish with a dollop of sour cream, if you like, and serve immediately.

Potato-Leek Soup
with Parsley and Chives

Unlike mushrooms, firm vegetables with little moisture, such as carrots, winter squash, cauliflower, sweet potatoes, broccoli, turnips, and rutabagas, have enough body to thicken soup when they are pureed. When making this potato soup or any other pureed vegetable soup, feel free to substitute a medium onion and/or 3 medium garlic cloves for the leek.

Soups like this one can also be varied by flavoring them with dried herbs and spices ($1\frac{1}{2}$ teaspoons curry powder, or $\frac{1}{2}$ teaspoon ground cumin, or $\frac{1}{2}$ teaspoon dried thyme leaves, or $\frac{1}{2}$ teaspoon ground ginger), which are best added to the heating broth. Other fresh herbs may be used as well and should be added when pureeing the soup. This soup can be doubled or tripled but obviously must be pureed in batches. It's equally good hot or cold.

2 cups chicken broth, in a carton, canned, or homemade, plus more if needed
1 medium leek, white and light green parts quartered lengthwise, cut into medium dice, and thoroughly rinsed in a sink full of cold water
1 pound baking potatoes (about 2 medium-large), peeled and cut into large dice
1 cup whole milk or half-and-half
2–3 parsley sprigs
4–5 chives or 2 tablespoons chopped scallion greens
   Salt and freshly ground black pepper

1 Bring broth to a simmer in a large pot over medium heat. Add leek and potatoes to broth. Cover and simmer until tender, about 10 minutes.

2 Add milk or half-and-half, parsley, and chives or scallions to broth mixture and transfer to a blender (or a food processor, but soup will not be as velvety in texture) and puree. (Soup can be cooled to room temperature, refrigerated, seasoned with salt and pepper, and served chilled.) Return soup to pot, season with salt and pepper, and thin with additional broth or water if it is too thick. Heat until soup starts to bubble. Serve.

Exceptional Ham and Split Pea Soup, When You Don't Have a Ham Bone

Ham is as much a part of my culinary past as boneless, skinless chicken breasts are to my present. Hardly a month went by that my mother didn't roast one of those big water-added grocery-store hams. She'd stick it in the oven and roast it for hours. The thick rind would crisp up, the fat would render, and the water would evaporate, leaving the meat irresistibly rich and dense. For days, we'd have sliced ham for dinner, ham sandwiches for lunch, and fried ham for breakfast. When the ham was picked nearly clean, it was time to make a pot of soup.

My mom's bean and pea soups were hardly recipes. She simply dropped the ham bone in a pot, dumped in a package of overnight-soaked beans or peas, and covered them with water. This simple concoction cooked until the meat fell off the bone, the fat discreetly melted into broth, and the beans became creamy enough to thicken the soup. Minced fresh onion and corn bread were the only accompaniments needed.

I still love split pea soups, but times have changed. Except for the occasional holiday, I rarely buy a bone-in ham, opting more often for the thin-sliced deli stuff. But convenience comes with a price. With every one of my deli ham purchases, I lose another pot of soup. I had tried to figure out ways to cheat the soup of its crucial ham bone — ham hocks or canned chicken broth porked up with bacon, sausage, or ham — and had almost convinced myself that I'd succeeded, until I remembered the tender shreds of flavorful ham in my mother's soup. Was it possible to make the same soup without buying a huge ham? I sure hoped so.

THE PROOF'S IN THE BROTH

In order to confirm or disprove my belief that ham broth is crucial to split pea soup, I made several pork broths and pork-enhanced canned chicken broths from pork hocks (fresh and smoked), smoked ham shanks, and smoked pork necks. I also made cheater broths — kielbasa simmered in canned chicken broth, kielbasa simmered in water, bacon simmered in chicken broth, and bacon simmered in water. And finally, for purposes of comparison, I made a pot of broth from a meaty ham bone.

Broths made with hocks were more greasy than flavorful. Worse, they yielded very little meat, making it necessary to purchase an additional portion of ham to fortify the soup. Ham shanks, which include the hock portion as well, made a pleasant but lightweight broth that was greasy and salty — both fixable problems had the broth been more promising. Though not widely available, pork necks made a fairly flavorful but salty broth. Both the kielbasa- and bacon-enhanced chicken broths tasted strongly of overly processed meat, while the water versions — especially the bacon broth — were weak.

The ham broth, however, tasted meaty and full-flavored; rich, but not greasy; seasoned, but not overly salty; and smoky with no artificial overtones. Unlike any of the other broths, this one sported bits of meat. And not just good meat — great meat. The tender pieces of ham that fell away from the bone during cooking were not just a nice by-product of the broth. They were a must in my split pea soup.

But was there a way around buying half a ham (with an average weight of about 8 pounds) just to make a pot of soup? I made a trip to the grocery store to find out. After checking out the ham and smoked-pork cases at two different stores, I discovered the much smaller smoked-pork picnic shoulder half. After making a couple of pots of soup, I found that this shoulder — with its bones, fat, rind, and meat — makes outstanding stock, and after 2 hours of simmering, the meat was meltingly tender, yet potently flavorful.

Since I didn't need the full picnic half to make soup, I pulled off and roasted two of its meatier muscles for other meals and used the remaining meat, bone, fat, and rind for the soup. At around 99 cents a pound, picnic shoulders are usually cheaper than a ham, and at my grocery store, picnics were even cheaper than pork hocks, shanks, and neck bones. For less than five dollars, I could make a pot of soup and still have a couple of pounds of extra smoked-pork meat for sandwiches, omelets, and casseroles.

Although not as common as picnic halves, picnic pieces are also available. These 2-to-2½-pound portions are ideal for the soup — simply throw the whole piece in the pot.

NO SOAKING, PLEASE

To determine whether or not the split peas needed to be soaked before cooking, I made soups in three ways: with peas soaked overnight, with peas soaked in boiling water for 10 minutes, and with unsoaked peas.

Happily, the soup made from the unsoaked peas was the best. These peas

LET'S HAVE A PICNIC

Unlike the ham, which comes from the back legs of the pig, the picnic comes from the shoulder and front legs. Smaller than the ham, a picnic half weighs only 4¹/₂ pounds. Why the name? According to the National Pork Board's vice president of quality, Dr. David Meisinger, it comes from the fact that cooks originally opted for this cut for informal summer meals. Not only was it less expensive than ham, it was nearly half the size, making it much more convenient to slip into a picnic basket. Accordingly, this hamlike cut was soon dubbed "picnic ham." The United States Department of Agriculture, however, objected to calling a shoulder cut "ham." So ham was dropped, but picnic stuck.

Picnic, I've observed, is more intensely flavored than ham. This finding made sense to Meisinger, who confirmed that shoulder muscles are higher in flavor than those of the hind legs.

Besides slicing the picnic and making sandwiches with it or frying it and serving it with eggs, I dice picnic slices and use them to flavor all kinds of dishes. I start by browning the diced picnic in oil to intensify its flavor. Then I add a little onion to the pan. From there, I may add eggs to make a frittata, Arborio rice to make risotto, greens or beans to make a vegetable side dish, or soft vegetables, such as bell peppers, mushrooms, or summer squash, to toss with cooked pasta.

cooked the quickest, and they melded into the broth, making the soup delicious, thick, and creamy. The peas that had been soaked overnight tasted washed out and bland, while the soup made with the briefly soaked peas was only a slight improvement.

ORDER IN THE POT

There are several ways to make ham and split pea soup. You can throw everything — ham bone, peas, and diced aromatic vegetables such as celery, carrots, and onions (or whole vegetables, which you fish out at the end) — into a pot and simmer it until everything is tender. Or you can sauté the vegetables, then add the remaining ingredients and cook the soup until the ham and peas are tender. Alternatively, you can cook the ham bone and peas (or give the ham bone a little bit of a head start) until the meat and peas are tender, then add raw, sautéed, or caramelized aromatic vegetables to the pot and continue cooking until the vegetables are tender and flavors have blended.

Although I had hoped to keep the soup a simple one-pot operation, I found out pretty quickly that dumping everything into the pot at the same time resulted in gloppy peas and tired, mushy vegetables by the time the ham was tender. Soups were best when the vegetables spent enough time in the pot to blend their flavors, but not so long that they had lost their individuality. The sweet taste of the caramelized vegetables gave this otherwise straightforward soup a richness and depth of flavor that made the extra step and pan worth the trouble.

Adding the ham, peas, and vegetables to the pot at different intervals turned out to be the way to go. After the meaty picnic shoulder had simmered about 2 hours, or until a fork stuck in the meat came out with some resistance, I added the peas and simmered until they disintegrated and the ham was falling-off-the-bone tender, about 45 minutes longer. I fished out the ham and shredded the meat, discarding the bone, rind, and excess fat. Then I added the vegetables and cooked them until they were just tender.

Although my split pea soup looked perfect, it needed a little something more. Many bean and pea soup recipes call for an acidic ingredient — vinegar, lemon juice, fortified wines such as sherry or Madeira, Worcestershire, or sour cream — to bring balance to the richness. After tasting all of the above, I was drawn to balsamic vinegar. Unlike any of the other ingredients, its mildly sweet, mildly acidic flavors perfectly complemented the soup. Now all I needed was some minced red onion for a garnish and a skillet of corn bread, and I was back home again.

Hearty Ham and Split Pea Soup
with Caraway and Potatoes

If you can't find a portion of picnic (see page 17), get a picnic half, remove the large outer muscle and reserve it for making sandwiches or flavoring eggs, frittatas, pasta, and greens (see illustration, page 20). This recipe works with a ham bone as well: simply substitute a meaty ham bone for the picnic half. The cooking time will be reduced, since the ham will not take as long to become tender.

1   piece picnic (about 2¹/₂ pounds)
4   bay leaves
1   pound (2 cups) split peas
1¹/₂ teaspoons caraway seeds, toasted in a small, dry skillet
        until fragrant, then crushed to a powder with a
        rolling pin
2   tablespoons olive oil
2   medium onions, cut into medium dice
2   medium carrots, cut into medium dice
2   medium celery stalks, cut into medium dice
1   tablespoon butter
2   medium garlic cloves, minced
    Pinch sugar
    Freshly ground black pepper
4   new potatoes, cut into medium dice

    Minced red onion for passing (optional)
    Balsamic vinegar for passing (optional)

Bring 3 quarts water, picnic, and bay leaves to a simmer over medium-high heat in a large pot. Reduce heat to low, cover, and simmer until ham starts to pull away from bone and a fork stuck in meat comes out with some resistance, about 2 hours. Add split peas and caraway, and continue to simmer, partially covered, until peas are tender, about 45 minutes.

2   Meanwhile, heat oil in a large skillet over high heat. Add onions, carrots, and celery, and sauté, stirring frequently, until most of their liquid evaporates and they start to brown, 5 to 6 minutes. Reduce heat to low; add butter, garlic, sugar, and pepper. Spread out vegetables in a single layer so they brown, and continue to cook, stirring once or twice, until vegetables are a rich brown color, about 20 minutes; set aside.

3   Remove picnic from soup. When cool enough to handle, shred meat; discard bone and rind. Add vegetables and potatoes to soup and simmer until tender and peas have just dissolved and started to thicken soup, about 15 minutes longer. Add shredded ham to soup; simmer to heat through. Ladle into bowls. If desired, serve with minced red onion and balsamic vinegar passed separately at the table.

If using a picnic half, pull the largest muscle out of the picnic and reserve for another use. Use the remaining 2½ pounds of meat, bone, rind, and fat to flavor the soup.

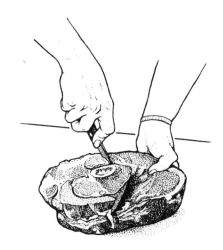

Weeknight Warriors

Simplified
Chicken Parmesan

Up until a couple of years ago, I hadn't made anything "Parmesan" except for the very occasional eggplant. But the first time I made Chicken Parmesan, it became an instant family favorite — meaning, of course, that the kids loved it. Why should I be surprised? Chicken Parmesan is little more than a plain cheese pizza, with boneless, skinless chicken breast standing in for the crust.

Chicken Parmesan isn't a particularly hard dish to make, but there are a lot of piddly steps that can bog you down if you're in a hurry. First, you must prepare and pound the chicken breasts. You have to make an egg wash for dipping and a crumb mixture for dredging. Unless you buy them pre-grated, the mozzarella and Parmesan cheese must be grated as well. You also need to make a quick tomato sauce and boil water for pasta. And then you're left with an impressive stack of pots, pans, and plates to wash and dry after dinner.

Since chicken Parmesan was such a family favorite, my goal was to ensure this dish was the best it could be and doable for weeknight supper — on the table in less than 30 minutes.

HOW TO TREAT THE MEAT

Since the bread-crumb coating on the chicken breasts usually burns before the meat is done, it's necessary to pound the breasts to a uniform thickness so they cook more quickly and evenly. Up to this point, I had bought and pounded standard (6-to-8-ounce) boneless, skinless breasts.

Using full-size breasts, however, results in massive cutlets that you need to cook in batches (which is time-consuming), cook in two skillets (which makes an even bigger mess), or oven-fry (which doesn't brown the cutlets as well). Loosely attached to either side of the breasts are long, thin, extra-tender pieces of meat called tenderloins, which fall apart during pounding.

Reducing portion size was a step in the right direction. A boneless, skinless breast half is too much for the average appetite when served with a side of spaghetti, a ladle of tomato sauce, and a topping of rich mozzarella cheese. Cut in half horizontally and with the tenderloin removed, these cutlets are perfect for two people, and the entire meal can be cooked in a single skillet.

"Specially trimmed chicken breasts" — a relatively new product on the market — also work well for chicken Parmesan. Fully trimmed, with the tenderloins removed, these boneless, skinless breast halves weigh four to five ounces each.

POUND SOFTLY AND WITH A FLAT SURFACE

Regardless of whether you buy boneless, skinless breasts and split them or choose the specially trimmed ones, both need a little pounding to make them thin enough for cutlets. I tried several different pounding gadgets — makeshift as well as purchased — and found that the best chicken-breast pounders were relatively lightweight with large flat surfaces. Unlike tough red meat, which can stand sharp, heavy blows, chicken breasts are delicate and need only gentle coaxing to thin out.

Rolling pins and wine bottles are large but not flat, producing inconsistently pounded meat. (Glass is a little unsafe, especially on granite or other hard kitchen work surfaces.) Frying pans and saucepans are relatively lightweight, but their unusually wide pounding surface makes control difficult.

Though a little heavy for chicken pounding, the disk-style pounder with a handle in the center is my favorite. Light pounding quickly and efficiently transforms breasts into cutlets. I've found that when I'm in a hurry, the palm of my hand makes a pretty good pounder, too.

It matters which side of the chicken breast is pounded. I soon discovered that the pliable cut side of the breast is more pounder-friendly, easily flattening to perfection, while the skin side often splits, resulting in an unsightly cutlet.

I also determined that pounding the breast directly with no protection is messy and damages the cutlet. Flattening the chicken breast between two sheets of plastic wrap ensures perfectly shaped chicken cutlets. Waxed paper, by comparison, disintegrates during pounding, causing bits of paper to stick to the breast.

EGG DIP, BREAD DREDGE

Traditionally, chicken cutlets are dipped in an egg wash before the crumb coating. Some recipes go even further, dredging the cutlet in flour before the egg dip. Was this extra flour step necessary? I thought not. Although the coating of the flour-dipped cutlet was thicker, it tended to separate from the cutlet, peeling off in sheets. The simple egg and bread crumb coating forms an almost inseparable skin.

Although I tried other dips — buttermilk, yogurt, even mayonnaise — I did not find anything better than just plain egg. Mayo-coated chicken sautéed into a greasy cutlet, while buttermilk and yogurt ones were too distinct and didn't blend with the Parmesan flavor.

A cutlet dipped in egg white was not an improvement over one dipped in whole egg — at least not enough of an improvement to warrant the extra step of separating the egg. Since one egg perfectly coats four cutlets, I didn't see the need to extend the egg with water or milk as some recipes did.

Although some coatings were more interesting, none was as neutrally flavored, as crisply textured, and as readily available as dry bread crumbs. Cutlets coated with fresh bread crumbs absorbed more fat and were less crisp than I preferred.

The crushed-potato-chip coating was surprisingly good, but a little too distinctly flavored for chicken Parmesan. Corn-flake crumbs were perfectly textured — fine and beautifully crisp — but, like the potato chips, they tasted too distinct. The matzo-meal cutlets were too bland, while the crushed-saltine cutlets were too soft. The cracker-meal-coated cutlets rivaled the ones made with dry bread crumbs

IS CHICKEN WORTHY OF THE BEST PARM?

Having determined that good Caesar Salad warranted good Parmesan (see page 177), I decided to see if cheese quality mattered as much with a dish like chicken Parmesan.

After sampling seven different chicken cutlets topped with Parmesan cheeses ranging in quality from the unaged, pre-grated stuff in the can to aged imported Parmigiano-Reggiano, tasters found the differences so minimal, they couldn't even rate them in order.

Based on these test results, will I start buying unaged, pre-grated cheese in a jar or can? Probably not. I buy Parmigiano-Reggiano in large blocks from my local food warehouse club for $7.99 per pound. When I do the math, I find it's not that much more expensive than canned cheese. Plus, when purchased in a block, Parmesan cheese can be thin-sliced for eating, shaved with a potato peeler for salads or elegant garnish, or grated coarsely or finely.

Those who can't get the real thing at a good price might consider buying a small block of Parmigiano-Reggiano for when it matters and lesser quality Parmesan cheese for cooking.

but were not good enough to warrant a special purchase. Although Japanese bread crumbs (panko) are exquisite — fine-textured, neutrally flavored, and brittle-crisp, they have the downside of being less readily available. If you have them, use them.

Many chicken Parmesan recipes season the bread crumbs with dried herbs and/or Parmesan cheese. After making cutlets dredged in crumbs seasoned with dried basil and oregano and another batch flavored with Parmesan cheese, I preferred the simplicity of the plain breaded cutlets. Although the cheese and herb flavors are key to the dish, I found better places to add them: grated Parmesan cheese perks up the mozzarella cheese topping, while oregano and basil enliven the tomato sauce.

Of the three cooking methods — oven frying, broiling, and sautéing — I preferred sautéing. No other cooking method produces such evenly golden brown color or such rich, satisfying flavor, and you can cook four cutlets at the same time, eliminating the need for a second pan.

Oven frying is potentially unsafe, because lightweight roasting pans can warp in a hot oven, causing hot oil to spatter. Pulling a hot oil-coated shallow pan in and out of the oven can also be dangerous. Broiling, the final method tested, resulted in inconsistently and unimpressively browned cutlets.

Which fat should be used for sautéing cutlets? For a full-flavored dish like chicken Parmesan, I might have guessed that it didn't much matter. I would have been wrong. Cutlets sautéed in olive oil are markedly better than those sautéed in vegetable oil. The differences, however, between cutlets sautéed in extra-virgin and ordinary olive oil are minimal. Given the price difference between the two, save your extra-virgin for drizzling. Cutlets sautéed in a combination of olive oil and butter are not superior to those sautéed in olive oil.

Some recipes, especially older ones, call for topping the cooked cutlets with mozzarella cheese and baking them, covered, in tomato sauce until the cheese melts. This step not only adds several minutes to preparation time but destroys the crisp, delicious coating, turning the cutlet into a soggy mush. I simply sprinkle my cooked cutlets with mozzarella and Parmesan right after sautéing them and broil them until the cheeses melt and turn lightly brown. After that, they're ready for a simple tomato sauce and accompanying pasta.

Chicken Parmesan in half an hour — the time it takes to boil spaghetti. Now all you need is someone to do the dishes!

Simplified Chicken Parmesan

Though not widely available, panko (Japanese bread crumbs) makes an excellent coating. These crumbs are often available at Asian markets or health food stores. If you're using small chicken breasts with tenderloins attached, remove the tenderloins, bread them, and sauté them alongside the chicken cutlets. Or if there's not room in the pan, sauté them after you cook the cutlets.

SIMPLE TOMATO SAUCE WITH BASIL AND GARLIC

- 3 tablespoons extra-virgin olive oil
- 2 medium garlic cloves, minced
- 1 can crushed tomatoes (28 ounces), preferably Redpack, Progresso, or Muir Glen
- 1/2 teaspoon dried basil
- 1/4 teaspoon dried oregano
- 1/4 teaspoon sugar
- Salt and freshly ground black pepper

CHICKEN PARMESAN

- 1 large egg
- Salt
- 1/2 cup dry bread crumbs
- Freshly ground black pepper
- 2 large boneless, skinless chicken breasts (6–8 ounces each), or 4 small chicken breasts (3–4 ounces each), prepared as described on facing page

- 1 tablespoon salt
- 8 ounces spaghetti or linguine
- 1/4 cup olive oil
- 3 ounces part-skim mozzarella cheese, grated (3/4 cup)
- 1/4 cup grated Parmesan cheese (1/2 ounce), plus more for passing

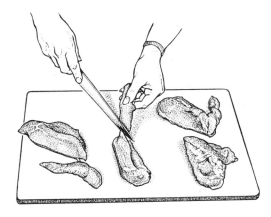

For large chicken breasts, remove the tenderloin and reserve for another use.

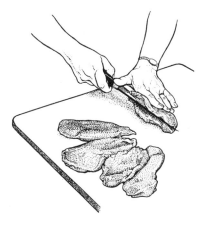

For easy slicing, partially freeze the chicken breasts. Cut them in half horizontally to form 2 chicken cutlets. When prepared this way, they need little or no pounding.

For small chicken breasts, place them, skinned side down, at least 2 inches apart on a large sheet of plastic wrap. Cover with a second sheet of plastic wrap. (Or lay them, 2 at a time, in a thin plastic produce bag.) Lightly pound the breasts to an even ¼-inch thickness.

FOR TOMATO SAUCE: Add oil and garlic to a large saucepan or Dutch oven and heat over medium-high heat until garlic starts to sizzle. Stir in tomatoes, basil, oregano, sugar, a pinch of salt, a couple grinds of pepper, and water, if necessary, to dilute tomatoes to a thin-sauce consistency. Bring to a simmer and continue to simmer until sauce thickens a bit and flavors meld, 10 to 12 minutes. Taste sauce, adjusting salt, if necessary. Cover and keep warm.

2 Bring 2 quarts water to a boil in a large pot.

3 FOR CHICKEN: Beat egg and a heaping $1/4$ teaspoon salt in a shallow dish until completely broken up. Mix bread crumbs, a heaping $1/4$ teaspoon salt and a grind or two of pepper in another shallow dish.

4 Preheat broiler. Working with 1 cutlet at a time, dip both sides of each cutlet in beaten egg, then in bread-crumb mixture. Place cutlets on a large wire rack set over a jelly-roll pan.

5 Add 1 tablespoon salt and the pasta to the boiling water.

6 Meanwhile, heat oil in a large (12-inch) skillet over medium-high heat. When oil starts to shimmer, add cutlets and sauté until golden brown on each side, about 5 minutes total. Wash and dry the wire rack and return to jelly-roll pan. Transfer cutlets to wire rack and top each with a portion of mozzarella and Parmesan cheeses. Place pan of cutlets 4 to 5 inches from heat source and broil until cheese melts and is brown-spotted. Drain pasta.

7 Transfer a chicken cutlet and a portion of pasta to each of four plates. Spoon 2 to 3 tablespoons sauce over part of each cutlet, then sauce the pasta as desired. Serve immediately, passing extra Parmesan separately.

I've always thought of oven-fried chicken as fried chicken manqué — only for those who were afraid to mess up their kitchen, or to eat too much fat, or to cook for a crowd. Although there was certainly nothing wrong with this style of chicken, there often wasn't a lot right with it. Depending on the liquid or crumb coating, it could be bland, soggy, rubbery-skinned, greasy, artificially flavored, dry, or crumbly. Was it possible to make oven-fried chicken that had the look and crunch of the real thing?

Good oven-fried chicken needs the right flavorings, oven temperature, and baking time. But after examining scores of recipes, I realized that what's most crucial are the coatings: both the moist one that helps the crumbs stick and the dry one that offers texture and crunch.

Since the moist coating comes first, I started there. A review of oven-fried chicken recipes revealed that this first coat could be as lean as water or milk, as rich as cream or butter, or as thick as mayonnaise, yogurt, or even sour cream. Before the test, I thought a wet dunk did little more than help the crumbs adhere to the chicken. After testing, however, it became clear that this initial coat played a larger role. A good coating, I discovered, should season the meat without being too obvious, attract the right proportion of crumbs to form an impressive uniform crust and, finally, help the crust stay crunchy during baking.

EGGS FOR THE LEGS

To determine the best moist coating, I baked thirteen drumsticks. The dry coating was constant — dry bread crumbs — but the moist coatings were all different: water, whole milk, evaporated milk, cream, buttermilk, yogurt, sour cream, egg beaten with milk, egg beaten with lemon juice, and egg beaten with Dijon mustard. In addition, I tried legs coated with ranch dressing, mayonnaise, and butter.

Since many oven-fried chicken recipes start by rolling chicken parts in butter, I thought the fat coatings would perform well. Not so. All of them — butter, mayonnaise, and ranch dressing — created a slick surface, which prevented the crumbs from adhering properly.

With the exception of buttermilk and evaporated milk, none of the dairy coatings was particularly good. While the sour cream version sported an impressively thick crust, its distinct, rich flavor overpowered the chicken. Yogurt, on the other hand, tasted downright sour. Milk and egg beaten with milk couldn't hold their crumbs. Chicken coated with an egg–lemon juice mixture tasted too distinctly of lemon with an overcooked-egg aftertaste.

Buttermilk and evaporated milk, however, deserved a second look. Both of these wet coatings attracted decent crusts — especially the buttermilk — and both contributed a subtle flavor dimension to the chicken. The beaten egg and Dijon mustard moistener was among my favorites. Not too thick and not too thin, it not only attracted a uniform, impressive layer of crumbs but also gave the meat a wonderfully subtle flavor. And unlike many of the wet coatings, which made the crumbs either soggy or barely crisp, this one took the crumbs to an almost crunchy level.

Although I was fairly certain about this one, I set up a runoff of my three favorites. In addition to egg and Dijon, I retested evaporated milk and buttermilk. And, since I liked the flavor of the Dijon so much, I also tried Dijon-flavored evaporated milk and buttermilk coatings.

In a crowded race, egg and Dijon won, giving the crunchiest crust and the best flavor. By comparison, buttermilk and evaporated milk tasted plain with a less impressive crust. Neither the Dijon-flavored buttermilk nor the Dijon-flavored evaporated milk scored well, either.

SO MANY COATINGS, SO LITTLE CRUNCH

For consistency, I had used dry bread crumbs in the moist-coating tests, but I had already noticed their lackluster texture and flavor. Now it was time to put those dry crumbs to the test. Considering there's an oven-fried chicken recipe on the back of many cracker and most good-for-you cereal boxes, I had scores of options. I started with twenty dry coatings or combinations, all from published recipes.

Corn flakes, unprocessed bran and bran flakes (both alone and mixed with flour), Grape-Nuts, and oatmeal took care of the cereal category. Saltines, cracker meal, and Ritz crackers were my nod to the cracker aisle. Stuffing mix (both bread and corn bread) as well as dry and fresh bread crumbs (and crumbs mixed with Parmesan cheese) represented bread. Flour and cornmeal, including a mix of the two, were on my list. And, of course, who could overlook the venerable Shake 'n Bake?

After baking and tasting them all, there wasn't a single one I thought was perfect. Of the cereal-coated chicken, corn flakes offered good color and good crunch but had too much sweet corn flavor for my taste. The flavor of bran flakes was even more pronounced. Grape-Nuts looked like crunchy little hamster pellets. Oatmeal tasted raw and chewy.

Crackers didn't work, either; both were too soft. The Ritz, in addition, were too sweet. Cracker meal delivered a bland blond shell. In the bread department, stuffing mix scored well in crunch but struck out in flavor. Fresh bread crumbs, on the other hand, tasted great but lacked the crunch I had come to like. The addition of Parmesan cheese did nothing to promote crunch.

The meals and flours did not show well. Cornmeal tasted raw and chipped off the chicken like flecks of old paint. I tried two brands of commercial chicken coating, and they were vile.

A TOAST TO MELBA

Although this first round of tests did not produce a strong winner, it became clear what I wanted — a coating that was crunchy (not just crisp) and flavorful (but not artificial-tasting), and that baked up a rich copper brown.

With this ideal in mind, I found a whole new range of coatings to try in the specialty/international cracker section of my grocery store. Melba toast, pain grillé (French crisp toast), Swedish crisps, lavash (crisp flatbread), two varieties of bread sticks, two brands of bagel chips, Italian toasts, and pita chips presented new possibilities. I also located some plain croutons and dry bread cubes for stuffing.

Although many of these coatings were good, Melba toast scored the best in texture, flavor, and color. Pain grillé, the most expensive of the coatings, tasted of dehydrated onion. Lavash and Swedish crisps were too hard. One brand of bread stick was soft like a cracker with a chemical aftertaste; the other tasted heavily of dehydrated onion.

One variety of bagel chips made an excellent chicken coating, while the other was dry and tasted of artificial garlic. Since I couldn't recommend all bagel chips, I decided not to recommend them at all. Italian toasts, much like crackers, were a tad pale and soft. Pita crisps had the right crunch but were light in color. Dry bread

TOAST OF THE TOWN

The thin, crispy toasts we know as Melba were named after Nellie Melba, a famous late-nineteenth-century opera diva. Ms. Melba, who was apparently concerned about her figure, had ordered pâté, but when she was served, she sent the accompanying toasts back to the kitchen, complaining they were too thick. The renowned Parisian chef Auguste Escoffier obligingly sliced them more thinly and returned them to the plate, naming the new "diet" toasts in her honor.

Why, I wonder, did no one think to take away her thick slab of pâté?

cubes for stuffing, ground in a food processor, delivered a respectable coating but are available only around the November/December holidays at my grocery store. Plain croutons are even rarer, and the brand I tried was a little softer than I wanted.

STRIP THE SKIN

Over the course of testing, I found that I much preferred legs and thighs to breasts. For chicken-breast lovers, however, the egg and Melba toast coatings work well. I also discovered that I didn't like the skin on oven-fried chicken. With fried chicken, the hot oil causes the fat to render and the skin to crisp up, but oven heat simply softens the skin and makes it rubbery.

Choosing an oven temperature was simple. I started baking at 400 degrees, and all the chicken parts were cooked through and rich golden brown in about 40 minutes. As a check, I baked one batch at 375 degrees and another at 425 degrees. At the lower oven temperature, the chicken was too blond, and at the higher oven temperature, the chicken looked and tasted overly brown by the time it was done.

Setting a wire rack over a foil-covered jelly-roll or shallow baking pan allows heat to circulate during baking, resulting in crisp chicken without the bother of turning. The foil protects the pan, making the cleanup of this crunchy masterpiece a breeze.

Oven-Fried Chicken That's as Good as Fried

Serves 4

A food processor is the cleanest, quickest way to get the toasts to a sand-and-pebble consistency, but you can also leave the Melba toast in the packaging, let out any excess air and crush them with a rolling pin.

- 2 large eggs
- 1 tablespoon Dijon-style mustard
- 1 teaspoon dried thyme
- 3/4 teaspoon salt
- 1/2 teaspoon freshly ground black pepper
- 1 package (5 1/4 ounces) plain Melba toast, pulsed to sand-and-pebble texture
- 4 drumsticks and 4 thighs, skin removed
  Spray bottle filled with vegetable oil or vegetable-oil cooking spray

1 Adjust oven rack to upper-middle position and heat oven to 400 degrees. Mix eggs, mustard, thyme, salt, and pepper in a shallow dish. Put Melba toast crumbs in another shallow dish. Set a large wire rack over an 18-by-12-inch foil-lined jelly-roll pan.

2 Using one hand for dry ingredients and the other for wet, lay chicken pieces, 4 at a time, in egg mixture; roll to coat. Then lay 1 piece at a time in Melba crumbs. Press a mix of crumbs into top of chicken. Turn piece over and repeat, pressing crumbs into other side. Gently shake off excess.

3 Set chicken on rack. Spray top portion of chicken pieces evenly with oil. Bake until chicken is nutty brown and juices run clear, 30 minutes for drumsticks and 35 minutes for thighs. Serve immediately.

One summer vacation nearly six years ago, my then twelve-year-old daughter decided she wanted to become a vegetarian. After a weeklong debate, we finally reached a compromise. She was excused from lamb, beef, and pork as long as she would eat fish and fowl. Hamburgers were one of her weaknesses, so I figured she'd cave in pretty quickly. But what I thought was a teen fad has evolved into a way of life.

Since hamburgers are a regular summer supper for us, I needed to find a substitute for her. Ground turkey was the obvious first choice, but I found out pretty quickly that a lean, fully cooked, pan-fried turkey burger seasoned with salt and pepper was a weak stand-in for an all-beef burger. Simply put, it was dry, tasteless, and colorless.

Since my daughter's anti–red meat resolve is still rock-solid, I decided to see if I could develop a turkey burger that would rival her best burger memories and give the rest of us the option of a meal with less fat and cholesterol. I wanted a turkey burger with beef-burger qualities — dark and crusty on the outside, full flavored and juicy with every bite.

MANY CHOICES, LITTLE TASTE

Finding the right meat was crucial. According to the National Turkey Federation, I had two options: white meat (consisting of 1% to 2% fat), or a blend of white and dark (ranging between 8% and 15% fat).

Once I got to the grocery store, I realized there were multiple variations on the white meat/dark meat theme. Did I want my turkey frozen and packed in a tube, like bulk sausage? Or did I want it refrigerated on a Styrofoam tray, like hamburger? Would pre-formed patties — refrigerated or frozen — offer quality as well as convenience? Or would I get better results by buying individual turkey parts and grinding them myself in the food processor? To find out for sure, I bought them all and fired up a skillet.

The higher-fat (15%), commercially ground turkey — both the kind that's frozen in a tube and the kind that's refrigerated — cooked up into fairly respectable burgers. Given the mushy texture and deviled-ham look of the tubed frozen turkey, I was surprised at the quality of the burger. It developed an evenly dark brown crust and had a juicy gray interior, much like that of an overcooked beef burger. Frankly, it didn't need all that much help. On the other hand, I didn't see much point in eating it. Given that a really great beef burger contains only 20% fat, I didn't think a mere 5% fat difference was worth the compromise in taste. The solution lay ahead.

At the other extreme, the all-white-meat ground turkey breast was a long shot, but I had to give it a try. As I was mixing and forming these patties, I knew I had about as much chance of making these look, taste and feel like a real burger as I did of making a vanilla wafer taste like a chocolate chip cookie. They needed a binder to keep them from falling apart. They needed extra fat to keep them from parching and extra fat in the pan to keep them from sticking. And they needed flavor to save them from blandness. This was a fool's task that I wasn't about to take on.

Containing about 7% fat and composed of both white and dark meat, lean ground turkey fell almost exactly between the high-fat products and ground turkey breast. Burgers made from it were dry, rubbery-textured, and mild-flavored, but they were meaty enough, and with a little help in the flavoring department, they had potential.

After a quick test of pre-formed lean patties — both the refrigerated and the frozen kind — I ruled them out. They all had a week-old-roast-turkey-you're-still-carving-off-the-bone taste to them. A few bites from one of the refrigerated varieties turned up turkey debris: ground-up gristle, tendon, and bonelike chips.

Knowing that the best beef burgers are made from home-ground meat, I bought turkey thighs and revved up my food processor. Sure enough, the burgers made from boned and skinned turkey thigh ground in batches were far superior to any commercially ground turkey. Since they were made from all-thigh meat rather than a mix of light and dark, they were very meaty-flavored. And because they were pulsed in the food processor rather than pushed through a grinder, they actually had a beeflike chew.

As with beef, I found that turkey grinds best when it is partially frozen, cut into small chunks and pulsed in small batches. My butcher analyzed my home-ground skinless turkey thigh in his Univex Fat Analyzer, a machine he uses to check the fat content of each batch of meat he grinds. My turkey burgers contain just under 10%

fat. For those willing to take the time, the grind-your-own turkey thigh makes a low-fat turkey burger with great flavor and texture.

For those who don't have the time or energy to grind their own turkey, I decided to spend a little time seeing what I could do to improve the flavor and texture of the lean commercially ground variety.

To improve texture and juiciness, I started with milk-soaked soft bread crumbs. For comparison, I also made burgers with buttermilk- and yogurt-soaked bread as well. With these additions, all three burgers felt more like meat loaf. And since turkey is so mild to begin with, adding these milk-toast ingredients subtracted what meaty flavor I had. Much like a fair-skinned body after a few hours in the sun, these burgers, when cooked, looked at once pale and burned. Developing a good crust on them was impossible.

I tried other fillers to improve texture, including cornmeal mush, mashed pinto beans, and minced tempeh, all of which tasted too distinct. Heat-and-serve mashed potatoes from the grocery store refrigerator case didn't mix well with the meat. Combining a small amount of turkey sausage with the ground turkey moderately improved the burger, but it seemed a little silly to buy a whole package of turkey sausage for such a small gain.

Among all the lackluster candidates, two successful fillers emerged. Minced rehydrated dried mushrooms added the moist, chewy texture that the burgers so desperately needed. Additionally, they offered an earthy, meaty flavor without tasting too distinct. Minced sautéed fresh mushrooms improved texture as well, but for me, their milder flavor makes them a less attractive option than the dried ones. Ricotta cheese, the other winner, gave the burger the boost it needed.

Of the more than twenty-five different flavorings that I tried (fermented black beans, drained salsa, sun-dried tomatoes, smoked mozzarella and Cheddar, olive paste, canned black olives, prepared Mediterranean eggplant relish, tomato paste, teriyaki marinade, A1 steak sauce, ketchup, Worcestershire, Dijon mustard, anchovy paste, Parmesan cheese, annatto powder, miso, soy sauce, paprika, fresh thyme, fresh rosemary, sautéed onions, and garlic), only three enhanced the burger's taste without drawing attention to themselves. Miso, a fermented soybean paste often used as a vegetarian soup base, offered a subtle savoriness to the turkey that I liked. The more common pantry items, Worcestershire sauce and Dijon mustard, were equally good.

Next I turned to the cooking method. Since turkey burgers must be well done, cooking them can be tricky — too high a heat and they burn before they're done; too low and they look pale and steamed. I tried several cooking methods, from broiling to roasting, but nothing compared in quality and ease to the stovetop method. Browning the burgers over medium heat, then cooking them partially covered over low heat gave me a rich-crusted burger that was thoroughly done.

My generous cooking times should ensure a fully cooked burger, but as an extra precaution, you may want to test one for doneness by sticking an instant-read thermometer through the side and into the center. The burger is done at 160 degrees.

The bargain my daughter and I struck nearly six years ago has probably affected me more than her. The burger I developed for her is so good, we all opt for turkey instead of beef.

Beefed-Up Grind-Your-Own
Turkey Burgers

Serves 4

The texture and flavor of this home-ground burger are superior to patties made with packaged ground turkey. The extra three steps of cutting, freezing, and grinding are well worth it when you have the time.

1   **turkey thigh (about 2 pounds), skinned, meat sliced from the bone and cut into 1-inch chunks (about 1¹/₂ pounds trimmed)**

¹/₂   **teaspoon salt**

¹/₂   **teaspoon freshly ground black pepper**

SEASONINGS

2   **teaspoons Worcestershire sauce**

2   **teaspoons Dijon mustard**

OR

1   **teaspoon pure soybean miso, thinned with 1 teaspoon water**

OR

1   **ounce dried mushrooms, soaked in 1 cup hot water for 15 minutes, squeezed dry, and minced**

1   **teaspoon pure soybean miso, thinned with 1 teaspoon mushroom-soaking liquid**

1   **tablespoon vegetable or canola oil**

1   To ensure even grinding, place chunks of turkey in freezer, uncovered, on a plate, tossing occasionally, until partially frozen, about 30 minutes. Working in three batches, place chunks in a food processor. Process until they resemble ground burger meat, twelve to fourteen 1-second pulses.

2   Transfer ground meat to a medium bowl; add salt, pepper, and desired seasonings. Form meat into 4 portions. Working with 1 portion at a time, lightly toss from hand to hand to form a ball. With your fingertips, lightly flatten ball into a 1-inch-thick patty.

Heat oil in a large, heavy-bottomed skillet (cast iron works well) over medium heat until hot, about 5 minutes. Add burgers and cook until bottoms develop a rich brown crust, about 5 minutes. Turn burgers over and continue to cook until they start to brown, 4 to 5 minutes longer. Reduce heat to low and use a wooden spoon to prop lid open on skillet so steam can escape around the edges. Continue to cook, turning burgers once again if necessary to ensure even browning, until a meat thermometer inserted from the side into the center registers 160 degrees, 5 to 6 minutes longer. Remove from pan and serve immediately.

Darn-Good Quick Turkey Burgers

Serves 4

A small amount of ricotta adds body and richness to store-bought lean ground turkey for a first-rate burger on the nights when you don't have the time or energy to grind your own.

$^{1}/_{2}$ cup ricotta cheese
$^{1}/_{2}$ teaspoon salt
$^{1}/_{2}$ teaspoon freshly ground black pepper

SEASONINGS

2 teaspoons Worcestershire sauce
2 teaspoons Dijon mustard

OR

2 teaspoons pure soybean miso, thinned with 2 teaspoons water

OR

1 ounce dried mushrooms, soaked in 1 cup hot water for 15 minutes, squeezed dry, and minced
1 teaspoon pure soybean miso, thinned with 1 teaspoon mushroom-soaking liquid

$1^{1}/_{4}$ pounds 93% lean ground turkey from the refrigerated meat case
1 tablespoon vegetable or canola oil

Mix ricotta, salt, pepper, and desired seasonings in a medium bowl. Add ground turkey; lightly mix to combine. Form burgers and cook in oil as for Beefed-Up Grind-Your-Own Turkey Burgers (page 38).

Phenomenal Fajitas

My kids order fajitas nearly every time they see them on a restaurant menu, but I rarely make them at home. Marinating and cooking the meat, sautéing the peppers and onions, steaming the tortillas, and assembling the remaining condiments put this meal a step or two out of reach for weeknight suppers. And because of all the last-minute effort that fajitas demand, I don't cook them for company, either. Up until now, it was one of those dishes that had fallen through the culinary cracks.

Without using packaged marinades or jarred condiments, could I make this dish as quick to prepare as it is fun to eat? Since beef is the original fajita filler, I started there, hoping to apply what I had learned to other cuts as well.

JUMPING THE GUN

In exploring possible beef cuts for fajitas, I eliminated a few immediately. Because of their high price tags, I ruled out rib-eyes, strip steaks, and filet mignons. If I were going to pay ten to fifteen dollars a pound for beef, I wouldn't marinate it, slice it thin, wrap it in a flour tortilla, and top it with peppers, onions, guacamole, and sour cream.

Expecting flank steak to be the cheapest, most readily available fajita option, I made a costly mistake by purchasing fifteen of them a few days before the scheduled testing. After running a few initial tests, I was dismayed with the results. Although I had tried pan-searing the steak in a blistering hot cast-iron skillet, broiling it as close to the element as possible, gas-grilling it with the lid closed and all burners blasting, and charcoal-grilling it over an extremely hot fire, I managed only a spotty brown crust at best. To ensure more browning, one recipe suggested lightly scoring the meat on both sides in a diamond pattern. In fact, the raised diamonds browned well, but the meat in between the diamonds did not, and the half-soft surface made slicing difficult. To help it brown more evenly, I next tried weighting the steak with a small, heavy skillet during cooking. Although this technique made an improvement, the crust still wasn't very impressive — nor were the texture and flavor. Cooked to medium and sliced very thin on the diagonal across the grain, the meat was chewy and flavorless. Unless marinades worked miracles, flank steak was not the right cut.

With a dozen of the fifteen flank steaks left, I decided to see if a marinade could improve the texture and flavor. I made four marinades of equal parts lime juice, olive oil, and a little salt, then marinated one steak for 2 hours, and the others for 4 hours, 8 hours, and 24 hours. In just 2 hours, however, the meat had absorbed as much flavor as it needed. Longer marinating did not result in any noticeable tenderness, and marinating for less than 2 hours seemed possible.

SKIRTING THE ISSUE

I set out for the grocery store and butcher to see what other fajita cuts were available. With the strip, rib-eye, and filet steaks off-limits, I picked up a steak each of boneless top and bottom sirloin. Both sirloin steaks seared better and developed a better crust than the flank steak, but both were equally if not more chewy.

Just when I was about to despair, I rediscovered the skirt steak, and things started to be fun. According to Ortega Brand, manufacturers of Mexican food products, the very name "fajita" derives from the Spanish word for skirt steak, which looks like a belt, or *fajq*. I knew skirt steak was the traditional beef fajita cut, but I worried that it had become a precious commodity.

But skirt steaks weren't as expensive and hard to find as I thought. I was pleasantly surprised to find a freezer full of them at my local butcher and a decent

REAR-GUARD ACTION

Flank and skirt steaks have a similar look and feel: flank is long and thin, while skirt steak is even longer and thinner. They are both cut from the animal's underbelly but cook and taste quite different. Skirt steak, which is streaked with surface fat, sears well, while flank steak browns spottily at best and is chewy and tough. Those attempting to take a bite out of a fajita made with flank steak usually end up with the whole thing in their teeth.

The skirt muscle runs along the diaphragm at the animal's center, while the flank extends to the rear legs. The function of each muscle determines its texture. The skirt aids in breathing, while the flank's primary role is to assist in walking, a much more strenuous activity that renders meat fibers tighter and less tender.

If skirt steak is unavailable, I'd choose chicken breasts rather than another cut of beef. Provided that your pan or grill is hot, chicken breasts brown well, and best of all, they're tender.

supply of them at the supermarket — priced at $3.99 to $4.99 per pound.

It had been a while since I had cooked a skirt steak. Looking just like long, wide belts, the eight steaks I purchased ranged from 18 to 28 inches long and 3 to 6 inches wide. Regardless of the measurement variations, each steak was about $1/2$ inch thick at one end. Halfway down the length, the steak thinned to $1/4$ inch or even thinner. Since it had to be cut into pieces to fit into a pan or grill, uneven thickness wasn't a problem. Each section could be cooked independently and to perfection.

The generous patches of fat covering this steak caused it to sear beautifully. And because it was so thin, it seared very quickly — 3 to 5 minutes, depending on the end of the steak I was cooking. Its flavor and texture were unsurpassed. This is one of the richest, beefiest, most reasonably priced, and quickest-cooking steaks available. None of the other cuts came close. After testing all the different cooking methods, I preferred pan-searing, because it was so simple, and charcoal-grilling, because of the distinct flavor.

TRIAL BY MARINADE

Since skirt steak is so thin and tender, I was hoping to get away with marinating the meat for as little as 15 minutes. Limiting the marinade at this point to just lime juice and oil, I made marinades ranging from lime juice only to these combinations:

Lime juice diluted with an equal portion of water
4 parts lime juice to 1 part olive oil
2 parts lime juice to 1 part olive oil
Equal parts lime juice and olive oil

After just a few tests, I realized that the meat had indeed absorbed the marinade in minimal time. In the allotted 15 minutes, straight lime juice had penetrated the skirt steak so thoroughly that it tasted like lime-drenched meat instead of rich, beefy steak pleasantly flavored with lime. Oil in the marinades seemed to slow down or at least tame the acid, but it seemed silly to add oil only to pat it off before cooking.

I came to prefer the simple lime juice–water marinade. Like oil, water cushioned the hard acidic blow. With this marinade, I could pat the meat dry, then rub the surface with a little oil to ensure browning and help the seasonings adhere.

LIME JUICE GOOD — ANYTHING BETTER?

I liked the diluted lime juice marinade, but was there an acid better than lime? Some recipes called for lemon juice rather than lime. Others called for a mix of the two. Diluted lemon juice lacked the clear, clean effect that lime had on the meat, but I'd certainly feel free to use it in a pinch. And there was no benefit in sacrificing both a lime and lemon to the cause.

Substituting orange juice for the water, I marinated a piece of skirt steak in equal parts lime juice and orange juice. The orange juice wasn't sweet enough to balance the acidity, and the meat was slightly sour. Marinating in part vinegar had an even more souring effect on the meat than the orange juice. A couple of recipes included tequila in the marinade, which seemed to make little difference, so I left it out. After seeing soy sauce in a number of recipes, I mixed equal parts lime juice, soy sauce, and water. Soy definitely helped with browning and made the meat taste well seasoned, but since the pan-seared skirt steak browned nicely and tasted beefy enough without it, I left it out, too.

ONE SEASONING SUCCEEDS

Because there were so many potential marinade flavorings, I divided them into two categories: dry and moist. Starting with dry, I added a little sugar to the marinade, but much like the orange juice, it didn't balance the tart lime. Dried herbs and ingredients like hot red pepper flakes had very little impact, and they had to be brushed off before cooking, since they burned if left on.

Powdered spices fared better, but not all were successful. Ground cumin was the only one that I liked. For the taste to come through, however, the spice needed to be rubbed directly onto the meat rather than added to the marinade. Paprika made the meat taste like barbecued potato chips. Spices like cayenne, garlic salt, and chili powder tended to cheapen the flavor of the meat. Because of ground coriander's citric overtones, I had hoped it would reinforce the lime juice marinade. Instead, it felt redundant.

Of the three moist ingredients I tried, minced garlic was the only one that had promise. Hot red pepper sauce, generously shaken into the marinade, barely registered on the cooked steak. The meat flavored with Worcestershire sauce tasted good — but not like fajita.

Although I liked it on the meat, minced garlic caused the same problem as the herbs and pepper flakes: it had to be brushed off before searing or it would burn. To get garlic flavor without the charred bits, I brushed the steak with a strained garlic oil that I had made in the food processor. But wrapped in a tortilla with peppers, onions, and condiments, the flavor was lost.

MARINATE AFTER, NOT BEFORE

I was starting to like my marinade less and less. A straight lime juice marinade was clearly too strong, but marinating in water-diluted lime juice seemed to compromise the rich beefy cut, giving it more of a squeaky-clean flavor. But an idea came to me. If it worked, it would eliminate the marinade and allow for the garlic.

While the skillet preheated, I lightly oiled a piece of skirt steak, rubbing both sides of the meat with salt, pepper, and ground cumin. After searing the meat on both sides, I removed it from the skillet and poured lime juice and minced garlic over it as it rested and the peppers and onions cooked. I sliced the steak thin and then returned it to the lime-garlic mixture.

The steak tasted better this way. Meat juices rather than water diluted the lime juice, making the marinade taste balanced but full-flavored. The heat of the steak softened the garlic enough to keep it from tasting raw, yet I didn't have to worry about burning the bits as I did when cooking the garlic with the meat.

Returning the sliced meat to the marinade caused one small problem — the acid eventually turned the steak gray. For that reason, if you don't plan to eat it all in a single sitting, don't return the meat to the marinade, and pass the marinade separately at the table.

I liked this technique equally well for chicken breasts, and since they are fully cooked and will not change color, the chicken can be sliced and returned to the lime-garlic sauce with no problem.

HOW TO COOK THE VEGETABLES? IT DEPENDS

How I cooked the peppers and onions for fajitas depended on how I cooked the steak. For pan-searing, I decided to cook the peppers and onions in the same skillet I cooked the steak or chicken in. There's enough rendered fat from the meat to sauté the vegetables, and since some of the cumin inevitably stays in the pan, the vegetables pick up that flavoring as well.

So that I didn't end up trying to cook simultaneously indoors and out, I grilled the vegetables for grilled steak or chicken. Since the vegetables need to be cut larger to keep them from falling through the rack, they take a little longer to cook. I grilled them before cooking the meat, then transferred them to the coal-less side of the grill to keep them warm.

Besides the peppers and onions, I liked only two toppings: sour cream and a bit of mashed avocado seasoned with salt and a little lime juice. Salsa just wet-blanketed the wonderful flavors of the meat, marinade, and vegetables.

Success! I had developed a fajita so streamlined that it can easily be served for weeknight dinners but special enough to please guests.

- Start by preheating a large (12-inch) cast-iron or heavy-bottomed nonstick skillet over medium-low heat for about 10 minutes.

- While the skillet heats, season the steak or chicken, cut 2 peppers and an onion into wedges, and make the lime-garlic marinade.

- A few minutes before cooking, increase the heat to high and turn on the exhaust fan. When the skillet starts to send up wisps of smoke, add the steak or chicken. While it cooks, prepare the mashed avocado and set out the sour cream.

- Pour the lime juice and garlic over the cooked steak or chicken and let it rest while cooking the peppers and onions.

- Heat the tortillas while slicing the meat, then serve immediately.

Fajitas with Pan-Seared Skirt Steak and Peppers and Onions

Serves 4 to 6

There are many ways to warm tortillas, but heating them briefly in the microwave is the simplest. Stack the number needed for the first round between paper towels and place them in a microwave-safe plastic bag. Microwave on high for 20 to 30 seconds. Repeat when everyone is ready for more. By following the steps on the opposite page, you can be sitting down to dinner in 30 to 40 minutes.

1 skirt steak (about 1¹/₂ pounds), cut into 4 pieces (see page 48)

Vegetable oil

Salt and freshly ground black pepper

3–4 teaspoons ground cumin

3 medium garlic cloves, minced

3 tablespoons lime juice

1¹/₂ medium red onions, root end left intact, halved lengthwise, each half cut into 6 wedges

1¹/₂ each medium red and green bell peppers, halved, seeded, and cut into 6 wedges

8–12 large flour tortillas, warmed (see note above)

1 cup sour cream

2 avocados, mashed and seasoned with lime juice and salt

1   Heat oven to lowest setting; at the same time, heat a large (12-inch) cast-iron or heavy-bottomed nonstick skillet over medium-low heat.

2   Meanwhile, coat both sides of each piece of steak with just enough oil to get the seasonings to stick. Sprinkle each side with salt, pepper, and some cumin.

3   Mix garlic and lime juice in a shallow, nonreactive baking pan, such as a Pyrex, and set near stove.

4   A few minutes before cooking, increase heat to high and turn on exhaust fan. When pan starts to send up wisps of smoke, add the 2 thickest pieces of steak. Cook until seared on first side, about 3 minutes. Turn and cook on other side until seared, 2 to 3 minutes longer for medium. Transfer to marinade; turn to completely coat and place in warm oven. Add remaining 2 pieces of steak to hot skillet. Cook until seared, about 2 minutes per side for medium doneness. Transfer to marinade and turn to coat. Place in warm oven.

5   Pour off all but 2 tablespoons fat from skillet. Add onions and peppers, and sauté until crisp-tender, about 8 minutes.

6   Slice meat thinly against the grain. Transfer to a platter, along with peppers and onions. If you are planning to eat everything at one sitting, pour lime marinade over meat. If not, pour marinade into a small bowl and pass separately, along with tortillas, sour cream, and avocado.

If pan-searing, halve the skirt steak into four 5-to-7-by-4-inch pieces.

Pan-Seared Chicken Fajitas

Serves 4 to 6

If you can't find skirt steak, chicken fajitas are far superior to other cuts of beef.

Follow preceding recipe, substituting 4 boneless, skinless chicken breasts, tenderloins removed and breasts lightly pounded to an even thickness (see page 23). Pan-sear breasts until crusted on one side, about 3 minutes. After turning chicken breasts, add tenderloins and cook, turning once, until cooked through, about 3 minutes. Continue cooking chicken breasts until other side has crusted and cooked through, 2 to 3 minutes longer. Continue as directed.

Fajitas with Charcoal-Grilled Skirt Steak and Peppers and Onions

Serves 4 to 6

Most gas grills don't produce enough heat to sear the steaks well. It's better, I think, to sear the steaks in a hot skillet rather than try to cook them on a gas grill.

1 skirt steak (about 1¹/₂ pounds), halved to make 2 pieces
Vegetable oil
Salt and freshly ground black pepper
3–4 teaspoons ground cumin
3 medium garlic cloves, minced
3 tablespoons lime juice
1¹/₂ medium red onions, root end left intact, halved lengthwise, each half cut lengthwise into thick wedges
1¹/₂ each medium red and green bell peppers, halved, seeded, and cut into large wedges

8–12 flour tortillas, warmed (see note on page 47)
1 cup sour cream
2 avocados, mashed and seasoned with lime juice and salt

1 Build a hot fire by heating 5 pounds of charcoal (I use a large chimney starter) until covered with white ash. Remove grill rack and pour or rake coals onto one half of grill. Return grill rack and put lid on grill to let rack get hot.

2 Meanwhile, coat both sides of each piece of steak with just enough oil to get the seasonings to stick. Sprinkle each side with salt, pepper, and some cumin, rubbing seasonings into meat.

3 Mix garlic and lime juice in a shallow, nonreactive baking pan, such as a Pyrex; set near grill.

4 Drizzle onions and peppers with enough oil to coat, and sprinkle with salt and pepper. Place onions on grill rack along edge of fire and place peppers on rack directly over coals. Grill peppers, turning once, until brown-spotted and crisp-tender, 4 to 5 minutes; move peppers to opposite, cooler side of grill when cooked. Grill onions, turning once until brown-spotted on both cut surfaces and crisp-tender, about 10 minutes.

5 While onions finish cooking, place steak over coals and grill until seared on both sides, about 4 minutes total for thinner portion, and 5 to 6 minutes total for thicker portion. (Because of hot fire and steak's surface fat, fire may flare. If so, place lid on grill until flames subside or make sure you have a squirt bottle handy.)

6 Place steak in lime-garlic marinade and turn to coat evenly; let meat rest in marinade for 5 minutes. Transfer peppers and onions to a serving platter.

Slice meat thin and transfer to platter of peppers and onions. If you plan to eat everything in one sitting, pour lime marinade over meat. If not, pour marinade into a small bowl and pass separately, along with tortillas, sour cream, and avocado.

Charcoal-Grilled Chicken Fajitas

Serves 4 to 6

Follow preceding recipe, substituting 4 boneless, skinless chicken breasts, tenderloins removed and breasts lightly pounded to an even thickness (see page 23). Grill chicken breasts and tenderloins, turning once, until crusted and cooked through, about 3 minutes per side for breasts and about 2 minutes per side for tenderloins. Continue as directed.

My mixed pedigree includes no Italian ancestors. Yet, when I need to serve supper for a crowd, spaghetti and meatballs is among the dishes that naturally come to mind. And why shouldn't it? Except for cooking the pasta, spaghetti and meatballs is do-ahead and a festive, fun (and economical!) way to serve a crowd. But this dish is not without its problems. Without an Italian mama's guiding touch, many who attempt to make meatballs end up instead with rubber balls, mushy balls, bland balls, blond balls, dry balls, or balls that fall apart.

For those who ultimately master the meatball, there's still the rich meat sauce, often called Sunday gravy, to consider. Needing hours of simmering time to tenderize the tough hunks of pork and beef that richly flavor it, the sauce may be the real barrier to making spaghetti and meatballs. To perfect this dish, I wanted to develop a foolproof meatball that was light and tender, yet meaty-flavored and substantial. And I wanted a rich sauce that tasted as if it had simmered all day rather than the 30 minutes I actually spent making it.

THE MEAT PART OF THE BALL

From the many recipes analyzed, I developed a composite meatball formula — one that represented the typical recipe. As I made my way down the list, I tested the extremes of each ingredient, but here's the formula from which I began:

1   pound ground meat
$\frac{1}{2}$ cup fresh bread, soaked in $\frac{1}{4}$ cup milk and squeezed dry
1   egg
$\frac{1}{4}$ cup grated Parmesan cheese
1   garlic clove, minced
2   tablespoons minced fresh parsley
Salt and freshly ground black pepper

Since meat makes up the largest percentage of the ball, I started by making meatballs from every meat and meat combination I had seen in my research, including:

Ground beef

Ground pork

Ground veal

Ground turkey

Ground beef with the addition of minced prosciutto

$^2/_3$ ground beef and $^1/_3$ sweet Italian sausage

$^1/_2$ each ground beef and veal

$^1/_2$ each ground beef and pork

$^1/_2$ each ground veal and pork

$^1/_2$ ground beef and $^1/_4$ each veal and pork

$^1/_3$ each ground beef, veal, and pork

$^1/_3$ each ground turkey, beef, and ham

As I suspected, none of the meats alone produced the perfect meatball. All-beef balls were dark, coarse, and chewy. Despite their firm, substantial texture, all-pork meatballs lacked flavor and color. Ditto for the meatball made with all veal.

Those who don't eat red meat will be pleased to know that the turkey meatballs were assertively flavored, if a bit gamey, with decent texture. And although I thought it tasted unappetizing plain, the turkey meatball's flavor was much improved after simmering in tomato sauce. Not my ideal, but a good option. The beef/prosciutto combination sounded like a good idea, but the resulting meatball was coarse-textured and livery, with hard bits of prosciutto getting in the way. I also wanted to like the mix of Italian sausage and beef, but blended together, the competing flavors sent a confusing message. Much like surf and turf, beef and sausage may belong on the same plate, but not in the same bite.

Except for the veal/pork mix, which was too mild, most of the beef/veal/pork combinations made good meatballs. But because of its wide availability, I ultimately chose equal parts beef, pork, and veal, also known as "meat loaf mix." Meatballs need a mix of meat: beef for meatiness, pork for subtle, supporting flavor and fine, yet toothsome texture, and veal for tenderness.

In addition to determining the right meat mix, I made three observations from that first set of tests. Up to this point, for convenience, I had roasted the meatballs in a 450-degree oven rather than browning them in a skillet. The roasted meatballs, however, lacked a flavorful, meaty crust. It appeared the perfect meatball would have to be pan-fried. All the meatballs were too dense. And finally, adding raw rather than cooked garlic gave the meatballs a harsh biting flavor.

Many cookbook authors joke about the large quantities of bread added to stretch meatballs during hard times. Meatballs made without any filler, however, are dense and coarse-textured. To determine how much and which bread, crumb, or cracker ideally softened the meatball without interfering with its meaty flavor, I ran a series of tests. A few recipes used ricotta or mozzarella cheese in the filler role, and I tried them, too.

Although I found no published meatball recipes calling for saltine crackers, I knew from experience they made a great filler, and they made flavorful, tender meatballs as well. Meatballs made with the day-old and fresh Italian bread were good, the ones made with the older bread seemingly more tender than those made with fresh. For so little improvement, however, I didn't want to have to "stale" bread for twenty-four hours. Meatballs made with store-bought dry bread crumbs were a little dense, but flavorful. I could neither complain about nor recommend the meatballs made with soft white bread or the firmer sandwich bread. Both the mozzarella- and ricotta-filled meatballs were dense and rubbery.

Since cracker crumbs bordered on heretical in a meatball recipe, I decided to perform another round of tests before declaring it the winner. Working with the three finalists — dry bread crumbs, fresh Italian bread crumbs, and saltine crackers — I made meatballs with differing quantities of filler to determine the correct ratio of bread to meat. Up to this point, I had been testing meatballs with a ratio of $1/2$ cup fresh bread (or $1/4$ cup dry bread crumbs) per pound of meat. This time, I tried increasing the fresh bread to $3/4$ cup and to $1^1/2$ cups per pound of meat, and I upped the dry bread crumbs and crackers to $1/2$ cup and to 1 cup per pound.

From these tests I confirmed that the higher the ratio of bread — whether dry or fresh — the softer, mushier, and blander the ball. Once again, crackers scored high, enhancing rather than diluting the ball's meaty flavor. Since meatballs made with $1/4$ cup cracker crumbs seemed a little dry and $1/2$ cup bordered on mushy, the ideal quantity of cracker crumbs seemed somewhere in between — $1/3$ cup, I suspected.

Which liquid moistened the best, and how many, if any, eggs did the mixture need to bind?

Although some meatball recipes called for as many as 4 eggs per pound of meat, I found that even 2 eggs resulted in an overly soft meatball with no bite or chew. Since meatballs made with no egg fell apart when cut with a fork, I stuck to the 1 egg per pound of meat that I had been using all along.

A meatball needs some liquid to keep it moist, but must the liquid be distinctively flavored? Happily, I discovered that it does not. Of all the liquids — milk, buttermilk, lemon juice, red wine, and chicken broth — none allowed the flavors of the meat, Parmesan cheese, garlic, and herbs to shine more than just plain water.

Regardless of the liquid, I faced one consistent problem. Up to this point, I had soaked all of the fillers, and the resulting meatballs were mushy and so tender that they were apt to fall apart during cooking. To remedy the problem, I tried mixing the crushed cracker crumbs with the meat, cheese, herbs, and flavorings and mixing the water with the egg. It worked. The meatballs were light and tender, yet meaty.

Nearly all Italian-style meatballs call for Parmesan or Romano cheese or a mix of the two. Was one better than the other? How much was right? Did an $18 per pound aged Parmigiano-Reggiano wedge produce a better meatball than the domestic pre-grated variety? Since the differences were minor and since I always have Parmesan cheese on hand, I chose Parmesan. And the meatballs made with the fresh-grated aged Parmigiano-Reggiano weren't any better than the pre-grated aged cheese that most grocery stores sell in a tub or plastic bag.

My original meatball formula called for $1/4$ cup cheese per pound of meat. One half cup cheese did not improve the formula, and an excessive 1 cup gave the meatballs a hard, gritty texture, so $1/4$ cup it was.

AROMATICS AND FLAVORINGS

Since the raw garlic was too obvious, I made meatballs flavored with sautéed garlic, raw and sautéed onions, raw scallions, and raw and sautéed green and red bell peppers. None of the aromatics I tried was satisfying. The sautéed garlic was too mild. Same with onion: raw was too strong, sautéed was too sweet. Scallions gave the meatballs an Asian feel, as though they should be served with sweet and sour sauce. I was reminded of stuffed green peppers when I tasted both the raw and sautéed green pepper–flavored meatballs, while the red bell pepper was barely noticeable.

I was happy to give up on all of the aromatics except garlic. Toasting the unpeeled garlic cloves in a small, dry skillet for just a few minutes took away the raw bite without excessively taming the flavor.

In addition to the aromatics, there were other meatball flavorings to consider as well: fresh and dried basil, fresh and dried oregano, dried thyme, sun-dried tomatoes, spinach, anchovies, Worcestershire, roasted peppers, tomato paste, and mozzarella (not grated, but as a cube inside the ball). Buying fresh herbs for meatballs isn't worth the money, since small quantities of the dried ones come through more clearly. And although dried thyme tasted fine, basil and oregano won for authenticity.

I also tried spinach, which added moisture, but its flavor was barely recognizable. Anchovies made saltier but not better meatballs. Worcestershire was clearly out of place. As the mozzarella cube melted and oozed out of the meatball, I declared it a gimmick. Sun-dried tomatoes and roasted red peppers tasted nice, but were too distinct. Other than dried basil and oregano, tomato paste was the only flavoring that enhanced the meatball without overpowering it.

"MEATMALLOWS"

I still needed to figure out the best way to shape and cook the meatballs. Roasting the meatballs at 450 degrees for 15 minutes was certainly simple and required no extra fat, but they tended to overcook and dry out before they browned.

Pan-fried meatballs developed an impressive brown crust and remained moist and tender, but round balls need endless flipping, rolling, turning, and general babying to brown evenly. Since I preferred pan-frying, I slightly altered the meatball's shape from round to a cylindrical marshmallow shape. Cooked in a generous film of oil, the bottom, top, and most of the sides brown with just one turn.

Forming meat into this squatty cylinder is simple. A 2-tablespoon coffee scoop is the ideal tool for the job. Fill the scoop with the meat mixture, then tap it out. As with ice cream, if the meat starts to stick to the scoop, just dip the scoop in water and continue.

Some meatball recipes call for coating the balls with flour or bread crumbs before cooking them. This extra step does indeed produce a crisp ball . . . until you drop it into the tomato sauce. And I did not prefer the smothered texture of the coated balls simmered in sauce.

FULL-FLAVORED SAUCE IN A FLASH

For developing a sweet, meaty-flavored sauce quickly, I knew I had only a few options. Some cooks flavor the sauce with ground meat, but I wanted a relatively smooth sauce. That left me with Italian sausage links, bacon, and prosciutto. While I was at the butcher's, I spied beef jerky and decided to give it a try as well.

After making a sauce with each meat, it was clear that beef jerky had very little impact. Even if I had increased the quantity, I'm not sure I would have liked the result. Bacon also made for a thin-flavored sauce with undesirable cured, smoky undertones. Italian sausage and prosciutto, however, were a different story. The sausage offered big, sweet, spicy meat flavor. Though more subtle, the prosciutto was very effective at seasoning the sauce as well. A combination of the two, I concluded, would give me a meaty-flavored sauce — quick.

With the Italian sausage addition, this recipe for spaghetti and meatballs serves four people for two meals: spaghetti and meatballs the first night, sausage with tomato sauce over polenta the next — or one large spaghetti and meatball dinner for eight.

Spaghetti and Meatballs
with Quick Meat Sauce

Serves 8

To make two meals, each serving four, out of this dish, change the recipe as follows: cool and refrigerate the fully cooked sausage and half of the sauce. Heat 2 quarts of water for the spaghetti in a large pot. Add 1 tablespoon salt and cook 1 pound of spaghetti. Drain and toss with half of the sauce and turn into a large serving bowl. Top with the remaining sauce and meatballs and serve. Serve the sausages for another meal. I like them with polenta.

MEATBALLS

3 garlic cloves, unpeeled

1/4 cup olive oil for frying

1 pound meat loaf mix (equal parts
    ground beef, pork, and veal)

1/4 cup grated Parmesan cheese

9 saltine crackers, finely crushed

Heaping 1/2 teaspoon salt

1/4 teaspoon freshly ground black pepper

1/2 teaspoon dried basil

1/4 teaspoon dried oregano

1 large egg

1 teaspoon tomato paste

QUICK TOMATO SAUCE

1 1/2 pounds Italian sausages, cut into approximately
    4-inch lengths

Pan drippings and oil from meatballs and sausage

5 garlic cloves, minced

2 ounces thinly sliced prosciutto, diced

2 cans (28 ounces each) crushed tomatoes

Salt and freshly ground black pepper

1 tablespoon chopped fresh parsley (optional)

2 tablespoons salt

2 pounds spaghetti

Use a 2-tablespoon coffee scoop to form the meatballs, rinsing the scoop occasionally, if necessary, to keep the meatballs from sticking.

Or, to shape the meatballs by hand, form a circle with your thumb and index finger and press 2 tablespoons of the meat mix into a drum shape.

1 **FOR MEATBALLS:** Heat a small skillet over medium-high heat. Add garlic cloves and toast until skins are brown-spotted and garlic flavor has softened, about 5 minutes. Remove from skillet, peel, mince, and set aside.

2 Heat oil over low heat in a large Dutch oven. In a medium bowl, break up meat into small clumps to facilitate mixing. Add garlic, cheese, cracker crumbs, salt, pepper, basil, and oregano; mix lightly with a fork to combine. In another bowl, whisk $^1/_4$ cup water, egg, and tomato paste until paste dissolves. Add egg mixture to meat mixture; mix lightly with fingers until thoroughly combined. Following illustration, form meat into drum shapes (you should have 20 to 24 meatballs).

3 A couple of minutes before frying meatballs, increase heat to medium-high. Add meatballs to pan in batches, if necessary, to avoid overcrowding. Cook, turning once with tongs, until browned on both sides, about 5 minutes total. Transfer to a plate and set aside. Meanwhile, bring 4 quarts water to a boil for spaghetti in a large pot.

4 **FOR TOMATO SAUCE:** Using the same pan that you cooked meatballs in, reduce heat to medium. Add sausages and cook, turning frequently, until nicely browned but not fully cooked, about 5 minutes. Transfer to a plate and set aside. Add garlic and prosciutto to drippings in pan. Cook, scraping brown bits from pan, until garlic is fragrant and starts to turn golden, about 2 minutes. Stir in tomatoes and enough water ($1/2$ to 1 cup, but additions will vary depending on brand of tomatoes) to make a sauce that is neither gloppy nor watery. Return sausages to pan, bring to a simmer, partially cover pan, then cook over low heat until sauce tastes sweet, rich, and meaty, 15 to 20 minutes. Season to taste with salt, if necessary, pepper, and parsley, if using.

5 Transfer sausages to a plate; cover and keep warm. Add meatballs to sauce and return to a simmer. Partially cover and simmer until meatballs are fully cooked and flavors blend, about 10 minutes. While meatballs cook, add salt and spaghetti to boiling water and cook spaghetti until tender, 7 to 9 minutes. Transfer meatballs to a plate. Drain spaghetti and return to pot. Toss with half of sauce, then transfer to a large, shallow serving bowl. Top with remaining sauce, arranging meatballs on top and sausages around the perimeter. Serve immediately.

8 STEPS TO DINNER

You can make this dish and sit down to enjoy it in less than 1½ hours. Here's how:

1. Start by toasting the garlic in a small, dry skillet for 5 minutes.
2. While the garlic toasts, gather and prepare the meatball ingredients.
3. While making and forming the meatballs, put the pan for cooking them on low heat. When you're a few minutes away from cooking the meatballs, increase the heat to medium-high.
4. Working in two batches, brown the meatballs on both sides.
5. While the meatballs fry, bring the spaghetti water to a boil and cut the sausages into 4-inch lengths.
6. Set the cooked meatballs aside and brown the sausages in the skillet. Remove them and add the minced garlic and prosciutto, and cook until the garlic softens. Then add the tomatoes, water, and seasonings, and bring to a simmer.
7. After the sausages have cooked in the sauce for 15 minutes, remove and keep them warm, and simmer the meatballs in the sauce for about 10 minutes.
8. While the meatballs cook, boil the spaghetti, then drain and dump it into a large pasta bowl. Toss with a little of the tomato sauce, arrange the sausages around the edge, then spoon the meatballs and remaining sauce on top.

used to love pot roast. It seemed that no matter how long or at what temperature I cooked it, the roast was always beefy-flavored, moist, and fall-apart tender. Or at least, that's the way I remember it.

My recent roasts have not measured up to memories. More often, they taste anemic and dry, with weak, flavorless gravy. Unfortunately, it's the beef, not my cooking ability, that has changed. In recent decades, cattle ranchers have bred so much fat out of the beef that pot roast has become a dish we fondly remember but can't seem to replicate.

This fat reduction may look good on paper, but in reality, it has dramatically changed the way many of our once favorite roasts cook and taste. Because of bad cooking experiences, many of us have gradually shied away from cuts we used to buy regularly, including those for pot-roasting. After cooking one too many failures, I had almost decided to add pot roast to my growing list of extinct classics.

Starting this project, I wasn't sure perfect pot roast existed, but at the very least, the meat had to taste beefy and be tender and well lubricated (no sawdust-textured meat for me), and the pan juices had to be simply but intensely flavorful. The technique had to be easy, and although I was prepared for long cooking, I hoped the roast wouldn't take the better half of a day to get done.

WHERE HAVE ALL THE CUTS GONE?

Since there were so many pot-roasting candidates, I decided to start with the various cuts to see if some were better than others. Based on recipe research, I set out to find fifteen or so different ones. Besides sirloin tip and brisket, most of the pot-roasting candidates came from the round (top round, bottom round, rump, eye of the round) and from the chuck (7-bone, blade, under blade, cross rib, mock tender, boneless shoulder roast, arm pot roast, chuck eye roast, and neck pot roast).

After talking with the National Beef Council, I disqualified top round as too lean for braising. I had no problem locating the sirloin tip, the brisket, or any of the cuts from the round. But after checking with several supermarkets and butchers, I discovered that in many areas of the country, the individual cuts of chuck are no longer as common as they once were and have been replaced by the generic "boneless chuck roast."

With four roasts from the round, the sirloin tip, the brisket, and a couple of boneless chuck roasts, I spent the first day trying to settle on the right cut. My method was standard: Coat the meat with oil and season it liberally with salt and pepper. Brown the meat on each side until a solid crust has formed. Remove meat, add 2 cups onions, and sauté until tender and golden brown. Add $1/2$ cup wine; return the roast to the pan. Cover and cook over very low heat until tender.

I simmered the pot roasts on the stovetop, rather than in the oven. Cooked by this method, however, they took forever to get tender. At an internal temperature of 200 degrees, the roasts were finally approaching fork tenderness, but by this time, the meat was dry and chalky-textured. The exception was the sirloin tip roast, the only one that was tender at a relatively low 160 degrees. But it had the look and taste of overcooked roast beef instead of pot roast. After cooking twenty-five pounds of meat, I hadn't made a single successful roast.

The brisket's thin, large, awkward shape made it difficult to cook. Bottom round was lean and as dense as a rock. The meat from the rump shredded rather than sliced and was dense and dry. The eye of the round was the least tasty of all. Although far from perfect, the chuck roast had promise, however. At least it was relatively beefy-flavored and the most tender of the lot.

MUSCLE PROFILING

BRISKET: Located just below the chuck near the front leg, brisket tastes beefy and braises well but isn't the cut most associated with pot roast. Its long, thin shape makes cooking awkward, and its large quantity of connective tissue makes the meat chewier than most people like for pot roast.

ROUND: From the animal's hindquarters, the round is generally not good for pot-roasting. Whether top round, bottom round, rump, or eye of the round, the fibers in these muscles are tightly bound with virtually no marbling. With the fibers tightly packed and very little fat to lubricate them and distribute the flavor, cuts from this area tend to make dry, flavorless pot roasts.

CHUCK: Located in the shoulder, the chuck is made up of more individual muscles, which are smaller than those of other cuts. And since most muscles are surrounded by fat, smaller muscles mean more fat. Many of the most tender muscles on the animal are located in the chuck.

CHECK THE CHUCK

Not all chuck roasts are good for pot-roasting. The following visual cues are helpful in making a selection. To choose a roast with the right look, see the illustration on page 63.

- Choose a chuck roast that's flat and steak-shaped. There are only two large sides to a steak-shaped roast, which means you'll need to turn it only once to brown it. Torpedo-shaped roasts need 4 turns. Box-shaped roasts need as many as 6 turns.
- Choose a thin roast. The thinner the roast, the more quickly and evenly it cooks.
- Choose a roast that's well marbled. Each muscle should be well streaked with fat throughout. Without it, even served with pan juice or gravy, the roast itself will still taste dry.
- Choose a roast with a substantial amount of fat between each muscle.
- Choose a roast with as few muscles as possible. (You can recognize a muscle easily, for it's a distinct section of meat with a particular grain. Individual muscles are usually encased in a thin frame of fat that separates them from other muscles.) Different muscles cook at different rates, so the fewer muscles a roast has, the more likely it will be to cook evenly.

BLAST THE SUCKER

Even though my cooking method wasn't perfect, I had at least selected the pot-roasting cut with the most potential. Having grown up on roasts simmered in the crock pot, I thought this method might produce a tender, succulent roast, but it didn't. Although convenient, cooking the beef in this way produced a bland, dry roast with relatively flavorless pan juices.

Since low heat seemed a dead end at this point, I headed in the opposite direction, trying an unusual technique and cooking method described in Madeleine Kamman's *The New Making of a Cook* (Morrow, 1997). After seasoning and browning the roast, cooking the onions, adding the wine, and returning the roast to the pot, I covered the pot with foil, as she instructed, pressing on it to form "an upside-down dome lid." Following her directions, I tucked the edges of the foil tightly against the outside of the pot, then covered the pot with the lid, creating an almost airtight environment.

Sealed in foil and cooked in a 350-degree oven, my 1³/₄-pound roast reached an internal temperature of 205 degrees in about an hour. Although I saw that I would have to tinker with the method, the roast was far better than any I had prepared up to this point — and it was fast. The pot roast liquid caught my attention first. Instead of watery pan juices that needed beefing up and enlivening, I had a gorgeous pan reduction. Although the roast was slightly chewy, it was relatively moist and tender. And unlike many of the cardboard-textured pot roasts I had tasted in the past few days, this one was clearly beef.

Just to see if the inverted foil dome mattered, I cooked another roast at 350 degrees without the foil. Clearly, it did make a difference. Compared with the roast cooked under the concave dome, the meat crept to doneness. And the resulting roast was dry, with a significantly less intense gravy.

Fascinated with this technique, I tried it several times at oven temperatures ranging from 200 degrees to 500 degrees. Cooked at any lower temperature, the roast was chewy and anemic, with watery juices and mediocre flavor. The higher the temperature, however, the better — up to a point. Cooked in a 500-degree oven, the roast was tender but overly brown. And since the roast had cooked on the bottom oven rack, the high direct heat caused the liquid to evaporate and some of the onions to burn. By lowering the oven temperature to 450 degrees and adjusting the oven rack to the center position, I made one of the most delicious pot roasts I had ever tasted. Best of all, it didn't require any special equipment. All I needed was an oven, a pot, and a piece of heavy-duty foil.

Testing the roast several times, I realized that its internal temperature was less important than the oven time. In cooking several chuck roasts (2 to 2¹⁄₂ pounds on average), I never went wrong with 1¹⁄₂-hour oven time. Smaller, thinner roasts can be pulled a little sooner; larger roasts may need a few minutes more.

WHY HIGH-HEAT POT-ROASTING WORKS

Long, low heat is the most common cooking method for pot roast. So how can pot roast cooked at 450 degrees be so tender and juicy? According to Melvin Hunt, professor of Animal Science at Kansas State University, the airtight foil dome, in combination with the high oven temperature, creates a modified pressure cooker. The higher pressure increases the temperature at which water boils, allowing the meat to cook to a higher temperature before the water starts to evaporate, resulting in a juicier roast. Pressure also increases the humidity in the pot. The higher the humidity and the temperature, the more quickly the tough connective tissue known as collagen gelatinizes, or softens.

Be careful cooking the roast much longer, however. To create intense pan juices, minimal liquid is used. If the roast is cooked for another 20 to 30 minutes, the pan juices will evaporate and the onions will caramelize and eventually burn.

Marinades of beer, wine, or wine/vinegar did not improve the roast's texture or flavor. Coating the roast with flour before browning, as some recipes suggest, did nothing but prevent the formation of a good crust. Studding the meat with garlic, however, made the roast even better. If slipped far enough into the meat, the garlic slivers soften, giving a sweet flavor and a soft, creamy texture. Cooked under such high heat, any exposed slivers tend to char and taste burned, so they must be buried deep.

After four long days of pot-roasting, I had finally found the ideal cut and cooking method that gave me a great dinner in about 90 minutes.

90-Minute Pot Roast with Rich Red Wine and Onion Gravy

You'll need a roast that is visibly streaked with fat not just around but throughout each muscle. If your pan is not heavy-bottomed, brown the roast and onions on medium-high rather than high heat. If you like vegetables with pot roast, steam the vegetables of your choice (carrots, celery, turnips, and potatoes are obvious candidates) until tender. Add them to the gravy in step 5 while you are slicing the roast, and cook until heated through.

2 tablespoons vegetable oil, plus more if needed
1 flat, boneless chuck roast (2–2½ pounds), with as few muscles as possible, a generous amount of fat separating those muscles, and as much marbling as possible, patted dry with a paper towel
   Salt and freshly ground black pepper
2 medium-large onions, halved and thinly sliced (about 2 cups)
1¼–1½ cups dry red wine
1 tablespoon cornstarch *or* 2 tablespoons flour
2 cups chicken broth

Choose a chuck roast that is flat and boneless, with as few muscles as possible, a generous amount of fat separating the muscles, and as much marbling as possible.

1   Adjust oven rack to middle position and heat oven to 450 degrees. Set a heavy-bottomed, nonreactive Dutch oven over medium heat while you prepare meat and onions.

2   Pour oil into a medium bowl (or onto Styrofoam tray, if roast came with it), add roast, and turn to coat. Generously sprinkle both sides of roast with salt and pepper. A couple of minutes before you plan to brown roast, turn heat to high.

3   Add roast to Dutch oven, cook on one side until a solid brown crust forms, about 5 minutes. Turn roast over, and cook until other side also forms a crust, about 5 minutes longer. Remove roast from pot. Tilt pot. If meat has not rendered 1 tablespoon fat, add enough oil to the pot to equal about 1 tablespoon. Add onions and sauté until soft and golden brown around edges, about 5 minutes. Add wine (the smaller amount if Dutch oven is $9^1/_2$ inches in diameter, the larger amount if it is wider than $9^1/_2$ inches); simmer for about 1 minute to burn off alcohol.

4   Return pot roast to pot and turn off heat. Following illustration, cover pot with heavy-duty foil. Place lid snugly on pot. Return pot to burner and cook over medium-high heat until you hear juices bubbling. Set pot in oven and cook for 1 hour and 20 minutes for a small roast, or about $1^1/_2$ hours for a larger roast, until roast is dark brown and tender and onions and pan juices are nicely brown and caramelized. Remove from oven and let stand, covered, for 10 to 15 minutes.

Use a potholder or towel when covering the pot with a sheet of heavy-duty foil, pressing on the foil so that it is concave and touches the roast. Seal completely around the edges.

5 Carefully remove lid and foil from pot, then remove roast to a plate. Skim fat from surface, if you like, and heat onions and drippings over medium-high heat. Mix cornstarch or flour with chicken broth and add to drippings. Simmer, scraping pot sides and bottom to loosen brown bits, until thickened slightly, 2 to 3 minutes. Return roast to pot to simmer for a minute or two. Remove roast from juices. Cut into thin slices, making sure that you are cutting against, not with, grain. Transfer meat to a platter or individual plates and spoon some juices over meat. Serve immediately, passing remaining juices separately.

Most of us like the idea of pork tenderloin. Like beef tenderloin, it's elegant enough to serve to guests. Like chicken breast, it's moderately priced and healthful enough for a weeknight dinner. It's mild enough to be rubbed, sauced, or marinated like fish or chicken. And it's meaty enough to be treated like the big boys: lamb and beef.

In reality, though, pork tenderloins are not all that easy to cook, especially if you want to cook them whole. Their convenient size turns out to be part of the problem; they're too small to be treated like a roast and too large to be treated like a steak. They need a combination of direct and indirect heat — direct heat to give them a tasty, thick crust for flavor; indirect heat to finish cooking them gently all the way through.

No indoor method supplies that. Roasting certainly doesn't. Unlike the average roast, the tenderloin weighs no more than a pound and is fully cooked before a crust has even begun to develop, regardless of oven temperature. Pan-searing takes forever and involves frequent turning. Most broiler heating elements are too weak, taking 20 to 30 minutes to do the job and cooking the pork unevenly.

COOK PORK TENDERLOIN LIKE A STEAK, THEN LIKE A ROAST

Cooking the tenderloins on a covered grill is the ideal solution. And since I don't usually go to the trouble of lighting a charcoal fire for two pork tenderloins, the gas grill is my

PORK TENDERLEAN

Pork tenderloin was a cut developed in the late 1970s, when processors started to market boneless pork loin. Attached to the pork loin along the pig's back, the tenderloin is one of the least exercised and therefore most tender of muscles. Because of its location at the leaner end of the loin (as opposed to the fattier rib end), it is also quite low in fat. A 3-ounce portion of tenderloin contains only 4.1 grams of fat, compared with 3.1 grams for a boneless, skinless chicken breast of the same size.

choice. Unlike a broiler, a gas grill preheated to high with the lid down can effectively cook a pork tenderloin with direct heat (like a steak) and indirect heat (like a roast) simultaneously.

To develop an impressive crust, it's best to turn the tenderloins only once. If the grill has been preheated for 10 minutes and all burners are on high, the tenderloins should be fully seared with impressive grill marks on one side in just 7 minutes. The second sides don't take as long as the first and brown in 6 minutes.

At this point, the pork tenderloins are so close to being done and the grill is so hot that it can be turned off and the lid closed. In just 5 minutes, the residual heat will fully cook any tenderloin.

For me, fully cooked means that a meat thermometer, inserted into the thickest section of the tenderloin, registers a safe 145 to 150 degrees (see below).

Cooked this way, pork tenderloins are as simple as 7, 6, 5 — 7 minutes on the

IS PINK PORK SAFE?

When I teach cooking classes, I'm always surprised at the number of students who won't touch pork that's been cooked to a pale pink, medium-well stage. They shy away from it for one of two reasons. Some simply prefer the texture of well-done food, whether it's lamb, beef, salmon, eggs, or pork. That I understand.

Those in the second group are simply afraid to eat pink pork. I understand that, too. After all, most of us were taught to cook by a generation that had good reason to cook pork beyond doneness. The pigs of our parents' or grandparents' time weren't fed a controlled grain-based diet as are today's pigs, so trichinosis was a real threat. Long cooking was the standard solution. If 2 hours was good, 3 was even better. In fact, "pork" was the last notch on the old meat thermometers, and the standard suggested internal temperature was 180 degrees. Nor was overcooked pork a problem back then, because there was enough fat on the meat to lubricate and flavor it.

Today's pork is different. It's safer, so there's no need to overcook it. It's also leaner, and overcooking will result in dry, sawdust-textured meat, particularly if you overcook cuts from the loin. There just isn't enough fat to trap and retain moisture.

The USDA lowered the recommended internal temperature for pork from 180 to 160 degrees, a temperature still too high for a lean cut like tenderloin. And there's no reason to cook tenderloin to that temperature. Trichinosis is virtually a nonissue today and, in any case, is killed at 137 degrees. In fact, according to the Pork Board, as long as the outside of the roast reaches 140 degrees within 4 hours, the pork tenderloin poses no risk. Since my pork tenderloins are seared over a hot fire and cooked to an internal temperature of between 145 and 150 degrees, they're safe.

If you don't eat pink pork because you don't like its texture, feel free to cook the pork tenderloins to 160 degrees or beyond. If you've avoided pink pork for safety reasons, fear no more.

first side, 6 minutes on the second, then 5 minutes with the grill turned off and the lid down. The method is so reliable that I can set a timer and go about my business. The tenderloins are so lean that there's no threat of a grill fire. For those who prefer charcoal grilling, the technique is similar.

Even when you cook them right, the flavor of tenderloins is fairly nondescript. Soaking them in salt/sugar brine causes them to absorb the sweet, salty water, making them juicy and seasoned throughout. When I'm in a hurry, I use a stronger solution and soak the tenderloins for 45 minutes. With this brine, the tenderloins taste a little salty on the surface, so I make sure I rinse them and pat them dry.

If it's Saturday or Sunday afternoon and I've got time, I halve the sugar and salt quantity and soak the tenderloins for 1$\frac{1}{2}$ hours. With this weaker brine, the tenderloins don't need to be rinsed but can simply be patted dry.

Painting the tenderloins with concentrates of fruit juice not only further flavors the pork but creates a subtly sweet surface that browns and caramelizes, resulting in an even more impressive crust. I've developed three different concentrates: orange, apple, and pineapple. Feel free to change and interchange the concentrates, spices, and herbs. For example, rosemary is equally good with orange or pineapple. Chili powder and cumin are great with orange juice. Try sage or herbes de Provence with any of the concentrates.

Quick Brined Pork Tenderloins

Makes 2 tenderloins

Tenderloins come two to a package. If you need just one, halve this recipe and freeze the other. Or since the meat is wonderful cold, cook, refrigerate, and serve in sandwiches.

If you have time and want to use less salt and sugar, you may want to let the tenderloins brine for 1½ hours instead of the 45 minutes recommended below, and omit the rinsing step. They can be brined in advance, as long as they're drained, rinsed, patted dry, and refrigerated. A little of the water that they absorbed during the soak may leach out, but they will still taste wonderfully seasoned.

½ cup kosher salt
½ cup sugar
1 package (about 2 pounds) pork tenderloins

Mix salt and sugar in 1 quart water in a medium bowl until dissolved. Place pork tenderloins in brine; let stand about 45 minutes. Remove tenderloins from brine; rinse thoroughly and pat dry. Continue with individual recipes on following pages.

Grilled Pork Tenderloins
with Curried-Apple Crust

For an optional drizzling sauce, mix $1/3$ cup Major Grey chutney with 4 teaspoons rice wine vinegar, adding freshly ground pepper and an optional teaspoon of minced fresh cilantro. Pass the sauce separately.

2　teaspoons vegetable oil
1　tablespoon curry powder
$1/4$　cup apple juice concentrate
　Quick Brined Pork Tenderloins (page 69), rinsed and
　　patted dry
　Freshly ground black pepper

1　Heat oil and curry powder in a small saucepan over medium heat. When mixture starts to sizzle and spices are fragrant, add concentrate. Simmer until mixture reduces to 2 to 3 tablespoons, 1 to 2 minutes. Brush each tenderloin all over with curry mixture, then sprinkle with pepper.

2　Meanwhile, heat gas grill, with all burners turned on high, until fully preheated, 10 to 15 minutes. Use a wire brush to clean grill rack, then brush lightly with oil; close lid and allow grill to return to temperature.

3　Place pork tenderloins on hot grill rack; close lid and grill-roast for 7 minutes. (Grill marks should form.) Turn tenderloins, close lid, and continue to sear until dark brown grill marks have formed on the other side, about 6 minutes longer. Close grill lid, turn off grill heat, and let meat continue to cook for 5 minutes longer. A meat thermometer inserted into thickest end of tenderloin should register between 145 and 150 degrees. If you don't like your pork pale pink (or if you want the pork well done), close lid and continue to cook until meat registers desired temperature, but not higher than 160 degrees. Remove tenderloins from grill and let rest for 5 minutes. Internal temperature will continue to rise during resting period.

4　Cut tenderloins into $1/2$-inch-thick slices and serve.

CHARCOAL-GRILLED PORK TENDERLOINS

If you don't own a gas grill or would rather charcoal-grill the pork tenderloins, the timing is the same. Simply heat 5 pounds of charcoal (a large chimney full of briquets) until covered with white ash. Remove grill rack and pour coals onto half of grill. Return grill rack and put lid on grill to let rack get hot. While coals are heating, prepare pork following instructions in step 1 of desired recipe. Place pork tenderloins over hot coals; with vent open, close lid and grill-roast for 7 minutes. At this time, grill marks should have formed. Turn tenderloins, close lid and grill-roast for 6 minutes longer. Transfer tenderloins to charcoal-less side of grill and continue to cook with vent closed and grill lid in place, 5 minutes longer. A meat thermometer inserted into thickest end should register between 145 and 150 degrees. If not (or if you want pork well done), close lid and continue to cook until meat registers desired temperature, but no higher than 160 degrees. Remove tenderloins from grill and let rest 5 minutes. Cut tenderloins into 1/2-inch-thick slices and serve immediately.

Grilled Pork Tenderloins
with Rosemary-Orange Crust

Serves 4 or 5

This pork is equally good made with 2 teaspoons dried rubbed sage instead of the rosemary.

1/4 cup orange juice concentrate

1 teaspoon brown sugar

4 teaspoons minced fresh rosemary

Quick Brined Pork Tenderloins (page 69), rinsed and patted dry

Freshly ground black pepper

OPTIONAL DRIZZLING SAUCE

1 teaspoon vegetable oil

2 garlic cloves, minced

1/2 teaspoon minced fresh rosemary

1/3 cup orange marmalade

4 teaspoons balsamic vinegar

1   Bring concentrate, brown sugar, and rosemary to a simmer in a small skillet. Simmer until mixture reduces to about 2 tablespoons. Brush each tenderloin all over with orange-herb mixture, then sprinkle with pepper.

2   Continue as directed in steps 2 and 3 of Grilled Pork Tenderloins with Curried-Apple Crust (page 70).

3   **FOR SAUCE, IF USING:** Heat oil, garlic, and rosemary in a small skillet over medium heat, stirring, until fragrant and sizzling. Stir in marmalade and vinegar and heat, stirring occasionally, until warm.

4   After tenderloins have rested, add any accumulated juices to sauce, cut tenderloin into 1/2-inch-thick slices, and serve, accompanied by sauce.

Grilled Pork Tenderloins
with Sweet Chili Crust

Serves 4 or 5

Even though commercial chili powders contain ground cumin, I find that adding a little extra improves and reinforces the flavor of most brands.

2   teaspoons vegetable oil
2   teaspoons chili powder
1/2 teaspoon ground cumin
1/4 cup pineapple juice concentrate
    Quick Brined Pork Tenderloins (page 69), rinsed and
        patted dry
    Freshly ground black pepper

1   Heat oil, chili powder, and cumin in a small skillet over medium heat. When mixture starts to sizzle and spices are fragrant, add concentrate. Simmer until mixture reduces to 2 to 3 tablespoons. Brush each tenderloin all over with mixture, then sprinkle with pepper.

2   Continue as directed in steps 2–4 of Grilled Pork Tenderloins with Curried-Apple Crust (page 70).

Grilled Pork Tenderloins
with Dijon–Black Pepper Crust

Serves 4 or 5

Mustard and pepper are a superb complement to pork.

Quick Brined Pork Tenderloins (page 69), rinsed and patted dry
3 **tablespoons Dijon mustard**
1¹/₂ **tablespoons coarsely ground black pepper**

1 Brush the tenderloins all over with mustard, then sprinkle with pepper.

2 Continue as directed in steps 2–4 of Grilled Pork Tenderloins with Curried-Apple Crust (page 70).

All-Purpose Salsa

Serves 4 or 5

This salsa can accompany any of the preceding pork tenderloin dishes and can be made with nearly any fruit.

1¹/₂ **cups fruit (peaches, nectarines, grapes, oranges, apricots, plums, pineapple, mangos, tomatoes, *or* avocados), cut into small dice, *or* 8 ounces frozen corn, thawed (about 1¹/₂ cups), *or* ³/₄ cup corn and ³/₄ cup black beans**
¹/₄ **medium red onion, cut into small dice, *or* 2 scallions, sliced thin**
¹/₄ **yellow or red bell pepper, cut into small dice**
1 **jalapeño or other hot pepper, stemmed, seeded, and minced**
1 **tablespoon minced fresh cilantro or parsley leaves**
2 **tablespoons juice from 1 lime or 2 tablespoons rice wine vinegar**
¹/₂ **teaspoon ground cumin or chili powder (optional)**
Salt and freshly ground black pepper to taste

Mix all ingredients in a medium bowl. Let stand so juices release and flavors blend, 10 to 15 minutes. (Salsa can be made up to 2 hours in advance.)

Blue-Ribbon Chili

grew up eating the same chili that almost everyone else of my generation did. You know the style. Sauté onion with a little garlic — maybe some green bell pepper. Add ground beef, canned tomatoes, water, chili powder, and salt and pepper. That's it. Made this way, chili is one of the friendliest dishes I know.

Then there's serious chili. The process of making it generally begins with toasting and grinding dried chile peppers and spices into homemade powder. Often the chili is made with little cubes of chuck roast or pork that must be carefully seared. These chilies usually require more time and effort than I can give.

The chili I hoped to develop would borrow from both styles. I wanted one that busy people like me could pull off with grocery store ingredients in a reasonable amount of time. I also wanted a chili that was a step up from the norm — one that would be special enough to serve to company on Super Bowl Sunday.

PORK 'N BEEF

The array of meat possibilities, spices, herbs, liquids, acids, sweeteners, aromatics, flavorings, techniques, tips, and lore was daunting. I started with a basic formula consisting of:

1^1/$_2$	cups chopped onion
6	minced garlic cloves
3	pounds meat
6	tablespoons chili powder
1^1/$_2$	teaspoons cumin
1^1/$_2$	teaspoons oregano
4	cups crushed tomatoes
2^1/$_4$	cups water

From previous experience, I knew that chuck is the most flavorful and succulent of all the cuts. Sirloin, flank, and skirt steak are tasty and tender and cook quickly, so I left them in the running, too. After selecting a range of ground meat and cubed meat, I tested the following:

Ground chuck, regular grind
Ground chuck, chili grind
Ground chuck and ground pork
Ground chuck and Italian sausage, removed from the casing
Ground meat loaf mix (equal parts ground beef, pork, and veal)
Ground turkey
Chuck roast, ground in the food processor
Chuck roast, cut into $1/2$-inch cubes
Chuck roast, cut into $1/2$-inch cubes, along with bacon
Chuck roast, cut into $1/2$-inch cubes, and ground beef
Sirloin, cut into $1/2$-inch cubes, and pork sausage
Sirloin, cut into $1/2$-inch cubes, and pork shoulder, cut into $1/2$-inch cubes

Searing a whole steak, then cutting it into cubes had potential as a timesaver, so I tried:

Flank steak, seared, then cut into cubes
Flank steak, seared, then cut into $1/2$-inch cubes and stewed with a pork chop, pork removed from the bone and shredded
Skirt steak, seared, then cut into strips

I couldn't argue with the chili made with regular ground chuck. It was comforting, familiar, and totally acceptable. The coarse chili-grind beef tasted partially chewed. Chuck ground in the food processor was good, but not worth the extra step. Both ground turkey and the meat loaf mix were too mild for the chili I hoped to develop.

Although chili made with beef cubes was more flavorful than chili made with ground beef, the little cubes were dry. The partnership of cubed and ground meat was confusing. Both sirloin and flank steak were dry and chewy. Skirt steak was tender and beefy and cooked quickly but felt a bit contrived. Bacon, Italian sausage, and bulk sausage were too distinct for my tastes, but plain cuts of pork added a compelling, rich, sweet flavor to the chili.

At this point, only ground chuck was satisfying — with pork support to be determined. For the moment, I decided to stick with ground chuck, but I would give my meat choice more thought as my chili took shape.

Onions and garlic were essential, but I had seen recipes calling for other aromatic vegetables: celery, bell peppers of all colors, carrots, pickled and fresh jalapeños, canned green chiles, and scallions. Could any of these improve the chili's flavor?

Sautéed at the beginning with the onions and garlic, vegetables like carrots, celery, and bell peppers cooked into the chilies, giving them a beef stew–like quality. Unlike garlic and onions that invisibly supported the chili, all three of these vegetables distracted from the meat and flavorings. Because of their distinct flavor and their dramatic effect on the chili, I decided to sauté the bell peppers and offer them at the table as a condiment. I felt the same about jalapeños, scallions, and canned green chiles. Treated like aromatics, they distracted from the chili's pure flavor. Used as condiments, they added life and color to an otherwise rich dish.

I got my best chili tip from Michael McLaughlin's *The Manhattan Chili Co. Southwest American Cookbook* (Crown, 1986). Instead of sautéing the garlic at the beginning, he stirs in raw minced cloves at the end. Added in this way, the garlic is potent and clear.

It's a good thing I didn't rely on my experience when choosing a liquid for the chili. Given a choice of canned beef or chicken broth, beef bouillon cubes, coffee, water, beer, or a water-wine combination to moisten the chili, I would have guessed chicken broth. And I would have guessed wrong.

I discovered that if you put enough beef, aromatics, tomatoes, and spices in the pot and simmer them long enough, the chili eventually creates its own flavorful broth. Therefore, water is good enough. If the chili needs help, however, bouillon cubes diluted in water are decent, as is a red wine–water combination (at a 1–3 ratio).

Canned beef broth, on the other hand, made the chili taste like a chain restaurant offering, while beer-enhanced chili tasted like the smell of a frat house on Saturday morning. Chicken broth, often the great unifier, stuck out. Strong coffee, I thought, might offer subtle complexity. Instead, it made the chili acidic and bitter.

Thus far, I had been using canned crushed tomatoes, but I'd seen chili recipes calling for nearly every variety of canned tomato product on the shelves. After testing representatives of each category, I stuck with the canned crushed kind. Diced canned tomatoes didn't break down in cooking. Diluted tomato paste, alone and in combination with tomato sauce, was reminiscent of Mom's spaghetti sauce — not bad, just not right.

Chili made with tomato juice was thin-textured and thin-flavored. Tomato sauce tasted tart, bordering on sour, while stewed tomatoes, much like the aromatic vegetables, made the chili taste too vegetal. Several recipes called for jarred salsa, but that chili was too zippy for my taste.

UNITY FROM CHOCOLATE

If I had tried all the herbs, spices, and flavorings I'd seen in chili recipes, I would have needed to pull every jar from the cabinet and still would have had to run to the store. Recipes made for chili competitions call for such unlikely spices as ginger, curry powder, turmeric, and mustard, as well as untraditional herbs such as basil, rosemary, and sage. Should I bother testing ingredients like orange liqueur and milk chocolate bars? I decided not to.

Instead, I tested common flavorings as well as those in the spirit of tradition. Although many were interesting, none panned out. Basil didn't clash, but it certainly wasn't essential. Thyme was too distinct and clearly didn't belong. Paprika added heat but little flavor. Coriander as well as fresh cilantro gave the chili a distinctly Thai feel. I decided to leave coriander out and add cilantro to the list of condiments.

A number of chili cooks add some form of chocolate to their chili. I tried cocoa powder, unsweetened chocolate, and bittersweet chocolate. All added a flavor depth that I found attractive. I ultimately decided on bittersweet (semisweet can be used instead), because it did double duty, rounding out the chili, as well as adding a hint of sweetness that kept me from having to add the granulated sugar, brown sugar, molasses, or honey called for in some recipes.

But I liked the chocolate only when it was added at the end of cooking. Stirred in up front with the spices, tomatoes, and water, it gave the chili a mole-like feel. One spoonful, I'd like it; the next, I'd be scratching my head. Stirred in at the end, however, it miraculously pulled the dish together.

Many chili recipes include an acid, such as cider, red wine, or balsamic vinegar or lemon or lime juice, which can be added at the beginning or end of the cooking process. I didn't think the chili needed the acid kick, but other tasters found that a squirt or two of lime juice worked for them. Rather than squeeze it into the entire pot, I decided to add a bowl of lime slices to the condiment tray.

GIVING UP THE HUNT FOR CHILE PEPPERS

Clearly, the quantity and kind of common chili spices I used would make a difference. I had almost ruled out making my own chili powder, and a trip to the grocery store confirmed my decision. I had a choice of three dried peppers in the produce department. The first package was labeled "habaneros," one of the hottest peppers in the world. One of the remaining two varieties was labeled "long hot peppers," and the others were strung on a rope and not labeled at all. Given the inconsistent availability, poor labeling, and extra toasting and grinding steps, I decided to stick with commercial chili powder. It helped a little to toast it in a small skillet, stirring constantly over very low heat, until it was hot and fragrant.

In the end, I increased the chili powder, cumin, and oregano from my initial quantities. Although toasted and ground cumin seeds were more pronounced in flavor than store-bought powder, and although Mexican oregano was bright and distinct, I liked my chili just fine with ground cumin and regular oregano, especially when I finally figured out just how to treat the meat.

THE GOOD MISTAKE

The week before I started testing chili, my oldest daughter graduated from high school, and we threw a huge party for her — 150 guests in all. Since I was getting ready to test chili (and had twenty-one pounds of frozen chuck roast left over from testing pot roast), I decided to serve chili as part of the buffet.

The party warranted a serious effort, so I hand-cut all the beef into ¹/₂-inch cubes and seared every piece until well browned. The recipe I decided to use suggested commercial chili powder but offered a formula for making my own. Given the quantity of chili I had to make, I opted for store-bought.

For each 3 pounds of meat, the recipe called for 1 cup of chili powder. It seemed like a lot, but since the book was very reputable, I followed the recipe, adding 7 cups of chili powder to 21 pounds of beef. Needless to say, the chili was potent, but by simmering it for hours and hours, thinning it with extra water, thickening it with cornmeal, then serving it with a huge bowl of sour cream on the side, I managed to patch it up.

I decided to freeze the leftovers for comparison in my tests. While reheating the chili, I noticed that with the extra-long cooking the first time around, the freezing and thawing, and the reheating, the chunks of meat were so tender that they started to shred. Compared with beef cubes, this meat was soft and tender — a pleasure to eat. Compared with the ground-beef chili I had been making, it was rich and beefy-flavored. Here was my answer, I thought — until I remembered how long beef had to cook to fall apart like that. For the meat to achieve that texture, the chili would have to simmer all day.

A MEAT TRICK

Then I remembered my 90-minute pot roast (page 59). In just 1¹/₂ hours (nearly all of it unattended cooking), I could have chuck roast tender enough to shred.

Following that technique, I seared a 2-pound chuck roast, sautéed the onions, then put everything in the pot, sealed it with foil, reinforced the seal with a tight lid, and cooked the chili for 1 hour and 20 minutes in a 450-degree oven. Cut into short pieces and shredded, the meat in this chili was far superior to the ground chuck. Having cooked under pressure for so long, however, the tomatoes, spices, and aromatics tasted old and spent. The solution wasn't far off, though.

I decided to try pressure-cooking the chuck separately in the oven. While it cooked, I made the rest of the chili on top of the stove, adding a pork chop to the pot to give it some flavor. Once the beef was done, I removed the chop from the chili, shredded all the meat and added it to the pot, and simmered the chili for another 45 minutes.

All I needed now was a different cut of pork. The rib-end chops I had selected were relatively lean and dry. Switching to country-style ribs, a more flavorful, fatty cut, helped immensely. Cooked under pressure in the oven, the chuck cooked more quickly than the pork. Cooking the two together in the oven, then simmering the meat in the chili on the stovetop, was the final piece of the puzzle.

Blue-Ribbon Chili

Serves 6 to 8

Other flavorful pork cuts, especially from the pork shoulder, can be substituted for the country ribs. If using boneless pork for the ribs, you may want to reduce the quantity from 1¹/₄ pounds to 1 pound. Although this chili may take 3¹/₂ to 4 hours to make, it requires very little attention. If you prefer to cook your own beans for chili, pour 3 cups boiling water over 1 cup dried kidney or pinto beans that have been rinsed and picked over. Let stand until beans have nearly doubled in volume, about 1 hour. Drain and rinse, then place in a large saucepan with water to cover by 2 inches. Bring to a boil, reduce the heat, and simmer until tender, about 45 minutes, adding salt to taste during the last 15 minutes.

¹/₄ cup vegetable oil

1 flat, boneless chuck roast (2 pounds), patted dry

4 country-style ribs (about 1¹/₄ pounds), patted dry

1 tablespoon plus 2 teaspoons ground cumin
   Salt and freshly ground black pepper

9 tablespoons mild chili powder

2 teaspoons dried oregano

2 large onions, cut into medium dice to make about 4 cups

4¹/₂ cups (one 28-ounce can, plus an additional scant cup) crushed tomatoes

1 ounce bittersweet or semisweet chocolate

6 garlic cloves, minced

2 cans (15¹/₂ ounces each) canned pinto or kidney beans (optional)

   Suggested condiments: Tabasco sauce, sliced scallions, minced jalapeño, canned green chiles, sautéed green and yellow bell peppers, minced fresh cilantro, lime slices, sour cream

1   Adjust oven rack to middle position and heat oven to 450 degrees. Set a large Dutch oven or ovenproof pot over medium heat while preparing roast and ribs.

2   Pour 2 tablespoons of the oil into a medium bowl, add roast and ribs, and turn to coat. Generously sprinkle both sides of meats with 1 tablespoon cumin and salt and pepper.

3 A couple of minutes before searing meats, increase heat to strong medium-high. Add chuck roast to pot and cook until a solid brown crust forms on one side, about 5 minutes. Turn roast over, and cook until a crust forms on other side, about 5 minutes longer. Remove from pot. Add ribs; cook until crust forms, 4 to 5 minutes. Turn ribs over and cook until crusty, 4 to 5 minutes longer.

4 Return roast with ribs to pot; add 1$\frac{1}{4}$ cups water (if using a pot that is more than 9$\frac{1}{2}$ inches in diameter, increase water to 1$\frac{1}{2}$ cups) and turn off heat. Following illustration on page 64, use a potholder or dishtowel to cover pot with a sheet of heavy-duty foil, pressing on foil so that it is concave and touches roast. Seal completely around edges. Place lid on pot. Turn on heat again until you hear juices bubbling. Set pot in oven and cook without checking until roast and ribs are dark brown and very tender, about 1 hour and 20 minutes.

5 Meanwhile, heat chili powder, oregano, and remaining 2 teaspoons cumin in a small, dry skillet over low heat, stirring constantly, until spices are warm, fragrant, and darker in color, being careful not to burn them. Set aside. When roast and ribs are done, remove from pot and set aside until cool enough to handle. Pour meat juices into a measuring cup; add enough water to equal 6 cups. Set pot (which will be very hot from oven) over medium-high heat; add remaining 2 tablespoons oil. Add onions and sauté until soft, 7 to 8 minutes. Add toasted spices, tomatoes, and meat juice–water mixture; stir to combine. When roast and ribs are cool enough to handle, tear meat into shreds and add to chili; discard pork bones.

6 Simmer chili until flavors are deep, rich, and unified, about 1$\frac{1}{2}$ hours. Add chocolate and garlic and simmer to blend flavors, about 5 minutes longer. Add beans, if using, and heat through. Chili can be served immediately, but it's better if it is allowed to stand 20 to 30 minutes before serving, and even better if it can be cooled, covered, refrigerated overnight and reheated before serving. Pass condiments at the table.

Weekend Classics

As local caterers, my husband and I taught cooking classes together in the early eighties. We both recall the time we included stuffed mushrooms on a list of proposed recipes for a "Cater Your Own Party" class. As the cooking-school owner reviewed the menu, she wrinkled her nose at the mushrooms. "Too common," she sniffed.

Common they are, and for good reason. Stuffed mushrooms are a virtual necessity for every cocktail party — comfortingly familiar, easy to eat, and mingling well in the society of flashier offerings. What the school's proprietor failed to recognize was that just because everyone makes them doesn't mean everyone knows how to cook them to perfection.

Over the years, I've sampled stuffed mushrooms that were almost raw, or dry and shriveled, or wet enough to drench a cocktail napkin. I've had them firm or fall-apart fragile. The ideal stuffed mushroom is full-flavored and sturdy enough to be easily eaten with one hand while a glass is balanced in the other. It's tender but not parched or soggy, with a filling that's nicely moist, not gummy.

To get them right, do you pre-cook the caps? And what's the proper temperature for baking? Is broiling them at the end the key? Surprisingly, the simplest technique for stuffed mushrooms turns out to be the best, though the pan you choose and where you place the oven rack will make all the difference.

ROASTING RULES

I started with the most straightforward method, stuffing raw mushrooms with a basic filling of sautéed stems, onions, bread crumbs, and binder and roasting them at temperatures ranging from 350 to 450 degrees. Cooked at the lower temperature, the caps were weak-flavored and spongy-textured, while at the highest temperature, the stuffing burned. Roasting on the lowest rack of the oven gives the mushrooms the right amount of strong heat, and a temperature of 425 degrees is sufficient to evaporate their liquid, intensify their flavor and turn them a nutty golden brown. But this browning occurs only when the roasting pan is low- (or no-) sided and when the pan is not overcrowded.

It's important to butter or oil the mushroom caps before filling them. Without some lubrication, the caps wrinkle unattractively. Before brushing them, I whirl the oil with garlic in a food processor, which produces a smoother blend than does chopping and mixing the garlic by hand.

A number of recipes suggest roasting the mushrooms before filling them. I pre-roasted mushrooms in several ways: stem side up, stem side down, and then starting them on one side and turning them. I discovered that as long as you roast the mushrooms on the bottom rack on the right baking sheet, this extra step is unnecessary. Nor is broiling stuffed mushrooms either before or after stuffing them a good idea. The mushrooms require constant tending and turn leathery. Sautéing them before roasting doesn't give superior results, either.

Simmering or soaking the mushrooms in boiling lemon water is another first step in a few recipes. This hot bath is supposed to jump-start the cooking process, but it gives the mushrooms an unpleasant canned flavor. To draw out some of their liquid and season them throughout, I tried salting a batch. Again, no luck: the salt made the mushrooms tough and rubbery.

THE BIG SCOOP

Scraping out the dark brown gills with a melon baller (or a teaspoon) helps in four ways. It reduces the amount of moisture released by the mushroom. It creates a larger area for stuffing. Although hollowing out the mushroom takes a little more time, it makes the stuffing process easier. Finally, the filling can be spread over the entire bottom of the cap, resulting in a mushroom that's easier to eat.

Regardless of the kind of filling, it makes sense to use the mushroom stems as a base. Bold flavorings work well in combination with them, and strong cheeses, such as blue, feta, and goat, can double as flavoring and binder. For the filler, crushed cracker crumbs are superior to fresh and dry bread crumbs, offering better texture than fresh and better flavor than dry.

These stuffed mushrooms are now a common — and much requested — feature of my cooking classes.

Roasted Stuffed Mushrooms

Serves 6 to 8 as a
side dish, 12 to 15
as an appetizer

Roasting the mushrooms on the bottom oven rack is important for flavor development. Be sure not to crowd the pan. Cremini mushrooms, also known as brown mushrooms or baby bellas, can be substituted for domestic white mushrooms. Twelve extra-large mushrooms (measuring about 2¹/₂ inches in diameter) can also be roasted by this method but are better as a side dish than an hors d'oeuvre. If you don't have a food processor, make the garlic oil in a blender.

20   ounces domestic white mushrooms (24 large or 30 button)
4   large garlic cloves
¹/₄   cup olive oil
     Salt and freshly ground black pepper
     Mushroom Filling of choice (pages 88–91)

1   Line a cookie sheet or low-sided roasting pan at least 12¹/₂ by 17¹/₂ inches with foil and spray with vegetable-oil cooking spray.

2   Remove mushroom stems. Finely chop; set aside in a small bowl for use in one of the stuffings on following pages. Use a melon baller or a teaspoon to scrape out gills as shown and add to bowl. Place mushrooms in a separate large bowl, stem side down.

To create a larger surface area for the stuffing, scrape the gills from each mushroom cap after removing the stem.

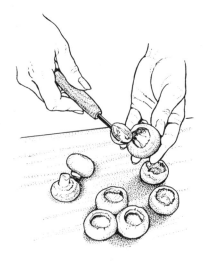

3   With food processor running, drop garlic cloves through feeder tube, one at a time. With machine still running, slowly pour oil through. Drizzle 3 to 4 tablespoons garlic oil over mushroom caps, along with a generous pinch or two of salt and several grinds of pepper. Toss to coat mushrooms evenly. Arrange mushrooms on pan; do not crowd.

4   Meanwhile, adjust oven rack to lowest position and heat oven to 425 degrees. Stuff each mushroom cap with a portion of filling. Lightly brush mushrooms with remaining garlic oil and roast until caps and filling are well browned, about 20 minutes. Let cool for 5 minutes. Transfer to a serving platter or individual plates and serve.

Mushroom Filling with Parmesan and Thyme

Makes enough for
20 large or 30 button
mushrooms

You can substitute Madeira or port for sherry. Since you're already using the food processor to make the garlic oil, chop the mushroom stems in it as well.

2 tablespoons butter or olive oil

1/2 medium onion, finely chopped

2 garlic cloves, minced

Chopped stems and gills from 24 large or 30 button mushrooms (see Roasted Stuffed Mushrooms, step 2, page 86)

3/4 teaspoon dried thyme leaves

Salt and freshly ground black pepper

3 tablespoons sweet sherry

1/2 cup plus 1 tablespoon crushed saltine crackers

2 tablespoons minced fresh parsley leaves

4 tablespoons grated Parmesan cheese

1. Heat butter or oil in a medium skillet. When butter starts to turn golden brown and smells nutty or oil is hot, add onion, and sauté until soft and golden, 3 to 4 minutes, adding garlic at last minute. Add chopped mushrooms and thyme; lightly season with salt and pepper. Cook until liquid evaporates and mushrooms start to brown, 3 to 4 minutes. Add sherry and simmer until alcohol burns off but mushrooms are still moist, about 15 seconds.

2. Transfer mixture to a medium bowl. Stir in crackers, parsley, and 3 tablespoons Parmesan cheese. Stuff mushrooms and sprinkle with remaining 1 tablespoon Parmesan cheese.

Mushroom Filling with Blue Cheese and Walnuts

Makes enough for
20 large or 30 button
mushrooms

Blue cheese and toasted hazelnuts are also a good combination. Toast nuts in a 300-degree oven until fragrant, about 10 minutes.

2   tablespoons butter or olive oil

1/2 medium onion, finely chopped

2   garlic cloves, minced

     Stems and gills from 24 large or 30 button mushrooms (see
         Roasted Stuffed Mushrooms, step 2, page 86)

     Salt and freshly ground black pepper

3   tablespoons port wine

1/2 cup plus 1 tablespoon crushed saltine crackers

2   tablespoons minced fresh parsley leaves

1/2 cup crumbled blue cheese

4   tablespoons walnuts, toasted (see note above), chopped

Proceed as directed in Mushroom Filling with Parmesan and Thyme (opposite page), omitting thyme and substituting port for sherry in step 1. Transfer mixture to a medium bowl. Stir in crackers, parsley, blue cheese, and 3 tablespoons walnuts. Stuff mushrooms and sprinkle with remaining 1 tablespoon walnuts.

Mushroom Filling with Goat Cheese and Pesto

Makes enough for
20 large or 30 button
mushrooms

Use any type of prepared pesto for this stuffing, either the jarred kind or the kind in the refrigerated case of your supermarket.

2 **tablespoons butter or olive oil**

¹/₂ **medium onion, finely chopped**

Chopped stems and gills from 24 large or 30 button mushrooms (see Roasted Stuffed Mushrooms, step 2, page 86)

Salt and freshly ground black pepper

¹/₂ **cup plus 1 tablespoon crushed saltine crackers**

¹/₄ **cup prepared pesto (see note above)**

1 **log (3¹/₂ ounces) fresh goat cheese (scant ¹/₂ cup packed)**

2 **tablespoons pine nuts (optional)**

Proceed as directed in Mushroom Filling with Parmesan and Thyme (page 88), omitting garlic, thyme, and sherry in step 1. Transfer mixture to a medium bowl. Stir in crackers, pesto, and goat cheese. Stuff mushrooms and top with pine nuts, if desired.

Mushroom Filling with Arugula and Feta Cheese

Makes enough for
20 large or 30 button
mushrooms

This updated filling gets a bit of a bite from arugula, but you can substitute spinach if you like.

2 tablespoons butter or olive oil

1/2 medium onion, finely chopped

2 garlic cloves, minced

Chopped stems and gills from 24 large or 30 button mushrooms (see Roasted Stuffed Mushrooms, step 2, page 86)

Salt and freshly ground black pepper

4 ounces arugula leaves, coarsely chopped (4 cups packed)

1/2 cup plus 1 tablespoon crushed saltine crackers

1/2 cup crumbled feta cheese

Proceed as directed in Mushroom Filling with Parmesan and Thyme (page 88), omitting thyme and sherry and adding arugula, cooking it until it wilts. Transfer mixture to a medium bowl. Stir in crackers and feta cheese. Stuff mushrooms.

Not long ago, I was asked to bring an hors d'oeuvre to a party. Since it was the holidays, I thought I'd prepare something festive and a little extravagant that everybody would love. So I cooked up several pounds of shrimp and made cocktail sauce.

Two other guests had been asked to bring an hors d'oeuvre. When I arrived at the party, I discovered I wasn't the only one who had thought shrimp cocktail was a good idea — all three of us had brought the same thing! A little more variety would have been nice, but the fact is, there weren't any shrimp left at the end of the night.

And that has always been my experience. Whether I plan two shrimp per guest or twelve, there are rarely leftovers. Guests may turn down a third chicken salad–stuffed cherry tomato, but not shrimp with cocktail sauce.

Not all shrimp cocktails are created equal, however. When I see dry shrimp curled up as tight as a roly-poly, I know I'm not in for a good eating experience. Often found on grocery store–arranged platters, these shrimp usually taste washed out and rubbery. Other shrimp may look inviting, but one bite and you often start searching for a cocktail napkin or trash can. These shrimp taste unbearably salty, muddy, or of chemicals.

Then there are the rare perfect shrimp: ice-cold, hook-shaped, and bright coral with a glistening, smooth surface. They are firm yet tender, of the sea but not salty. The cocktail sauce is bracing but not overbearing, lively but not distracting.

Having been raised on the Florida panhandle, with the Gulf of Mexico practically lapping at my front door, I grew up eating great shrimp cocktail. I knew that overcooking (or buying peeled and cooked varieties) generally produces dry, rubbery results. But having long since moved away from Florida (and having been introduced to the world of farm-raised shrimp), I also knew that buying the right kind was key.

Approaching the subject with a bit of experience, I began three days of cooking, eating, and analyzing shrimp. By the end, I not only had discovered a better way to cook them but had learned how to choose them as well. And if only mediocre varieties were available, I had learned how to improve them, too.

At first, it seemed as if there were dozens of ways to cook shrimp for cocktail, but after analyzing the recipes, I realized that most were simply variations on six basic techniques: blanching (boiling in a large quantity of water), shallow boiling, steaming, microwaving, broiling, and roasting.

Since blanching was the most common method, I started by testing various flavoring liquids, cooking times, and salt quantities. This dump-and-cook-until-pink approach worked well for large amounts. But regardless of how much salt I used, the flavoring ingredients, or how long I cooked the shrimp, they were relatively bland and tough compared with those prepared by other methods.

How about cooking shrimp in water to cover? I found three versions of this technique. The most straightforward instructed me to bring the shrimp to a boil, *uncovered,* with an occasional stir during the heating process. As soon as the water boiled, the shrimp were drained immediately.

In a similar technique, the shrimp were brought to a boil with the lid ajar, then drained and covered for 15 minutes. A final recipe suggested adding the shrimp to a small quantity of boiling water. Once the water returned to a boil, the shrimp were drained and left to stand, partially covered, for 10 minutes.

This trio of techniques offered pros and cons. Shrimp cooked by these methods were more flavorful and tender than those that had been blanched, but they could not be ideally cooked in large quantities. And compared with the simple, direct technique I ultimately chose, these methods were more complex and the shrimp more firm.

Rarely does the microwave produce superior results, and shrimp were no exception. Speed was the advantage (4 shrimp fully cooked in a mere 30 seconds). But no other method produced shrimp more rubbery and shrunken in their shells.

Broiling and roasting both worked, but the shrimp lacked that pristine fresh look, and the tails looked dried up and were unattractively spotted white. The oven's dry heat never dissolved the kosher salt with which they had been seasoned.

Steaming, I find, always works but rarely excels, so I was surprised when the steamed shrimp showed potential. As with the shallow-boil method, there were three different steaming techniques. For batch one, I brought ½ pound shrimp and 3 tablespoons water to a steamy state, then continued to steam until the shrimp were pink.

Cooked this way, the shrimp were flavorful and firm, but they also cooked a bit unevenly — those sitting in the water were ready more quickly and were firmer than those on top. Short of cooking them in a pot with a glass lid or frequently stirring and checking them, it was difficult to determine when the shrimp had started to steam and when they were done.

In a slight variation on this technique, I wanted to try "steaming" the shrimp in their own juice. Since I liked the idea of using the shells, I made a small amount of intense broth from them, then steamed the shrimp in the broth. The broth had very little flavor impact on the shrimp, and as with water steaming, the shrimp sitting in the broth were tougher than those sitting above it.

I sprinkled the next batch of shrimp with salt, placed them in a steamer basket, and cooked them over high heat until pink. I could season these shrimp directly, not just the water. And unlike with any previous technique, the flavor was not lost in the liquid. These were the best-tasting shrimp I had cooked thus far.

The direct seasoning and intense cooking method both contributed to the shrimp's flavor, but it was low heat that ultimately delivered perfect texture. Steaming the shrimp that way made them noticeably more tender and flavorful. The method, however, needed some work. For the initial tests, I had cooked only a few shrimp. Increasing the number, I tossed a full pound into the steamer basket only to find they cooked inconsistently — some tough, others tender.

I ultimately realized the shrimp could not be tossed carelessly into the basket. In order for them to cook evenly, they had to be arranged in a single layer. I thought this meant I could steam only in small batches, but I found I could arrange up to 1½ pounds at a time in a large steamer basket. Rarely would I do more than that quantity, and since each batch was ready in just 5 minutes, I could cook multiple batches back to back.

To cook the largest quantity of shrimp possible, I arranged them as close together as I could on a 12-inch collapsible steamer basket. Since shrimp were arranged all around the side of the basket, they needed to be cooked in the widest pan possible. Both my 11-inch deep skillet and a wide soup kettle worked well.

For consistently accurate cooking times, I found it best to bring an inch or so of water to a boil over high heat in the skillet or kettle. Once the pan was steamy hot, I removed the lid, set the shrimp in place, re-covered, then turned the heat to low and started the timer. Depending on the size of the shrimp, they were done in 4 to 6 minutes. (Since the burners on electric stoves take longer to cool down, it's best to decrease the heat before setting the shrimp in the pan.) If the shrimp were almost done when I checked them, I simply turned off the heat and let them slowly finish cooking.

I had always believed shrimp were more flavorful if cooked in the shell, but tasting peeled and unpeeled shrimp side by side, I could not tell the difference. Flavor aside, some cooks recommend cooking shrimp in the shells to keep them from curling (they look bigger and more impressive as well). But I found that if the shrimp were arranged in the basket and steamed over low heat, they held their shape as well as if they had been cooked in their shells. Since there were no benefits to cooking them in the shell, I decided to peel them before cooking.

To confirm that this firm yet tender texture from low-heat steam was not just in my mind, I boiled a few shrimp for comparison. The boiled, peeled shrimp cooked up into a tight curl, while the steamed ones had a loose half-heart shape. The boiled shrimp were tight and rubbery, while the low-steamed ones were firm and tender.

YOU GET WHAT YOU PAY FOR

I buy most of my shrimp at one of three places. When I have time or when I want something special, I make a trip to a local high-quality seafood market about twenty minutes from my house. I also shop at a local warehouse food club, where I occasionally pick up a 5-pound bag of extra-large white shrimp for the freezer. When I need shrimp quickly, I head to the grocery store five minutes away.

Shopping at all three of these places, I bought most of the widely available farm-raised shrimp varieties: tigers from Thailand, white shrimp from Mexico, and brown shrimp from Texas. Tiger and brown shrimp are cheap and are regulars at most grocery store fish counters. I purchased pink shrimp and wild whites from Florida, and I also found some pinks from Brazil as well as king shrimp imported from Australia.

I discovered that price is directly related to quality. The more expensive the shrimp, the better. Of the cheaper widely available farm-raised varieties, white shrimp from Mexico were the best I tasted. Although they were a bit bland, their taste was decent.

Lacking any ocean flavor, tiger shrimp were bland and muddy. My notes read: "Taste like they were raised on a river bottom. Remind me of catfish." I subsequently learned that tiger shrimp are, in fact, farm-raised in fresh water, so it made perfect sense that they tasted more like catfish than shrimp.

At the other extreme, brown shrimp from Texas were salty and almost inedible. Feeding on iodine-rich plankton, this variety tasted distinctly of iodine. Since I had (unfortunately) bought a 5-pound box, I was able to read the ingredients list: shrimp, water, salt, and sodium bisulfite.

Similar to the sodium tripolyphosphate with which scallops are treated, sodium bisulfite preserves and flavors the shrimp. The more solution absorbed, the heavier the shrimp, and the higher the price. In this case, the shrimp had either sat too long or in too strong a solution.

To see if I could cleanse tiger shrimp of their muddy flavor and infuse them with a little sea-like flavor, I made a brine of 1 cup kosher salt and ⅔ cup sugar dissolved in 2 cups boiling water. Once the salt dissolved, I added 6 cups ice water and the shrimp. I decided to test a few after 15 minutes of soaking and to cook a new batch every 15 minutes to check the progress.

I needed only two tries. In just 15 minutes, the brine had dramatically improved the flavor of the tiger shrimp. Thirty minutes was better, but borderline salty. Twenty to 25 minutes was perfect. By peeling the shrimp while they were brining, I could still have them soaked and cooked in about 30 minutes.

To confirm the need to brine, I taste-tested brined tigers and those that had been heavily seasoned with salt. By comparison, the brining process flushed out the muddiness and made this little river creature taste as if it came from the sea.

Brown shrimp had the opposite problem: they needed to be purged of their saltiness. Instead of the brine, I soaked them in fresh water. As with the brine, just 15 minutes of soaking time greatly improved these shrimp. And although I'd still try to avoid buying them, a 30-minute soak made them taste perfectly acceptable.

Of higher-quality shrimp, wild whites and pinks from Florida were very good. Pinks from northern Brazil were outstanding. King shrimp from Australia offered tender, clean, sweet meat. These varieties needed only a sprinkling of salt before steaming.

Browns are not the only shrimp that are treated, and not all shrimp are treated alike. Some may require a simple rinse. Others may require a full-fledged soak. If you want to know if the shrimp you plan to buy have been soaked in sodium bisulfite, ask. If the person at the fish counter doesn't know, then ask to see the box. Shrimp are usually sold to the retailer frozen in 4- or 5-pound waxed cardboard boxes. If the shrimp have been soaked in it, sodium bisulfite will be listed as an ingredient.

Whether you're working with less expensive grocery store varieties of shrimp or the top-notch kind from your local fish market, these preparation techniques, combined with the low-steam method, guarantee great shrimp, with or without the cocktail sauce.

Perfectly Cooked Shrimp for Cocktail

If you're unsure about the kind of shrimp you've purchased or uncertain whether they need to be brined, soaked, or salted, then start by microwaving just one of the shrimp (it should be fully cooked in about 15 seconds) and tasting it. If it is bland and muddy, follow brining instructions for tiger shrimp (page 96). If it tastes overly salty, follow soaking instructions for sodium bisulfite–treated shrimp (page 96). If it tastes sweet and pure with no off flavors, lightly season with salt and continue.

1–1¹⁄₂ **pounds shrimp, peeled and deveined**

¹⁄₂–³⁄₄ **teaspoon kosher salt, unless using tiger shrimp or any shrimp soaked in sodium bisulfite (see note above and opposite page)**

Cocktail Sauce (page 100)

1   Lightly sprinkle shrimp with salt.

2   Bring 1 inch water to a boil in a large (at least 10 to 11 inches in diameter) covered deep skillet or large soup kettle.

3   Arrange shrimp on a collapsible steamer basket as shown (shrimp will cling to side of basket as it collapses to fit into pan). If using an electric stove, reduce heat to low.

Arrange the shrimp close together in a single layer on a 12-inch collapsible steamer basket. If steaming in a skillet, unscrew the center handle of the steamer, which can prevent the lid from forming a tight seal.

4 Remove lid from pan, set steamer basket in pan, and replace lid. Turn heat to low. Depending on shrimp size, set timer as follows:

Colossal (12 or less per pound): 6–8 minutes

"16/20s" (16–20 per pound): $5^{1}/_{2}$–7 minutes

Jumbo (21–25 per pound): 5–6 minutes

Large/medium (31–35 per pound): 4–5 minutes

When timer goes off, lift pan lid. If shrimp are opaque throughout, remove basket from heat. If they are almost fully cooked, turn off heat, cover, and let stand for another 2 minutes.

5 Refrigerate until well chilled, then arrange on a serving platter or individual plates and serve with cocktail sauce alongside.

For Tiger Shrimp

Since tiger shrimp are farm-raised in fresh water, the muddy flavor needs to be replaced with the briny flavor of the sea. This can be accomplished by soaking the shrimp in a salt-sugar brine.

For $1^{1}/_{2}$ pounds shrimp, dissolve 1 cup kosher salt and $^{2}/_{3}$ cup sugar in 2 cups boiling water. Once salt has more or less dissolved, add 6 cups ice water. Soak shrimp, peeling them as they brine, for 20 to 25 minutes. Drain, rinse, and continue with step 2 of Perfectly Cooked Shrimp for Cocktail.

For Shrimp Heavily Treated with Sodium Bisulfite

Soak $1^{1}/_{2}$ pounds shrimp in room-temperature tap water for 25 to 30 minutes, peeling them as they soak. Drain, rinse, and continue with step 2 of Perfectly Cooked Shrimp for Cocktail.

Cocktail Sauce

Makes about 1 cup

The quality of cocktail sauce is dependent on good jarred horse-radish. If yours has started to turn brown with age, it will have lost its potency. For best results, discard it and buy a fresh jar for this sauce.

1   cup ketchup
2   tablespoons very fresh prepared horseradish
1¹/₂   tablespoons juice and ¹/₂ teaspoon zest from 1 lemon
¹/₄   cup finely minced celery
2   tablespoons minced fresh dill, parsley, or cilantro

Mix all ingredients in a small bowl and refrigerate until ready to serve.

| make crab cakes as often as I can afford them, and they're always the first thing to tempt me on a restaurant menu. But with the key ingredient costing twenty-five to thirty dollars a pound, this is not a dish you serve for a regular weeknight supper.

Despite the many good crab cakes I've eaten, I had never really thought about how the ideal crab cake should look and taste until I saw *Cooking with Crab* (QVC Publishing Inc., 2000) by Margie Kaufman, co-owner with her husband, Ron, of Chesapeake Bay Gourmet. Smack-dab on the cover were two of the most beautiful crab cakes I'd ever seen. These were not the typical kind — tiny lumps of crabmeat lost in bread filler and concealed by a thick fried coating. The jumbo lumps were clearly visible, held together by a minimal but substantial binder.

What was distinctive about this recipe was the binder: dry bread crumbs in combination with a couple of tablespoons of water and a few egg whites. I liked that concept, but I wanted more crab.

MAKE MINE JUMBO

The first step in developing the perfect crab cake was to find the right crabmeat. I knew canned crab was inferior to fresh and pasteurized crab, but I couldn't remember the last time I had tasted the canned variety from the grocery store shelf. I also thought perhaps it might play a role in a cheaper crab cake.

But after tasting seven different brands and styles of canned crab, I concluded these products were vastly inferior. Regardless of the variety — jumbo lump, fancy lump, claw, or the cheaper "white" — the canned crab tasted bleached, without even a hint of sweetness. The meat of the "white" kind looked more like shredded noodles and tasted like a combination of metal and overcooked shell.

Canned crab was also no bargain. Like tuna, crab usually comes in 6-ounce cans. Once you drain off the liquid, however, there are only about 4$^1/_2$ ounces of bad crabmeat left. Except for the cheap white crab, most of the other cans cost over four dollars — no cheaper than a tub or can of pasteurized crab. I moved on.

There were many varieties of pasteurized crab from which to choose. Starting from least to most expensive, I bought "special," claw, backfin or lump, and jumbo lump (see below) and started making crab cakes. For a more affordable version, I also tried combining the cheaper varieties with jumbo lump. From my experience, "special" on a can of crab is a code word for trash. Made up of tiny bits of meat and lots of shell, this crab must be picked through thoroughly. And for the price (about ten dollars a pound at my store), don't expect to find any lumps.

Costing a few dollars more than special, claw meat is nearly half the price of the most expensive jumbo lump. Using claw meat to make crab cakes, however, is the equivalent of using leg and thigh meat to make chicken salad. Perfect for soups

KNOW YOUR CRAB

You can't make good crab cakes with canned crabmeat. Instead, you'll need pasteurized crabmeat, available in the refrigerated case of your supermarket or fish store. Here's what's available in order of preference:

JUMBO LUMP: Like the pork tenderloin, jumbo lump is a relatively recent invention resulting from consumer and industry need for a shell-free product. Jumbo lump comes from the two muscles attached to the swimmer fin of the crab. They are the most used and most developed and therefore the largest muscles. Since there are only two muscles per crab, it takes forty to fifty crabs to make a 1-pound can of jumbo lump, thus the premium price.

BACKFIN, LUMP, SUPER LUMP, BACKFIN LUMP: Although there is no national standard, this grade is usually a perfectly acceptable blend of broken jumbo lump crabmeat, along with the remaining body minus the claw meat.

CLAW: Exactly what it sounds like, claw meat is extracted exclusively from the claw. There are, however, different extraction techniques that affect quality. In one method, rollers crush the claws, after which the shells and meat drop into a brine solution. In theory, the shells float and the meat sinks. Unfortunately, a significant amount of shell sinks as well, and meat extracted by this method must be picked over very carefully. Because the meat has been soaked in brine, it must also be rinsed, resulting in flavor loss. Handpicking, the more tedious of the two extraction methods, yields larger chunks of meat, with little or no shell.

SPECIAL OR REGULAR: This is meat extracted from the remaining crab, minus the lump and claw. Crab pieces are small in this grade, and if the quality is poor, there will be lots of shell mixed in with the meat.

and stews, this darker, richer meat was not right for the light, delicate crab cake I was looking for.

At only $15.99 per pound, lump (or backfin) was the grade I was hoping would win. Because of the smaller lumps, the cake held together well and tasted good, but it wasn't as impressive as ones made with jumbo lump.

Though it was difficult to bind, pasteurized jumbo lump crabmeat made the most tender, exquisitely flavored, impressive-looking cakes. Alone, the crab tasted as bland as a boneless, skinless chicken breast, but light seasoning and gentle cooking brought the meat alive.

Following my fishmonger's tip that mild-flavored fish are often used as filler, I also bought shrimp, scallops, salmon, and scrod and tried them in combination with the crab as well. If I was lucky, one of them might double as filler and binder. The cakes were interesting, but not the answer. Scallops, which I had always thought of as delicately flavored, completely dominated the crab. Shrimp's distinct flavor and rubbery texture were too prominent as well. Surprisingly, salmon wasn't a bad match, but it seemed silly to spend nearly thirty dollars on jumbo lump and not get pure crab flavor.

THE BREAD THAT BINDS

Keeping the recipe free of flavorings at this point, I established a composite recipe, which I made in quarter batches:

1 pound lump crab
2 teaspoons lemon juice
½ teaspoon salt
  Black pepper to taste

To this mixture I added:

1 egg
¼ cup mayonnaise

After reviewing fifty-three different crab cake recipes, I identified thirteen binding ingredients and techniques. Starting with the simplest, I tried crab cakes made with:

Dry bread crumbs
Panko (Japanese bread crumbs available at Asian markets, gourmet stores, and the ethnic section of many grocery stores)
Crushed common crackers
Crushed saltine crackers
Crushed butter crackers
Fresh bread crumbs from cheap white bread

Fresh bread crumbs from good-quality baguette
Fresh bread crumbs from a firm white bread (Pepperidge Farm)
Mashed potatoes made from instant mashed potatoes
No binder
Béchamel (thick white sauce made of butter, flour, and milk)
Fresh bread soaked in milk
Fresh bread soaked in sherry

Saltine crackers and Pepperidge Farm white bread led the pack. The crab cake with no binder held together better than I thought, but one bite and I knew something was missing. Dry bread crumbs made a downright bland filling as well. Panko, which is known for producing extra-crisp fried food, bound the cakes too tightly. Crushed common crackers were . . . ordinary. Crushed butter crackers didn't create enough of an effect to justify the special purchase. Mashed potatoes and béchamel made wet cakes, the mashed-potato cake being especially boring, while the béchamel, in addition to adding a step to the recipe, felt stodgy.

The cakes made with saltine crackers were among the best. The crackers' full but unobtrusive flavor bound the cakes without making their presence known. But fresh bread was good, too, particularly crumbs from an American-style sandwich loaf. Unlike the baguette crumbs, the soft sweet crumbs from the sandwich bread reinforced the crab's tenderness and sweetness.

Should the bread crumbs be soaked in liquid as some recipes suggest? Liquid-soaked bread turns to mush, and mushy bread makes mushy crab cakes. Still, trying to bind a crab cake without liquid is like trying to build a stone wall with dry mortar. The key was to add the liquid to the crabmeat rather than to the bread. In my original testing formula, I had freshened the crab with a couple of teaspoons of lemon juice, but after a few rounds of lemon-flavored crab cakes, I realized that the juice lost its freshness during cooking and was best squeezed onto the cooked cake.

My other moistener choices were sweet sherry, milk, and water. I thought crab and sweet sherry would be natural partners, but I was wrong. Because the crab cakes cooked so quickly, there wasn't enough time for the alcohol to evaporate, and the resulting cakes tasted of raw sherry. Water was fine, but milk was even better. Just a few teaspoons moistened the cakes and enhanced the crab's sweetness.

Most crab cakes call for some form of egg. I tried making eggless crab cakes as well as ones with just yolks and just whites and ones with a separated egg. Nothing beat one whole egg.

Most crab cakes call for an enrichment — usually mayonnaise, but some recipes call for cream, sour cream, or butter as well. I made six cakes: one with no additional fat, one with cream, one with sour cream, one with butter, and one each with higher and lower quantities than the ¼ cup mayonnaise per pound of crab I was using.

The crab cake with sour cream had a nice flavor but browned too quickly. The butter made the crab cake taste greasy. Cream wouldn't bind it.

I was pleased to find that cakes made with 2 tablespoons of mayonnaise — even less than what I had been using — were perfect. Using this quantity, the mayonnaise, bread, and egg were in sync, almost invisibly holding the crab together. With minimal binder and fat, I was starting to see crab chunks at the cake's surface. This was a good sign.

Since there were innumerable possible flavorings, I divided them into aromatics and flavorings. Starting with the aromatics, I made crab cakes with each of the following raw ingredients: garlic, scallion, bell pepper, celery, and jalapeño. I repeated the test with the same vegetables, sautéing them first (and substituting minced onions for the scallions), before adding them to the cakes. Providing both vivid green color and mild flavor to the pale delicate crab cakes, only scallions passed this first round of tests. Sautéing was unnecessary; chopped fine, they cooked by the time the cakes were done. Bell peppers made the cakes taste too deviled. I liked minced celery, but since celery salt is the key ingredient in most Maryland-style seasonings, I decided to withhold judgment. I also liked the kick that the jalapeño gave, but with Tabasco and cayenne still waiting for their chance, I held off that decision as well.

I tried thirteen other flavorings, including lemon zest, capers, garlic powder, and three different kinds of mustards (Dijon, spicy brown, and powdered). None passed muster. Parsley, Worcestershire sauce, nutmeg, and cayenne weren't bad. But in the end, only two flavorings triumphed, in combination with the scallions. Maryland-style seasoning (Old Bay) gave the celery taste I wanted, as well as pleasant hints of eleven other spices. Tabasco provided heat and sweet flavor.

Because crackers and crumbs add texture and help the cake bind, I had always dredged my crab cakes before cooking, but after making cakes with ten different coatings, I realized they tended to mask the crab's flavor. To various degrees, all the coatings — corn flakes, bread crumbs, flour, cornmeal, fresh bread crumbs, cracker crumbs, cracker meal, butter crackers, panko — made the cakes taste like cheap fried food. For twenty-eight bucks a pound, I wanted crab.

After pan- and deep-frying, broiling, baking, and sautéing crab cakes, I preferred those that were sautéed in a thin film of fat. The baked cakes looked delicate but tasted bland. Broiled crab cakes weren't bad, but the method was a bit testy. Like the coatings, deep-frying made the cakes taste like ordinary fried seafood. If the oil level is not high enough during cooking, a crumb-coated crab cake develops an undesirable pale ring around the circumference. Since my cakes weren't coated, however, the extra fat was not necessary, and just a generous film of oil in the pan is all that's needed to cook the cakes.

More important than the quantity is the kind of fat and its temperature. Like broiling, sautéing over relatively high heat caused the surface of the crabmeat to turn leathery. Medium heat, on the other hand, cooked the cakes to a beautiful golden brown.

Cakes fried in ordinary olive oil beat out all the others, including those fried in extra-virgin oil and those fried in vegetable oil. Many recipes talked of crab cake's affinity for butter and pushed it as the ideal cooking medium. This was not my experience. Butter foamed the entire cooking time, and the resulting cakes didn't taste significantly better. The foaming stopped when I used clarified butter, but the extra step didn't warrant the extra trouble.

PENNY-WISE, POUND-FOOLISH

Up until now, for purposes of economy, I had been testing with backfin lump crabmeat. With my newly developed recipe in hand, I was ready for a final run-through, this time with the preferred jumbo lump crabmeat. What a disappointment. Although I loved the big, sweet lumps of meat, the texture was all wrong. With no coating and the soft bread, these crab cakes barely held together and were mushy and soft. The filling that seemed right for the smaller lump crabmeat did not work with the larger lumps. I felt lost.

As it turns out, I was closer to my ideal crab cake than I thought. I picked up Margie Kaufman's *Cooking with Crab*. What did I need to do to make crab cakes that looked like hers? I studied the ingredients list again and noticed that she'd used a combination of cracker and bread crumbs as the binder. Cracker crumbs had been my other choice. After trying my recipe again with them, the difference was clear. Dry crackers, not soft bread, were the key. These crab cakes taste as good as they look.

Crab Cakes Worth the Price

Serves 8 as a first course,
4 as a main course

If pasteurized jumbo lump is not available or too expensive, this recipe works beautifully with backfin as well. From start to finish, these crab cakes are ready in about 20 minutes. Served with corn on the cob and coleslaw, they make a fast, yet special dinner.

  1 large egg, beaten
  2 tablespoons mayonnaise
  2 tablespoons minced scallion greens
 1/4 teaspoon Maryland-style seasoning, such as Old Bay
 1/4 teaspoon hot red pepper sauce, such as Tabasco
  1 pound pasteurized jumbo lump crabmeat (see note above)
  1 tablespoon plus 1 teaspoon milk
     Salt and freshly ground black pepper
 10 saltine crackers, crushed (about 1/2 cup)
  6 tablespoons olive oil, for frying

     Lemon wedges

1 Mix egg, mayonnaise, scallions, seasoning, and hot red pepper sauce in a small bowl.

2 Very carefully break up crabmeat in a medium bowl and pat with paper towels to remove excess liquid, making sure not to break up lumps (check for shells, but there should not be any). Add milk and season with salt and pepper to taste; toss gently to coat. Add saltines; toss gently to combine. Add egg mixture; gently toss once again to combine. Let stand for about 5 minutes so crackers have a chance to soften.

3 Meanwhile, heat oil in a large (11-to-12-inch) skillet (if using a smaller skillet, you may need to fry in batches) over medium-low heat. Using a standard 1/3-cup measure, scoop up a portion of crab, pressing it into cup to make a compact cake. Shake cake onto a large plate. Repeat process to make a total of 8 cakes.

4 A couple minutes before frying, increase heat to medium. Carefully add crab cakes to skillet. Sauté, turning once, until golden, about 3 minutes per side. Transfer cakes to a paper towel–lined plate. Serve immediately with lemon wedges.

Vegetable lasagna is one of my favorite dishes to serve when I entertain. For vegetarians and carnivores alike, it's a satisfying main course. And for larger spreads, it makes a perfect one-dish starch and vegetable alongside a meaty roast.

The problem with lasagna — particularly the vegetable variety — is that preparation is time-consuming and assembly tedious, and the results often don't seem worth the effort. The vegetables end up bland and overcooked, the noodles leathery, the dish either too dry or oozy rich. I wanted a lasagna that was simple, quick, and attractive with bright, flavorful vegetables.

Although I make tomato sauce–based vegetable lasagna more often than the white-sauce style, I like them both. Since the two dishes have so much in common, I wanted to tackle them both. I started with the components common to both dishes — the noodles and vegetables — then I figured out the sauces and cheeses for each style.

NOODLES OF NOODLES

Most purists say the only lasagna worth eating is made with homemade pasta. Since I've eaten plenty of fine lasagna from boxed grocery store noodles, I wasn't sure I agreed. Even if it was true, was it smart to develop a recipe that most people didn't have the time or equipment to make? I was willing to try homemade pasta. If it was superior, I could offer it as an optional step, but I was committed to finding a first-rate, easy option.

In addition to lasagnas with homemade pasta, I also tested four widely available dried commercial noodles: Mueller's, San Giorgio, Ronzoni, and the less widely available DeCecco, which I cooked al dente before assembly. I had also seen recipes calling for parboiled noodles (partially cooked in a large quantity of boiling water) and even raw, dry noodles, so I made pans of lasagna with those as well. Nor could I ignore oven-ready noodles, and I tested the only two grocery store brands I could find: Ronzoni and Barilla. Egg-roll wrappers were another quick and easy alternative, and of all the possibilities, I was most excited about these. A relatively easy ingredient to find in most grocery stores, egg-roll wrappers might offer the thin, refined texture of fresh pasta with all the convenience of dried.

A tasting of lasagnas made from all these different noodles revealed significant differences. The Mueller's, San Giorgio, and Ronzoni noodles produced ordinary lasagna. Besides having to be boiled, these clunky, curly-edged noodles baked up thick and doughy. Lasagnas made with parboiled or raw noodles from these brands were particularly unsuccessful.

As much as I wanted to like egg-roll wrappers, these sheer, delicate sheets blended in with the other ingredients and became invisible. The lasagna made from fresh pasta was superb. The thin layers were tender yet firm, delicate yet substantial. Were it not for the extra steps of making, kneading, rolling, and cutting the dough in an already tedious recipe, this lasagna would have been first-rate.

OVEN-READY TRIUMPH

The lasagnas made with "oven-ready" noodles were very different — one a clear winner, the other a dog. I knew I was in trouble when the Barilla package instructions called for a 1-hour baking. The vegetables in this dish would never survive the prolonged oven time. In an attempt to shave off some time, I baked the lasagna for 40 minutes, only to find that the noodles were still the texture of cardboard. On the other hand, Ronzoni oven-ready noodles were done in just 30 minutes. And like homemade pasta, these noodles were thin yet substantial.

Despite the oven-ready noodles' convenience and texture, I had three problems. The noodles may have been thin, but they were stiff, making it impossible to build more than three complete layers. I wanted at least four. Since the noodles were dry, I had to figure out some way to get additional moisture into the dish. I preferred to develop a recipe that didn't rely on thinning the sauce or adding water around the edges. And since these noodles weren't cooked, they weren't seasoned. Boiling the pasta may add an extra step to the recipe, but the salted water seasons the pasta. These from-box-to-pan noodles lacked flavor.

As I was weighing which direction to go, I picked up a package of the Ronzoni oven-ready lasagna and saw a recipe for Pasta Roll-Ups. To make the noodles pliable enough for rolling, the recipe called for soaking the noodles in hot water. I tried it, and in just 10 minutes, I had noodles that looked, tasted, and felt as if they had been boiled and had the wonderful texture of fresh — without all the hassle. If I added salt to the water, I figured they'd absorb it as well. And, sure enough, they did.

To figure out the best way to cook vegetables for lasagna, I made a large batch each of red and white sauce and tested eleven obvious lasagna vegetables: asparagus, broccoli, carrots, cauliflower, eggplant, mushrooms, onions, bell peppers, spinach, tomatoes, and zucchini. For each vegetable, I chose obvious cooking methods, prepared them accordingly, and then made a red and white lasagna with each style of vegetable.

Seventy-eight tests later, I was miserably full and stuck with test results that could not be easily categorized. I did learn, however, that all vegetables (except tomatoes, when you are using them in a white lasagna) need to be cooked before the lasagna is assembled. Once baked, raw vegetables taste bland, old, and stale, like canned vegetables.

I wanted to develop a cooking method that would work whether I was making a red or white lasagna. From subsequent tests, three techniques emerged — steam-sautéing, sautéing, or broiling — depending on which vegetable you choose.

⊱ **FIRM, HARD VEGETABLES** like asparagus, broccoli, carrots, and cauliflower are best steam-sautéed. By this method, the vegetable should be cooked by the time a small amount of salted water evaporates. A touch of oil not only flavors and enriches the vegetables but keeps them from scorching once the water evaporates. The result is a lightly cooked, well-seasoned vegetable that stands up to further cooking.

⊱ **TENDER VEGETABLES** like peppers, mushrooms, and onions are best sautéed. The high, dry heat draws out the water from these moist vegetables, intensifying their flavor.

⊱ **ABSORBENT VEGETABLES** like eggplant, which suck up oil if sautéed, and water-filled vegetables like zucchini and yellow squash, which turn to mush if cooked in an overcrowded pan, are better broiled.

No matter which vegetables you choose, you'll need the same quantity. For the most part, 1 pound of vegetables generally cooks down to about 2 cups. There are a few exceptions. Broccoli florets have more volume, so to get the right measure, either use heads (a combination of florets and stems) or measure the florets after cooking. Broiled vegetables tend to cook down to just under a couple of cups. So you may want to broil extra zucchini, yellow squash, or eggplant.

Regardless of the cooking method, it is important to season the vegetables with salt and garlic. A vegetable that tastes bland going into a lasagna will not be magically transformed during baking.

I started with the sauce for white lasagna. White sauce, or béchamel, is the flavored "glue" that unifies and moistens this lasagna and gives it character. The sauce is little more than fat, flour, and milk, but a lot can go wrong when combining these three ingredients. Depending on how much flour and fat are used, this sauce can be as thick as undiluted cream of mushroom soup or as thin as heavy cream. And depending on the milk's temperature when combined with the fat and flour, the sauce can turn out silky smooth or lumpy as oatmeal. But it's the flavor that's the biggest concern. Unless perked up in some way, white sauce is nothing more than a one-dimensional culinary glue.

Determining the kind of fat that should be used in this sauce was simple. It wasn't much of a contest between sauces made with butter and with olive oil. The butter-flavored béchamel was richer, moister, and more flavorful and full-bodied than the one made with oil.

After many experiments, I established flour/butter/liquid ratios that produced a smooth, velvety sauce. Whole and 2% milk deliver the fullest flavor. Only when I conducted this round of tests did I discover that the sauce is best when made with part chicken broth (or vegetable broth for vegetarians), which technically changes the sauce from a béchamel to a velouté. After making a lasagna with it, though, I realized it needed still more flavor. I returned to the stove and made six sauces. I flavored the first two with garlic — one with minced garlic that I added to the hot butter before whisking in the flour, the other with minced garlic cloves that I poached in the milk–chicken broth. In addition, I made sauces flavored with basil and nutmeg, sun-dried tomatoes, Parmesan cheese, and parsley.

Garlic dramatically improved the sauce, and of the two, I preferred the sauce with the poached garlic. Dried basil and tomatoes, on the other hand, gave the sauce a commercial feel. Nutmeg contributed a nice flavor but tasted too distinct. Parsley freshened up the sauce and made it more attractive but got lost in the baked dish. I worried that Parmesan cheese would make the sauce grainy, but it melted invisibly into the sauce, giving it complexity and flavor.

Mild, creamy ricotta and mozzarella were not good matches for this mild, creamy sauce. I wanted cheese with a little edge, so I went to the grocery store and picked out six varieties with potential — Swiss, Gouda, Gruyère, Edam, provolone, and fontina (a readily available semifirm cow's milk cheese) — and made lasagnas with each. Fontina, my favorite, offered unobtrusive color, flavor, and richness, and provolone was certainly acceptable. (See Choosing a Cheese for White Lasagna, page 112, for more details.) Swiss was too sweet, Gruyère and Edam were too distinct, and Gouda wasn't bad.

Tender noodles, a full-flavored béchamel, well-seasoned, perky vegetables, and a modest sprinkling of cheeses baked up into one of the simplest white lasagnas I've ever eaten.

Since the tomato sauce did not contain meat, how could I enliven it? I knew the dish needed mozzarella, but did it need ricotta? If so, did the ricotta need flavoring or textural improvements?

I began with a simple tomato sauce consisting of 3 tablespoons fat, 2 garlic cloves, and a 28-ounce can of crushed tomatoes. My first move was to increase the quantity of sauce — the 28-ounce can wasn't enough for a full pan of lasagna, but two cans were too much. To solve the problem, I added a 14$^{1}/_{2}$-ounce can of diced tomatoes. This chunky-style tomato gave the sauce substance, while the juice

CHOOSING A CHEESE FOR WHITE LASAGNA

Having made my white lasagna with ordinary grocery store brands of fontina and provolone, I decided to probe a little further. Would Italy's Fontina d'Aosta, declared one of the world's great cheeses by expert Steve Jenkins, author of *Cheese Primer* (Workman, 1996), improve my lasagna? Or might an imported or a mild provolone taste better than the sharp domestic provolone I had used in my first test?

I started by tasting three fontina cheeses: a Fontina d'Aosta from my local cheese shop and two grocery store varieties (a Danish import and a domestic fontina). At twelve dollars a pound, Fontina d'Aosta was firm-textured and straw-colored, with earthy depth and a barnyard bite. Clearly, this cheese commanded respect. By comparison, the Danish import was pale yellow with a red waxed border. Much flabbier in texture, it tasted pleasantly processed but hardly related to its Italian counterpart. The domestic fontina I tried was produced by Bel Gioioso Cheese in Denmark, Wisconsin. This nationally distributed cheese, pale cream with a Cheddar-like tang, was rubbery soft like the Danish import.

When melted, the domestic and Danish fontinas were pleasant, offering richness and flavor and mingling well with the remaining ingredients. Unlike the other two cheeses, Fontina d'Aosta took a lead role, taking on a clear Gruyère-like presence. If you serve this lasagna to a discerning crowd, Fontina d'Aosta might be your choice. For an intergenerational gathering, however, I'd recommend milder Danish or domestic fontina.

Choosing a provolone proved equally complicated. According to Steve Jenkins, provolone is made from mozzarella that has been rubbed with brine, bound with a rope and hung to dry in a temperature- and humidity-controlled environment. For this reason, the mild or unaged provolone offered little flavor depth for white lasagna. Sharp provolone cheeses, whether domestic or imported, vary. The forceful bite of one domestic provolone that I tried would have overwhelmed any dish. One imported aged provolone and another sharp domestic provolone offered flavor without hogging attention. The lesson: avoid mild provolone and taste the sharp ones before you go to the trouble of grating them.

thinned out the thick puree in which crushed tomatoes are usually packed. I now had a sauce that was the right quantity for the lasagna, but it tasted a little too thin and tangy. To sweeten the sauce and give it dimension, I sautéed a couple of onions until they were lightly caramelized.

In the absence of meat, ricotta makes lasagna feel pleasantly rich and substantial. After testing fourteen different flavorings and enhancements, I realized that the ricotta needed no embellishment whatsoever. Draining it did nothing but add a step to the recipe. Egg, egg yolk, egg and cream, and egg and water mixed with it only turned the cheese stiff and grainy, and stirring Parmesan cheese into it did the same thing. Flavoring it with garlic was too harsh; basil was okay, but I decided I preferred it in the sauce. Parsley wasn't all that helpful — even salt and pepper took away from the ricotta's natural sweetness.

Since cottage cheese and ricotta are cousins once removed, I tried substituting cottage cheese as well. After all, that's what my mom did. I had a soft spot for this one, but tasters immediately told me I was way off base.

PART-SKIM VERSUS WHOLE-MILK MOZZARELLA

A few final tests resulted in further refinements. To determine if there was any difference between fresh, part-skim, and whole-milk mozzarella, I made lasagnas with one of each. Surprisingly, the fresh mozzarella became almost invisible during baking and tasted bland. I detected very little difference between part-skim and whole-milk. Given their equality, part-skim is the obvious choice.

The same holds true for ricotta. I detected flavor and texture differences from brand to brand. Some were coarse and grainy; others (which I preferred) were creamy smooth. There's no way to know the texture until you open the container. But don't worry. If you want to make grainy ricotta smooth, just dump it in the food processor and press pulse.

Vegetable Lasagna
with Fontina Cheese and
Creamy Parmesan Sauce

Serves 8 to 12

Make this lasagna with the vegetables you like and have on hand. I've kept the recipe simple by calling for a pound each of two different vegetables, but feel free to use a pound each of four vegetables, making each of the four layers with one vegetable.

1 pound each of 2 vegetables (asparagus and mushrooms; spinach and zucchini; broccoli and carrots; eggplant and bell peppers, or other desired combination; see page 110)

1½ tablespoons salt

15 Ronzoni oven-ready lasagna noodles (from 2 packages)

½ pound fontina or provolone cheese, grated (2½ cups; see page 112)

¾ cup grated Parmesan cheese

PARMESAN-FLAVORED WHITE SAUCE

2½ cups 2% milk (whole and skim work as well)

1 cup canned chicken broth or vegetable broth

6 garlic cloves, chopped

3 tablespoons butter

5 tablespoons all-purpose flour

½ cup grated Parmesan cheese

¼ teaspoon salt

Freshly ground black pepper

1. Prepare vegetables (see pages 116–20) to yield about 4 cups; set aside.

2. Mix salt and 2 quarts very hot tap water in a 13-by-9-inch baking pan. Add noodles and soak until soft and pliable, 10 minutes. Drain and stack loosely. (Noodles tend to stick together as they dry but pull apart easily.)

3. FOR PARMESAN SAUCE: Microwave milk, broth, and garlic in a 1-quart microwave-safe container on high power until steaming hot, about 8 minutes. (Or slowly heat in a medium

saucepan over medium-low heat.) Melt butter over medium heat in a large saucepan. When foaming subsides, whisk in flour and continue to cook, whisking constantly, until well blended. Pour in hot milk mixture all at once and whisk vigorously until sauce is smooth and starts to bubble and thicken. Stir in Parmesan and season with $1/4$ teaspoon salt and pepper to taste. Remove from heat and place plastic wrap directly over sauce's surface.

4 Adjust oven rack to upper-middle position and heat oven to 425 degrees. Smear $1/4$ cup sauce over bottom of baking pan. Assemble next layers in the following order: 3 noodles, $2/3$ cup sauce, half of one of cooked vegetables (alternate layers of each kind), $1/2$ cup fontina or provolone, and 2 tablespoons Parmesan. Repeat 3 more times. Then make a final layer with remaining 3 noodles, sauce, and cheeses. (Lasagna can be covered and refrigerated up to 24 hours ahead or frozen for up to 3 months; thaw before baking.) Seal lasagna with foil and bake until bubbly, about 35 minutes. Remove foil, then broil until cheese is brown-spotted, 5 to 7 minutes longer. Let stand for 10 to 15 minutes to firm up lasagna. Cut and serve.

Vegetable Lasagna with Creamy Ricotta and Get-Rich-Quick Tomato Sauce

Serves 8 to 12

Any vegetable combination works with this lasagna, but eggplant and onions are a terrific pairing. If the ricotta you purchase is grainy-textured, whip it in a food processor to smooth it.

1   pound each of 2 vegetables (asparagus and mushrooms; spinach and zucchini; broccoli and carrots; eggplant and bell peppers; or other desired combination; see page 110)

GET-RICH-QUICK TOMATO SAUCE

3   tablespoons butter
2   medium onions, halved and thinly sliced
2   garlic cloves, minced
$1/4$ teaspoon dried basil
1   can crushed tomatoes (28 ounces)
1   can diced tomatoes ($14^{1}/_{2}$ ounces)
    Salt (optional) and freshly ground black pepper

$1^{1}/_{2}$ tablespoons salt
15   Ronzoni oven-ready lasagna noodles (from 2 packages)
$1^{1}/_{2}$ cups smooth ricotta cheese (see note above)
1   pound part-skim mozzarella cheese, grated (about 4 cups)
$3/4$ cup grated Parmesan cheese

1   Prepare vegetables (see pages 118–20) to yield about 4 cups; set aside.

2   FOR TOMATO SAUCE: Heat butter over medium-high heat in a large pot. Add onions and cook, stirring frequently, until soft and golden brown, about 10 minutes. Add garlic and basil and cook until fragrant, about 30 seconds longer. Stir in tomatoes; rinse out cans using about $1/4$ cup water and add it to pot. Bring to a simmer, reduce heat to low, and simmer to blend flavors, 10 to 15 minutes. Season with salt, if necessary, and pepper to taste.

Meanwhile, mix salt and 2 quarts very hot tap water in a 13-by-9-inch baking pan. Add noodles and soak until soft and pliable, 10 minutes. Drain and stack loosely. (Noodles tend to stick together as they dry but pull apart easily.)

4 Adjust oven rack to upper-middle position and heat oven to 425 degrees. Smear $\frac{1}{2}$ cup sauce over bottom of baking pan. Assemble next layers in the following order: 3 noodles, 6 tablespoons ricotta cheese spread over noodles, a heaping $\frac{2}{3}$ cup sauce, half of one of the cooked vegetables (alternate layers of each kind), $\frac{3}{4}$ cup mozzarella, and 2 tablespoons Parmesan. Repeat 3 more times. Then make a final layer with remaining 3 noodles, sauce, mozzarella, and Parmesan. (Lasagna can be covered and refrigerated up to 24 hours ahead or frozen for up to 3 months; thaw before baking.) Seal lasagna with foil and bake until bubbly, about 35 minutes. Remove foil, then broil until cheese is brown-spotted, 5 to 7 minutes longer. Let lasagna stand 10 minutes to firm up. Cut and serve.

Steam-Sautéed Asparagus, Cauliflower, Broccoli, Carrots, or Spinach

Makes about 2 cups

If only thick asparagus is available, halve it lengthwise before cutting it into pieces. To perk up cauliflower, add ¼ teaspoon dried basil to the pan.

1 **pound of one of the following:**
- ➤ **Thin asparagus, trimmed and cut into 1-inch pieces**
- ➤ **Cauliflower, cut into medium florets**
- ➤ **Broccoli, cut into florets, stalks peeled and cut into ¼-inch-thick coins**
- ➤ **Carrots, peeled and sliced into ¼-inch-thick coins**
- ➤ **Spinach, rinsed and stemmed**

2 **garlic cloves, minced**

2 **teaspoons butter or olive oil**

Scant ½ teaspoon salt

Place vegetable, ⅓ cup water (omit water if cooking spinach), garlic, butter or olive oil, and salt in a large deep skillet or Dutch oven. Set lid ajar and cook over high heat until steam starts to vent. Cover and steam until vegetables are brightly colored and just tender, 3 to 4 minutes. Remove lid and continue to cook until water evaporates. Turn vegetables onto a plate; set aside uncovered. So that broccoli and cauliflower lie flat, cut florets into thick slices before assembly.

Sautéed Mushrooms or Peppers

Makes about 2 cups

Roasting the peppers gives them a sweeter, more intense flavor and is an optional cooking method if you have the time. To roast peppers, place them directly on the flame of the burner on your stovetop (if you have a gas stove), and roast over medium-high heat, turning frequently, until the skins are blackened. Or, if you have an electric stove, roast them a few inches from the broiler element, turning as each side blackens. Place in a paper bag to cool, then rub off the skins and seeds, and cut into thin strips.

1 **tablespoon olive oil**
1 **pound of one of the following:**
  - **Domestic white or brown (also known as cremini) mushrooms, rinsed and sliced**
  - **Yellow or red bell peppers, stemmed, seeded, and cut into $1/4$-inch-thick bite-size strips**
  - **Red, yellow, or white onions, halved and sliced thin**
  Salt
2 **garlic cloves, minced**

1 Heat oil in a large (11-to-12-inch) skillet over medium-high heat. When oil starts to shimmer, add vegetable and a sprinkling of salt, and cook, stirring often, until vegetable is soft and liquid evaporates, 5 to 7 minutes.

2 Stir in garlic and cook until fragrant, about 30 seconds. Turn onto a plate and set aside until assembly.

Broiled Eggplant, Zucchini, or Yellow Squash

Makes about 2 cups

To perk up zucchini and yellow squash, sprinkle with ¼ teaspoon dried basil when tossing with the garlic.

1 pound of one of the following:
- **Eggplant or zucchini or yellow squash, trimmed and sliced into ⅓-inch-thick rounds**

1–2 tablespoons olive oil

Salt

2 garlic cloves, minced

1. Adjust oven rack to highest position and preheat broiler.

2. Lightly brush both sides of vegetable with oil and sprinkle with salt. Broil, turning once, until brown-spotted on each side, 7 to 10 minutes. Sprinkle hot vegetables with garlic, lightly toss, and set aside until assembly.

Salmon is one of my entrées of choice when I serve a crowd. It's elegant, readily available, and reasonably priced. Even guests who say they don't care for fish generally like salmon. And unlike any other large cut, a whole salmon fillet can be ready in about twenty minutes.

Cooking and serving a whole salmon fillet is obviously more efficient than twelve individual fillets or steaks, but handling, maneuvering, and finding the right equipment for this foot-and-a-half-long cut creates its own problems. The big question, of course, is how to cook it. Give me an individual salmon fillet, and I can pan-sear or grill it to perfection. But pan-searing a whole salmon fillet is impossible, and grilling one can result in a sticky, frustrating mess.

The challenges that confronted me were clear. The cooking vessel and the technique had to work with ordinary kitchen equipment. It wasn't worth purchasing special racks, pans, or poachers for a dish I make perhaps a couple of times a year. Since there was always trouble turning, inverting, and transferring the salmon to a platter, the method had to be as hands-off as possible. Ideally, I wanted a grilled version as well as one that was cooked indoors. I also wanted to figure out an easy way to serve the salmon. Hacking up the fish before bringing it to the table was unattractive. Yet presenting guests with a large whole fish was a little like setting an uncarved ham or turkey on the table. I knew from experience, they'd just as soon skip over the entrée as destroy a beautifully garnished perfection.

BROIL OR BAKE?

Before cooking whole sides of salmon, I started testing individual fillets to see which cooking methods worked best. To avoid flavor distractions, I simply seasoned the fillets with salt and pepper and a little oil when it made sense.

Starting with broiling, I cooked two pieces of fish — one with the oven rack adjusted as close to the broiler as possible, the other about 6 inches from the element. Cooked closest to the heat, the first piece of salmon developed a decent-looking crust and was done in just 8 minutes. But unlike the juicy, caramelized crust of pan-seared salmon, the crust of the broiled one was leathery. Cooking the salmon so near the heat without turning it caused the fish to sear on the outside, while remaining medium-rare at the center. And although I like medium-rare salmon, I knew from experience that most of my guests preferred their fish juicy but opaque.

Broiling a little further from the element resulted in a more evenly cooked but less crusted fish. Since my ultimate salmon might be marinated or glazed, I reasoned the more distant heat was probably strong enough to brown a sweetened coating, but I'd withhold judgment for now.

I decided to try baking and roasting while I was at it. Cooked at a wide range of oven temperatures — 350 to 500 degrees — the salmon tasted blah. Even at 500 degrees, the surface never browned. All the salmon cooked at these temperatures were acceptable, but none was superb.

GRILL OR BARBECUE?

Grilled salmon is a little tricky, especially when you're working with a whole fillet. Up to this point, I had always cooked whole salmon fillets skin side down, so that if the fish stuck, it would be the skin, not the flesh, that got left behind. Grilled this way, whether over direct or indirect heat, the fish picked up just a slight hint of smoke. If adding wood chips or chunks, I'd consider this method. Otherwise, developing a crust was crucial.

It was hard to argue with salmon cooked *flesh* side down over direct heat. Much like broiling, the searing added color and flavor depth. But at this point, I had one big problem: the fish was sticking. Anticipating the problem (and hoping to simplify removal of the fish), I had already taken precautions by cooking the salmon on a large cake rack set over the grill rack. Still it stuck.

Reasoning that the fish was less likely to stick to a hot rack, I preheated the cake rack on the grill rack. In addition, I tried spraying both racks with vegetable-oil cooking spray, to no avail. The cake rack, I finally realized, was the problem. Like many wire racks, this one had wires running in both directions in a grid pattern. Better to hold the salmon secure, I had reasoned. Not so.

Since I didn't own a large enough rack with wires running in only one direction, I started looking around the kitchen. Then I remembered the oven rack. I tried again, setting the oven rack on the grill, spraying both racks with vegetable-oil cooking spray, and heating the grill over the highest heat possible. To my relief, it worked. The oven rack offered enough support to guarantee the salmon's safe removal from the grill but not so much support that the salmon became hopelessly glued.

I marinate rarely and brine often. Marinating, I find, tends to mask rather than enhance meat's character, while brining can produce the opposite effect. But salmon was different. I tested three marinades: one pineapple juice–based, one orange/lime juice–based and an Asian-style one. At the same time, I soaked a salmon fillet in a salt-sugar brine. All three marinades improved the flavor. And because all contained some form of sweetener, they helped the surface color. Although I love salty smoked salmon and gravlax, I didn't want my fresh salmon to taste like either, but with the brine, it did. Generously seasoning the surface is sufficient.

The recipe for pineapple juice marinade called for cooking down a large can of pineapple juice, then cooling it to room temperature before adding the fish — too lengthy a process for my taste. But it gave me an idea. Why not just buy frozen pineapple juice concentrate? It worked so well that I tried it with the orange juice marinade as well.

I liked the fruit juice concentrate–based marinades because they penetrated and flavored the fish fairly quickly. Since they were relatively thick, they also adhered to the fish, doubling as a glaze during cooking. They even serve a third purpose. When cooked down, they are transformed into a wonderfully pungent dipping sauce. With my newfound marinating glazes, the salmon cooked beautifully and evenly about 6 inches from the broiler and at medium-high heat on the grill.

At this point, I had two simple cooking techniques with accompanying marinating glazes, but I had yet to figure out a guest-friendly way to serve the whole fillet. Thanks to a *Bon Appétit* recipe, I got my answer. The recipe recommended cutting deep portion-size slits in the fillet, without slicing through the skin. I tried this for both grilled and broiled fillets, and it worked beautifully. This scoring not only simplified serving but helped the salmon marinate and cook more quickly and evenly.

Having tried all of the dry-heat methods, I was ready for poaching and steaming. Steaming a small fillet on a rack set over a roasting pan of simmering water was quick — the piece cooked in just 6 minutes. While its texture was fine, this farm-raised salmon was tasteless. Since the fish cooked so quickly, the herbs and aromatics I'd put in the water had little time to impart flavor.

Poaching yielded similarly unimpressive results. After brewing a flavorful concoction of clam juice, wine, peppercorns, lemon slices, and dill sprigs, I added the salmon and let it slowly cook to doneness. As with some of the other cooking methods, the fish tasted fine but not exceptional. Little, if any, of the potent cooking liquid penetrated the fish. I suspected there was a better moist-heat method.

As it turns out, there was. Oven-steaming proved to be the simplest and best of the moist-heat methods. Following a recipe I found on allrecipes.com, I laid the whole salmon fillet on a sheet of heavy-duty foil, seasoned the fish with salt and pepper, and covered it with lemon slices and dill sprigs. To help with the steaming and add to the flavor, I drizzled it with a little dry vermouth, enclosed it in foil and steamed it in a 450-degree oven. Steamed in its own juices, the fish was tasty, and unlike the other methods, this one infused the salmon with the flavor of the aromatics, herbs, and vermouth.

Once the salmon had been transferred to the serving platter, I simply had to wad up and throw away the foil. But there was one remaining question. Was 450 degrees the ideal temperature? My instinct was no.

To find out, I made three foil packs, steaming one salmon at 450 degrees, one at 350 degrees, and another at 250 degrees. Cooked at the two higher temperatures, the fish were comparatively overcooked and dry. The high heat also took its toll on the herbs and aromatics, which looked faded, spent, and ready for the garbage can. In contrast, the salmon steamed at 250 degrees took an hour but was cooked evenly and to perfection, with bright, colorful herbs and aromatics.

Moist-cooked salmon releases scum during cooking. If the salmon is poached, the scum simply floats to the surface and can be skimmed off. But with oven-steaming, the scum remains on the flesh. It can be easily scraped off with a paring knife, however. At that point, the fish can be garnished with fresh herbs and aromatics (or with the cooked ones) and carried out to expectant guests.

Broiled Marinated and Glazed Whole Salmon for a Crowd

Serves 12 to 16

The marinade and broiling techniques work equally well for individual salmon fillets.

1 **whole skin-on salmon fillet (3–3¹/₂ pounds), pin bones removed**
Marinating Glaze of choice (page 128)
Vegetable oil
Salt (omit if using soy glaze) and freshly ground black pepper

1. Following illustration, cut salmon to form 12 to 16 pieces, depending on how many people you are serving. Place scored salmon in a 1¹/₂-to-2-gallon zipperlock bag; pour marinating glaze over salmon. Press as much air as possible from bag, then seal. Make sure salmon is evenly coated with marinating glaze, then lay it flat and refrigerate for 3 hours (you can reduce marinating time, but salmon will not absorb as much flavor).

2. About 15 minutes before cooking, adjust oven rack to 6 inches from broiling element. Line a large jelly-roll pan, or other shallow baking pan large enough to hold salmon, with foil. Brush or spray foil with vegetable oil to keep salmon from sticking. Remove salmon from marinating glaze, shaking off excess. Lay salmon skin side down on baking pan. Season with salt and pepper.

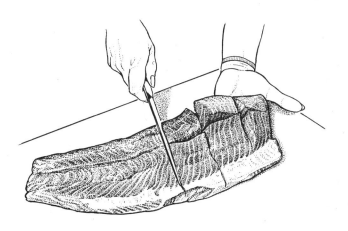

Cut the salmon lengthwise down the center seam, then make 6 to 8 crosswise cuts (depending on the size of the salmon), making sure to cut through the flesh but not the skin.

3 Meanwhile, transfer marinating glaze to a small nonreactive saucepan. Bring to simmer over medium-low heat and cook until marinade is a thick glaze (soy marinade will simply intensify in flavor), about 5 minutes. Remove from heat and keep warm.

4 Broil salmon, rotating pan if necessary to ensure even cooking, until glaze starts to caramelize and turns spotty brown, 10 to 12 minutes. Remove from oven, brush generously with glaze, then continue to broil until glaze starts to brown and salmon just turns opaque at its thickest point, another 1 to 2 minutes. (If fillet is exceptionally large and salmon is browned but not done, turn off oven and let salmon sit in oven for another 1 to 2 minutes.)

5 Slide salmon onto a serving platter. Garnish as desired and serve immediately with remaining dipping glaze.

Grilled Marinated and Glazed
Whole Salmon for a Crowd

Serves 12 to 16

Grill the salmon before guests arrive. Serve it at room temperature, if you like, or warm it in a 250-degree oven for 15 to 20 minutes before serving.

1   **whole skin-on salmon fillet (3–3¹/₂ pounds), pin bones removed**
    Marinating Glaze of choice (page 128)
    Vegetable oil
    Salt (omit if using soy glaze) and freshly ground black pepper

1   To prepare salmon, follow step 1 for Broiled Marinated and Glazed Whole Salmon for a Crowd (page 125).

2   About 15 minutes before cooking, remove rack from oven and set on gas grill rack. Brush or spray oven and gas grill racks with vegetable oil. Close grill lid and heat grill on high. Remove salmon from marinating glaze, shaking off excess. Lay salmon on a pan large enough to hold it. Season with salt and pepper.

3   While grill heats, transfer glaze to a small nonreactive saucepan. Bring to simmer over medium-low heat and cook until glaze is thick (soy marinade will simply intensify in flavor), about 5 minutes. Remove from heat; keep warm.

4   Place salmon, flesh side down, on oven rack, and close grill. Reduce heat to medium-high and cook for 8 to 9 minutes without opening grill cover. Check salmon. If it is nicely caramelized and brown-spotted on edges, reduce heat to medium and continue cooking until salmon is nicely browned, about 5 minutes longer. If salmon has not browned well, leave grill at medium-high heat and continue to cook for 5 minutes. If fillet is exceptionally large and salmon is browning too much but is not done, turn off grill and let salmon sit for another 1 to 2 minutes. Remove oven rack with salmon from grill. Let rest 3 to 5 minutes, then run a spatula under portions of salmon that touch rack to loosen. Place a platter over fish and carefully invert rack. Remove rack, then brush salmon generously with glaze. Serve with remaining dipping glaze.

Variations

Makes enough for one 3½-pound salmon fillet

Each of these mixtures starts out as marinade, penetrating and flavoring the fish. While the salmon cooks, pour the marinade into a small saucepan and reduce to a glaze to brush on the fish as it comes off the grill. Then pour the leftover glaze into a small bowl and serve alongside the salmon as a sauce.

To prepare the following glazes, mix all ingredients in a small bowl and set aside until ready to marinate salmon.

Pineapple-Soy Marinating Glaze

- 1 can (12 ounces) frozen pineapple juice concentrate, thawed
- 3 tablespoons soy sauce
- 1 teaspoon minced fresh ginger (optional)

Orange Red Pepper Marinating Glaze

- 1 can (12 ounces) frozen orange juice concentrate, thawed
- 1½ teaspoons hot red pepper flakes

Curry Chutney Marinating Glaze

- 1 cup Major Grey chutney
- 3 tablespoons red or rice wine vinegar
- 2 teaspoons curry powder

Soy-Sesame Marinating Glaze

- ³⁄₄ cup soy sauce
- ³⁄₄ cup rice wine vinegar
- 1 tablespoon sesame oil
- 3 tablespoons light or dark brown sugar
- 2 scallions, thinly sliced crosswise
- 1½ teaspoons hot red pepper flakes

"Poached" Salmon for a Crowd
with Orange Zest and Parsley

Cucumber Salsa with Lime (page 132) or Lemon-Parsley Relish with Capers and Shallots (page 134) is good with this salmon.

1	whole salmon fillet (about 3¹/₂ pounds), pin bones removed
1	teaspoon salt
	Freshly ground black pepper to taste

8–9	strips of orange zest, removed with a vegetable peeler from 1–2 oranges
6	parsley sprigs
¹/₄	cup clam juice
2	tablespoons lemon juice

Adjust oven rack to middle position and heat oven to 250 degrees. Place salmon on a sheet of heavy-duty foil as shown. Season with salt and pepper.

Arrange orange zest and parsley over salmon. Pour clam and lemon juices over salmon, enclose in foil as shown, and seal. Place in oven.

Cook until an oven thermometer registers 140 degrees at the thickest point, about 1 hour. Cool to room temperature, remove the herbs and aromatics from the cooked fish, scrape the scum from the surface, then replace the herbs and aromatics you removed (or garnish with fresh ones). Or refrigerate until well chilled, and serve.

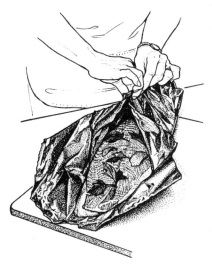

Place the salmon on a sheet of heavy-duty foil long enough to enclose it completely. After seasoning it and pouring liquid over it, enclose it in foil, rolling one edge of the foil over the other to make a tight seal.

"Poached" Salmon for a Crowd
with Ginger and Cilantro

Serves 12 to 14

Pineapple-Ginger Salsa (page 132) complements the flavors of this salmon.

1   whole salmon fillet (about 3¹/₂ pounds), pin bones removed

1   teaspoon salt

Freshly ground black pepper to taste

15–18   thin crosswise slices fresh ginger

6   cilantro sprigs

¹/₄   cup clam juice

1   tablespoon soy sauce

1   tablespoon sweet sherry

Proceed as for "Poached" Salmon for a Crowd with Orange Zest and Parsley (page 129), substituting ginger for orange zest, cilantro for parsley, and soy sauce and sherry for lemon juice.

"Poached" Salmon for a Crowd
with Lemon and Dill

Cucumber-Dill Cream (page 133), Mustard-Dill Cream (page 133), Lemon-Parsley Relish with Capers and Shallots (page 134), and Cucumber Salsa with Lime (page 132) are all good accompaniments.

1	whole salmon fillet (about 3¹/₂ pounds)
1	teaspoon salt
	Freshly ground black pepper to taste

10–12	strips of zest from 2 lemons
6	dill sprigs
¹/₄	cup clam juice
3	tablespoons lemon juice

Proceed as for "Poached" Salmon for a Crowd with Orange Zest and Parsley (page 129), substituting lemon zest for orange and dill for parsley.

Cucumber Salsa with Lime

Makes about 2 cups

A mix of grapefruits and oranges, sectioned and cut into medium chunks, can be substituted for the cucumber. If this is the only sauce you're serving with the fish, you may want to double it.

1 seedless cucumber, cut into small dice (about 2 cups)
$^1/_2$ small red onion, cut into small dice
$^1/_3$ medium red bell pepper, cut into small dice
$^1/_2$ medium jalapeño, stemmed, seeded, and minced
1 tablespoon each minced fresh parsley and cilantro *or* 2 tablespoons minced fresh parsley
2 tablespoons lime juice
Salt and freshly ground black pepper to taste

Mix all ingredients in a medium bowl. Let stand for at least 5 to 10 minutes so flavors blend. (Salsa can be covered and refrigerated for up to 2 hours before serving.)

Pineapple-Ginger Salsa

Makes about 2 cups

Buying pineapple that has already been peeled and cored simplifies this recipe considerably.

$^1/_2$ fresh pineapple, peeled, cored, and cut into small dice (about 2 cups)
2 scallions, thinly sliced
$^1/_3$ small red bell pepper, cut into small dice
$^1/_2$ medium jalapeño, stemmed, seeded, and minced
1 tablespoon minced fresh cilantro or parsley
2 teaspoons minced peeled fresh ginger
2 tablespoons lime juice
Salt and freshly ground black pepper to taste

Mix all ingredients in a medium bowl. Let stand for at least 5 to 10 minutes so flavors blend. (Salsa can be covered and refrigerated for up to 2 hours before serving.)

Cucumber-Dill Cream

Makes about 1½ cups

Because they're seedless, I like using hothouse cucumbers for cold sauces and salsas. A regular cucumber can be used, however, if you simply scoop out the seeds.

½ small hothouse cucumber, cut into small dice
    (about 1 cup)
  Salt
1 cup sour cream
¼ cup minced red onion
1 garlic clove, minced
1 tablespoon minced fresh dill
1 tablespoon red wine vinegar
  Freshly ground black pepper

Place cucumber in colander; sprinkle with ½ teaspoon salt. Place a weight on cucumber (a water-filled zipperlock bag works well). Let stand until cucumbers release about 2 tablespoons liquid. Rinse quickly and pat dry. In a small bowl, mix cucumber with remaining ingredients, seasoning with salt and pepper to taste. Cover and refrigerate until ready to use. (Sauce can be covered and refrigerated for up to 3 hours before serving.)

Mustard-Dill Cream

Makes about 1 cup

For a sweet-flavored sauce, substitute honey mustard for the Dijon.

1 cup sour cream
½ cup Dijon mustard
3 tablespoons minced fresh dill

Mix all ingredients in a medium bowl. Cover and refrigerate until ready to serve. (Sauce can be refrigerated for up to 4 hours before serving.)

Lemon-Parsley Relish
with Capers and Shallots

Makes about 1 cup

If you prefer a mayonnaise-based sauce to a relish, substitute mayonnaise for the olive oil.

1/2 cup chopped fresh parsley

1/4 cup capers

1 medium shallot, thinly sliced

1/2 cup extra-virgin olive oil

4 teaspoons finely grated lemon zest

2 tablespoons juice from 1 large lemon

Salt and freshly ground black pepper to taste

Mix all ingredients in a medium bowl. Let stand at least 10 minutes so flavors blend. Cover and refrigerate until ready to use. (Relish can be covered and refrigerated for up to 1 day before serving.)

For festive holiday parties, few cuts rival beef tenderloin. This elegant roast cooks quickly and serves a crowd, and its rich, buttery slices are tender enough for lap-top dining. Despite its many virtues, however, beef tenderloin is not without its liabilities. Price, of course, is the biggest. Even at my local warehouse-style super-market, the going rate for a whole beef tenderloin is $7.99 a pound — an average sticker price of about fifty dollars. But there are special occasions — Christmas and New Year's Eve among them — when only a beef roast will do.

The tenderloin's sleek, boneless form makes for quick roasting, but its torpe-do-like shape — thick and chunky at one end, tapering at the other — roasts unevenly. In addition, this roast, which is usually done to a bare medium-rare, does not cook long enough or to a high enough internal temperature to develop precious pan drippings for a sauce. And finally, there is a tradeoff for that tender texture: a rich but mild flavor, sometimes barely recognizable as beef. With these challenges in mind, I headed to the supermarket and brought home 550 dollars' worth of beef tenderloin — just eleven roasts.

LET'S GET IT OFF

Whole beef tenderloin is composed of three sections. The thicker end is dubbed the "butt tenderloin"; the middle portion, virtually even in thickness, is called the "short tenderloin." The tapered tip is sold as part of the whole tenderloin or removed and sold as "tenderloin tips." Rather than lop off the butt or tip end to solve uneven cooking, I decided to take on the challenges of preparing the whole roast.

A whole beef tenderloin can be purchased "unpeeled," with an incredibly thick layer of exterior fat left attached, but is usually sold "peeled," or stripped of fat. Because of previous bad experiences with today's overly lean meat, I purchased six of the eleven roasts unpeeled, determined to leave on as much fat as possible. After a quick examination of the unpeeled roasts, however, I realized that the excessively thick layer of surface fat had to go. Not only would such a large quantity of rendering fat smoke up the kitchen, it would also prohibit a delicious crust from forming on the meat.

I peeled, literally, the thick layer of fat from the six tenderloins. Even after I had removed the sheath of fat, large fat pockets were still there, as was significant surface fat. I started by leaving generous amounts on each roast but eventually preferred only minimal patches.

It doesn't make sense to buy an unpeeled roast and trim it yourself. I paid $6.99 a pound for the unpeeled tenderloins, each weighing about eight pounds. After they were trimmed, they weighed about five pounds, a whopping three pounds of waste. Since peeled tenderloins of similar quality cost $7.99 per pound, it's more economical to buy those.

FOLD IT UNDER AND TIE IT UP

Roasting a whole tenderloin is a little like cooking a whole fish. Both are thick at one end and tapered at the other. For people who want a range of doneness, this is not a problem, but for cooks who prefer a more evenly cooked roast, a solution is needed.

Folding the tip end under and tying it ensures that the tenderloin cooks more evenly. (Even so, the tail end is always a *little* more well done than the butt end.) Tying the roast at approximately 1½-inch intervals further guarantees a more uniformly shaped roast and more even slices of beef.

After watching roast after roast bow during cooking, I found it necessary to snip the "silverskin," or surface connective tissue, at the butt end of the tenderloin. Since this thin membrane almost completely melts during roasting, I decided its removal was unnecessary. On the other hand, snipping the membrane at a couple of points releases the tension caused when the silverskin shrinks more than the meat to which it is attached.

BETTER HIGH THAN LOW

After cooking many roasts, I've come to like slow-roasting for the larger ones. The lower the heat, the more evenly the roast cooks, so you don't overcook the outer meat while you wait for the deep center to reach an ideal temperature. To develop a rich brown crust on these slow-roasted larger cuts, I either pan-sear them in the beginning or increase the oven temperature during the last few minutes of roasting.

Even though beef tenderloin is a relatively large roast, its long, thin shape means a fairly quick cooking time. High-temperature roasting, I thought, might work better for this cut. To determine the ideal temperature, I started at the two extremes, roasting one tenderloin at 200 degrees, the other at 500 degrees. As expected, the rendering fat from the 500-degree tenderloin smoked up the kitchen. The roast was overcooked at each end and around the edges, but the high heat had formed the thick, flavorful crust that is crucial to this mild-flavored roast. The 200-degree beef tenderloin wasn't perfect, either. Though it had an even, rosy pink interior, it lacked the all-important crust.

A 450-degree oven still gave me smoke and uneven cooking, so I moved down a notch to 425 degrees. For comparison, I roasted another tenderloin at 200 degrees, this time increasing the temperature to 425 degrees at the end. Both roasts emerged from the oven looking beautiful, and the carved meat from each roast tasted almost identical. Since the tenderloin roasted at 425 degrees was done in just 45 minutes (as compared to the slow-roasted tenderloin, which took about 1 1/2 hours), I chose the high-heat method.

Although all roasts should rest 15 to 20 minutes after roasting, I found beef tenderloin improves dramatically if left uncarved even longer. If it's cut too soon, its slices are too soft and flabby. A slightly longer rest, however, allows the meat to firm up to a texture I find more appealing.

GETTING BETTER WITH AGE

The best beef is always aged, to give it a more pronounced beefy flavor. Aged beef is available only from good specialty markets, though, and you pay for that aging. It's easy — and perfectly safe — to age your own, simply by letting it sit, uncovered, in the coldest part of your refrigerator for a few days. I tried the technique with tenderloin by blotting the Kryovac-packed meat dry and refrigerating it on a wire rack set over a roasting pan. In addition, I salted another tenderloin and refrigerated it like the other roast. The salted roast tasted more like corned beef than tenderloin — at least a 50 percent loss on my big investment. The beef straight out of the plastic wrapping tasted washed out when compared with the dry-aged meat, which was stronger and gamier, with a pleasant tang and a buttery texture. Four days in the refrigerator was enough. Any longer and the meat would have been overly dry. Interestingly, other tasters preferred the milder, fresher flavor of the tenderloin roasted straight out of the package.

Since the roast yields few pan juices, I developed simple sauces, none of which are dependent on drippings. They work well with warm, room-temperature, or even cold beef tenderloin.

IS IT SAFE?

With the emphasis on meat safety, 160 degrees (the temperature at which potentially dangerous bacteria have definitely given up the ghost) has become the official safe internal temperature. It is clear why hamburgers must be cooked to this well-done stage. They are, after all, a ground concoction of hodgepodge beef scraps with potentially contaminated surfaces. Beef tenderloin, with an exposed surface and an unexposed interior, is different.

According to Sarah Reddington, director of the Beef and Veal Culinary Center of the National Cattlemen's Beef Association, beef tenderloin and other beef roasts and steaks are safe to cook medium-rare. Any bacteria on the roast's surface are killed during roasting. The unexposed interior is virtually sterile and therefore safe.

Taking it one step further, the research and technical department of the National Cattlemen's Beef Association wondered if the interior would offer a bacteria-friendly environment if somehow it were contaminated. To test the roast's safety, the researchers performed a series of experiments in which roasts were intentionally injected with bacteria. Their test results confirmed that, unlike hamburger, a roast's interior is not a breeding ground for bacteria.

At this time, the research team is presenting its findings to the USDA in hopes that the suggested internal temperature of roasts and steaks might be officially lowered to a temperature below 160 degrees.

Simple Roast Beef Tenderloin

Serves 12 to 16

Aging meat is optional, but if you purchase your beef tenderloin a few days before cooking it, you can intensify its beefy flavor simply by patting it dry, placing it on a rack set over a pan large enough to accommodate the roast, and putting it in the coldest section of your refrigerator. If you find yourself with an unpeeled roast, simply pull the fat from the roast. It will peel off in sheets. Trim remaining excess fat, but leave a few patches. They give the meat flavor and help it to brown.

1 **whole beef tenderloin, peeled of fat (5–6 pounds)**
2 **tablespoons olive oil**
1 **tablespoon kosher salt**
2 **tablespoons coarsely ground black pepper**

1 Two to 3 hours before roasting time, remove tenderloin from refrigerator, pat dry, and prepare and tie as shown.

2 Adjust oven rack to upper-middle position and heat oven to 425 degrees. Set meat on a sheet of plastic wrap and brush all over with oil. Sprinkle with salt and pepper, lifting plastic wrap up and around meat to press on excess seasonings.

3 Roast tenderloin on a wire rack set in a shallow roasting pan until a meat thermometer inserted into thickest part of roast

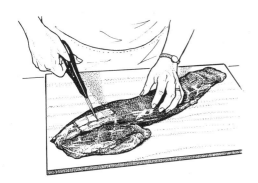

To keep the meat from bowing during roasting, snip the silverskin at 3 or 4 points.

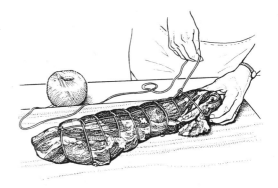

To ensure that the tenderloin roasts more evenly, fold the thin tip end of the roast under about 6 inches. For more even cooking and evenly sized slices, tie the roast every 1½ to 2 inches.

registers 130 degrees for medium-rare to medium, about 45 minutes. Let stand at room temperature 10 to 15 minutes. (Tenderloin can be wrapped in plastic, refrigerated for up to 2 days, sliced and served chilled.)

4 Cut meat into ¹/₂-inch-thick slices. Arrange on a platter and serve with one or more of the sauces that follow.

Peppercorn-Coated Roast Beef Tenderloin
Serves 12 to 16

Be sure to crush the peppers with a mortar and pestle or with a heavy-bottomed saucepan or skillet. Don't use a coffee or spice grinder, which will pulverize the green and pink peppercorns to a powder before the harder peppercorns begin to break up.

Coarsely crush 6 tablespoons mixed peppercorns (black, white, pink, and green) and proceed as for Simple Roast Beef Tenderloin, pressing peppercorns onto tenderloin, along with salt.

Chili-Rubbed Roast Beef Tenderloin
Serves 12 to 16

Mix 2¹/₂ tablespoons chili powder with 1¹/₂ teaspoons ground cumin and ¹/₂ teaspoon dried oregano and proceed as for Simple Roast Beef Tenderloin, pressing chili powder mixture onto tenderloin, along with salt and pepper.

Parsley Sauce with Cornichons and Capers
Makes about 1 cup

This sauce is particularly well suited to Simple Roast Beef Tenderloin.

³/₄   **cup minced fresh parsley leaves**
12   **cornichons, minced (6 tablespoons), plus 1 teaspoon cornichon juice**
¹/₄   **cup capers, coarsely chopped**
2   **medium scallions, light and dark green parts, minced**
    Pinch salt
¹/₄   **teaspoon freshly ground black pepper**
¹/₂   **cup extra-virgin olive oil**

Mix all ingredients in a medium bowl. (Sauce can be made up to a day in advance and refrigerated before serving.)

Mustard–Green Peppercorn Sauce

This cool yet piquant sauce goes well with Simple Roast Beef Tenderloin (page 139). Green peppercorns are usually available in the gourmet section of the grocery store or in specialty food shops, but they can be omitted if unavailable.

1   cup Dijon mustard
¹/₂   cup crème fraîche or sour cream
1   tablespoon green peppercorns (in brine), minced

Mix all ingredients in a medium bowl; cover and refrigerate until ready to serve. (Sauce can be made a day in advance and refrigerated before serving.)

Sour Cream Sauce with Roasted Jalapeños

3   medium jalapeños
¹/₄   teaspoon chili powder
4   teaspoons minced fresh cilantro leaves
1   cup sour cream

Broil peppers, turning once, until skin has blistered and blackened. Let cool, then peel, stem, seed, and mince.

Mix all ingredients in a medium bowl; cover and refrigerate until ready to serve. (Sauce can be made up to 4 hours in advance and refrigerated before serving.)

Chicken and dumplings is the humblest of comfort foods. A satisfying all-in-one meal, it's a real charmer to serve to company — the kind of thing that immediately makes guests feel right at home. Unpretentious though it may be, this dish is not exactly a looker. Its monochromatic ingredients give it a dowdy feel.

I wanted a dinner that would be easy, yet beautiful. I also wanted to discover the secret to foolproof dumplings that would be light and tender, yet substantial.

I grew up in the South, where dumplings are rolled thin and cut into strips. I lived nearly a decade in the Midwest, where dumplings are rolled thick and stamped out like biscuits. And I've spent nearly an equal amount of time near Pennsylvania Dutch country, where dumplings are pinched off and dropped onto the surface. Could these three styles be made from the same dough, or would I need to develop separate recipes to accommodate each style?

GETTING IN HOT WATER

Most flour-based dumplings are made of flour, salt, and one or more of the following ingredients: butter, eggs, milk, and baking powder. Depending on the ingredient list, dumplings are usually mixed in one of three ways. The most common mixing method is a biscuit or pastry style, in which cold butter is cut into the dry ingredients and then cold milk and/or eggs are stirred in until just combined. Some dumpling recipes instruct the cook to melt the butter first, then mix the wet ingredients into the dry ones. And finally, many of the egg-based dumplings are made like pâte à choux (cream puffs), by adding flour to hot water and butter, then whisking in eggs, one at a time.

I spent a full day preparing batch after batch of dumplings in some combination of the above ingredients and following one of the three mixing techniques. (I even made a yeast-based dumpling that, when cooked, tasted like soggy bread!) By the end of my tests, I hadn't made a single dumpling that I really liked. Dumplings made with eggs tended to be tough and chewy, while those made without eggs were too fragile, often disintegrating into the cooking liquid. Dumplings made without enough liquid were leaden, while those made with too much were particularly prone to fall apart.

I finally made progress after coming upon a recipe in *Master Recipes* (Clear Light Publishers, 1998). Author Stephen Schmidt cuts butter into flour, baking powder, and salt, but instead of the usual procedure of stirring cold liquid into the dry ingredients, he adds hot liquid to the flour-butter mixture. Dumplings made by this method were light and fluffy, yet held up beautifully during cooking. These were the firm yet tender dumplings I was looking for.

With the technique decided upon, it was time to test the formula ingredients. Looking for a tender dumpling, I made a batch each with all-purpose and cake flour. I would have guessed that cake-flour dumplings would be even lighter-textured than those made with all-purpose. In fact, just the opposite was true. They were tight, yet spongy, with a metallic, acidic aftertaste. Attributing this odd flavor to the baking powder, I called food-science expert Shirley Corriher for confirmation. According to Corriher, however, the problem lies with the cake flour, not the baking powder. The method by which cake flour is processed leaves it acidic. This acidity helps set eggs faster in baking, resulting in a smoother, finer-textured cake, but the flavor, which is hidden by a butter-sugar-egg-rich cake batter, is distinct in the simpler dumpling dough.

HOT MILK AND MELTED BUTTER FOR TENDER DUMPLINGS

Which fat best enriched the dumplings? Although I was certain that dumplings made with vegetable shortening wouldn't taste as good as those made with butter, I had high hopes for those made with chicken fat. After a side-by-side test with butter, shortening, and chicken fat, I selected those made with butter, which gave the dumplings the extra flavor dimension they needed.

The choice of liquids proved to be simple. Whole milk dumplings were tender, with a pleasant biscuity flavor. Dumplings made with chicken stock, much like those made with chicken fat, tasted too similar to the broth. Those made with water were dull. Since buttermilk tends to separate and even curdle when heated, buttermilk dumplings felt wrong.

Up to this point, I had made all the dumplings by cutting the fat into the dry ingredients, then adding hot liquid. Since I was adding hot milk, I questioned whether it was necessary to cut in the cold butter first. Why couldn't I simply heat the milk and butter together and stir the mixture into the dry ingredients? After a taste test, I determined that cutting the butter into the flour was indeed unnecessary. Simply adding the hot milk and melted butter to the dry ingredients yielded more substantial, better-textured dumplings.

I tested my new formula by shaping the dumplings into balls, cutting them with a biscuit cutter, and rolling them thin and cutting them into various shapes. Regardless of the style, I got the same consistent results: tender, sturdy dumplings.

Next I turned my attention to the chicken and vegetable part of the dish. My first few attempts were not a success. For the sake of convenience, I left the chicken pieces on the bone, cut the vegetables into long, thin strips and thickened the broth ever so slightly. As I ate, I realized that I needed a knife (to cut the chicken off the bone), a fork (to eat the vegetables, dumplings, and meat), and a spoon (for the broth). I wanted the dish to be eater-friendly — a one-utensil meal.

Could chicken and dumplings be made with boneless, skinless chicken breasts? I ultimately decided that it couldn't. Only a whole chicken could give the large chunks of light and dark meat that were needed. Because I wanted the dish to serve six to eight, and because I preferred bigger hunks of meat, I chose a large oven roaster over the small fryer hen.

From experiences with chicken noodle soup, I had already discovered the ideal method for making quick, flavorful broth, which also worked beautifully for chicken and dumplings. Rather than following more traditional methods of simmering chicken parts for an hour or two, I start by cutting a whole chicken into parts, then further hacking the bony back and wings into small pieces. I sauté the hacked-up pieces with an onion. Once they lose their raw color, I turn the heat to low and cover the pot to release and intensify the chicken flavor. Only after 20 minutes of stewing do I finally add water, as well as the remaining chicken parts. With just 30 minutes of simmering, I have flavorful chicken parts as well a rich, intense broth.

My updated chicken and dumplings needed vegetables, but where and how to cook them? In an attempt to streamline the process, I tried cooking the vegetables along with the poaching chicken. After fishing out hot, slightly overcooked vegetables from among the chicken parts and pieces, I decided this shortcut wasn't practical. Instead, I simply washed the chicken-poaching pot, returned it to the stove, and steamed the vegetables for 10 minutes while I strained the broth, removed the meat from the chicken parts, and made the dumpling dough. Since the vegetables would be heated again for a short time in the sauce, I wanted them slightly undercooked at this point. Steaming them separately gave me more control and resulted in brighter, fresher vegetables in the finished dish.

With the meat poached and off the bone, the broth degreased and strained, and the vegetables steamed to perfection, I was ready to complete the dish. To a roux of flour and chicken fat, I added the homemade broth and stirred it until thickened. Although I needed 6 cups of broth to poach the chicken parts, I found that this quantity of liquid made the dish much too saucy, so I removed 2 cups for another use. Then I added the chicken and vegetables to the thickened sauce and steamed the dumplings. As they cooked, the chicken and vegetables married with one another and the sauce.

A few peas and a little parsley make the dish beautiful, while sherry heightens the flavor. A touch of cream enriches and beautifies. The final dish is both eye-catching and palate-pleasing, and it's simple to make. Best of all, I can eat it with just a fork.

Chicken and Dumplings
with Aromatic Vegetables

Serves 6

A touch of heavy cream gives the dish a more refined look and rich flavor, but for weeknight dinners, you may want to omit it. Flat noodle-style dumplings or round, puffy ones create a more rustic feel, while the cut-out dumplings make a more sophisticated dish.

1   **large roasting chicken, 6–7 pounds**
1   **large onion, unpeeled, cut into large chunks**
2   **bay leaves**
    Salt
3   **celery stalks, trimmed and cut into 1-by-$^1/_2$-inch sticks**
4   **carrots, peeled and cut into 1-by-$^1/_2$-inch sticks**
6   **boiling onions, peeled and halved**

BAKING POWDER DUMPLINGS

2   **cups all-purpose flour**
1   **tablespoon baking powder**
$^3/_4$ **teaspoon salt**
3   **tablespoons butter**
1   **cup milk**

4   **tablespoons softened butter or skimmed chicken fat**
6   **tablespoons all-purpose flour**
1   **teaspoon dried thyme leaves**
2   **tablespoons dry sherry or vermouth**
$^1/_4$ **cup heavy cream (optional)**
$^3/_4$ **cup frozen peas, thawed**
$^1/_4$ **cup minced fresh parsley leaves**
    Freshly ground black or white pepper

1   Cut chicken into 2 breast halves, 2 thighs, 2 legs, 2 wings, and back. Cut wings and back into 1-inch pieces.

2   Heat a large Dutch oven over medium-high heat. Add back and wing pieces and onion chunks and sauté until onion softens and chicken loses its raw color, about 5 minutes. Reduce heat to low, cover, and continue to cook until chicken pieces give up

most of their liquid, about 20 minutes. Increase heat to medium-high, add 4 cups water, remaining chicken parts, bay leaves, and ¾ teaspoon salt; bring to a simmer. Reduce heat to low and simmer, partially covered, until broth is rich and flavorful and chicken pieces are just cooked through, 20 to 30 minutes longer. Remove chicken pieces with a slotted spoon and set aside to cool. When chicken is cool enough to handle, remove meat from bones in large chunks. Discard bones. Strain broth into a large bowl, discarding backs and wings. Skim and reserve fat from broth for sauce. Rinse out pot.

3   Add ½ inch of water to cleaned pot and fit with a steamer basket; return to medium-high heat. Add celery, carrots, and halved onions, and steam until just tender, about 10 minutes. Remove vegetables and set aside.

4   **FOR DUMPLINGS:** Mix flour, baking powder, and salt in a medium bowl. Heat butter and milk to a simmer, then add to dry ingredients. Mix with a fork until mixture just comes together. Following illustrations, form dumplings.

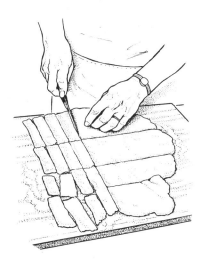

For flat noodle-like dumplings, roll the dough to a ⅛-inch thickness and cut into approximately 2-by-½-inch strips.

For round, puffy dumplings, pinch the dough off to form 18 pieces.

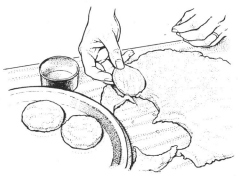

For biscuit-like dumplings, roll the dough to a ½-inch thickness and use a 2-inch biscuit cutter or a round drinking-glass top to cut the dough into rounds.

5 Heat butter and/or chicken fat in pot over medium-high heat. Whisk in flour and thyme; cook, whisking constantly, until flour turns golden, 1 to 2 minutes. Whisking, gradually add sherry or vermouth, then 4 cups chicken broth (reserving remaining broth for another use); simmer until gravy thickens. Stir in cream, along with the chicken and steamed vegetables; return to a simmer.

6 Add dumplings to simmering chicken; cover and simmer until dumplings are cooked through, about 5 minutes. Stir in peas and parsley. Adjust seasonings, adding a generous amount of pepper. Serve immediately in soup plates, ladling a portion of meat, sauce, vegetables, and dumplings into each dish.

Chicken and Herbed Dumplings with Aromatic Vegetables

Serves 6

Proceed as for Chicken and Dumplings with Aromatic Vegetables, adding a mixture of $1/4$ cup minced soft fresh herb leaves, such as parsley, chives (or scallion greens), and tarragon, along with milk in dumpling recipe. If other herbs are unavailable, all parsley may be used.

Chicken and Cornmeal Dumplings with Aromatic Vegetables

Serves 6

Proceed as for Chicken and Dumplings with Aromatic Vegetables, adding 1 teaspoon sugar and using $1 1/2$ cups flour and $1/2$ cup fine-ground cornmeal in place of 2 cups flour in dumpling recipe.

Ribs That Taste Like You Slaved All Day

If I had to think of one dish I could eat every day for the rest of my life, barbecued spareribs would come to mind. Maybe I feel this way because I cook them so rarely and enjoy them so much.

Up until this point, I'd always made "real ribs," meaning I'd sprinkle them with a rub, refrigerate them overnight and cook them ever so slowly over a charcoal fire with a couple of chunks of smoldering hickory. After they came off the grill, I'd wrap them tightly in foil, stick them in a paper sack, then set them in a turned-off warm oven to rest until they became succulent and tender.

I don't have time to cook ribs like that very often, and when I do, I can't cook many at a time. Because of the ribs' long, thin shape, I can barely fit two slabs on the grill. And since I cook my ribs over indirect heat, a third to a half of the grill is unused, giving me even less space for the ribs. I wanted to find out if there was a way to simplify the recipe, or at least make a large enough quantity so that I could eat them every day if I wanted.

I began by analyzing fifty mostly indoor-cooked rib recipes. I was almost overwhelmed with the number of times, temperatures, and combinations of techniques that guaranteed tender-to-the-bone ribs. I started by testing the major techniques to focus myself.

INDOOR/OUTDOOR EXERCISES

Baking was the most common rib method, so I started by cooking five slabs in a 300-degree oven. I cooked the first slab in the low oven until fork-tender. I pulled out slabs two and three when they were just shy of done and finished them on a gas grill, adding a handful of soaked hickory chips to the third slab. Slabs four and five I finished in a hot oven, broiling one and blasting the other at 500 degrees.

Although these ribs were acceptable, none was sensational. Both grilled slabs had developed a nice crust from their post-roast sear, but the smoke and grill flavors were almost imperceptible. All five slabs were on the dry side, with virtually no flavor depth.

Boiling is a common way of cheating on time, and as with baking, there were many variations on the theme. Because plain boiled ribs aren't very appealing, this method is always used in combination with another cooking technique. I tried them all: boil, then bake; boil, then broil; boil, then roast at a high temperature; boil, then grill; and finally, boil, then smoke. One recipe suggested that poaching — cooking the ribs at a low simmer — would result in more tender, juicy, succulent ribs than boiled ones. I tried that, too.

Regardless of how the boiled ribs were cooked the second time around, they couldn't shake their unmistakable boiled look and flavor. The moist heat prohibited color or crust development, and it was practically impossible to make up for that loss during the second round of cooking. Unlike the crusty-textured surfaces of oven-baked ribs, the boiled ribs' slick surface repelled the sauce. Poaching did, in fact, result in more juicy ribs, but like their boiled kin, they lacked flavor, color, and crust.

Other recipes suggested searing the ribs in a pan before further cooking. Following two published recipes, I tried two variations: searing and baking one slab, and searing, boiling, then baking another. Pleasant enough, the sear-and-bake ribs tasted like a nicely browned pork chop or roast. The extra boiling step, though, did nothing to justify the effort. Good results or not, the impracticality of trying to brown a couple of slabs of ribs in a skillet caused me to cross it off the list.

A final method suggested smoking the ribs *before* roasting them. After just 15 minutes of grill time and a handful of chips, these ribs were transformed, and I was pleasantly shocked at how much smoke and grill flavor permeated the meat in a short time. Unlike the ribs that I had baked, then smoked, these actually tasted as if they had spent some time outdoors. Smoking the ribs before cooking gave me plenty of color and flavor. When I smoked them after cooking, the smoke was virtually undetectable.

This outdoor-smoke/indoor-roast technique needed further refining. And for the times when I didn't want to go outside at all, I wanted a successful indoor method. For now, I was pleased to have found a technique that required so little and delivered so much.

Before fine-tuning the technique, I shifted gears. Since many recipes call for marinating the ribs first, I wanted to know if this step was effective. For testing, I selected three very different styles of marinades: one soy-based, another wine-and-vinegar-based, and the third plain barbecue sauce.

Though very different in style, all three marinades had the same effect.

Without penetrating the meat, they managed to overpower the character of the pork.

Brining pork makes the meat more tender, so I couldn't ignore that possibility. I assumed the thin ribs would absorb the salt solution relatively quickly. I made a brine of ¾ cup each salt and sugar for a half-gallon of water and brined a slab for 30 minutes. In just that short time, the ribs were fully seasoned, almost too much so. After comparing them with ribs that were just salted and peppered, I decided the extra step wasn't worth it.

Dry spice rubs were much more successful. The first few that I tried, designed for southern-style ribs, were too strong, but I liked the way their flavors enhanced the pork and their sandy texture crusted the meat. Wanting a rub that would work with any style of ribs, I pared the rub down to just five generic ingredients — salt, pepper, brown sugar, paprika, and garlic powder — all flavors that would complement not just barbecue-sauced ribs but nearly any glaze I chose.

During these tests, I also made another interesting discovery. A few recipes suggested brushing the slab with mustard — a secret, they claimed, of many award-winning recipes. Not only was the mustard supposed to help the rub to cling better; it was also supposed to quietly flavor the ribs. I was a little skeptical that ballpark mustard could be discreet, but I brushed two portions of ribs with mustard — one with ballpark, the other with Dijon. Not only did both mustards accomplish what the recipes claimed, they also bulked up the spice rub, resulting in an impressive crust. Those who are so inclined can stir a couple of teaspoons of liquid smoke into the mustard, though the ribs are so good, they don't really need it.

With the mustard-and-spice-rub coating now part of my recipe, I needed to determine when to start brushing the ribs with glaze. After smoking the ribs, then slow-roasting them, I tried brushing them after 30 minutes, 1 hour, and 1½ hours of roasting. I didn't like any of them. Even brushing the ribs during the last 30 minutes wasn't right and ruined the wonderful, flavorful crust.

Ultimately, I opted for roasting the ribs completely, then brushing them with the glaze, and briefly broiling them. Cooked this way, the meat was tender, rich, and distinct, the spice-rubbed exterior stayed crisp and flavorful, and the glaze was piquant and caramelized.

I had observed that the 300-degree oven temperature dried out the ribs before they were done, so I lowered the oven heat to 250 degrees and found subsequent slabs much more juicy.

I also noticed that the undersides steamed in their own juice rather than roasting. By cooking the ribs on a rack set over a pan, I solved one problem but created another. How could I oven-roast a large number of ribs without having to buy extra racks and pans?

Necessity brought forth a very clever invention. After staring at the ribs, the oven, and pans, I decided to try roasting the ribs right on the oven rack. I laid three whole slabs of ribs directly on the rack. Then I placed a jelly-roll pan on the bottom rack of the oven and covered it with a sheet of heavy-duty aluminum foil, extending the foil so it covered the entire surface of the rack.

The ribs roasted beautifully. At such a low heat, there was no spitting or smoking fat. And cleanup was a breeze — simply rinse the oven rack and toss the foil. Since the heating element of my gas oven is under the oven floor, I can use both oven racks and roast six slabs at one time, placing the foil-lined pan on the floor of the oven. Cooks who own electric ovens with heating coils mounted on the oven floor will need to place the foil on the bottom rack, leaving room for three slabs (or four slabs of baby back ribs) on the top rack.

AND SMOKE 'EM OUT

Through trial and error, I perfected the smoking process as well. Before turning on the grill, I removed the grill racks and lined the grill area over the burners with heavy-duty foil, pricked it with a fork and scattered the foil with the soaked hickory chips. I put the grill racks back in place, closed the lid and turned all the burners on high. In just 7 to 8 minutes, the grill was preheated, and the chips were just beginning to smoke.

While the grill preheated, I prepared the ribs, then placed them on the grill rack, turned the heat to medium and smoked them until the chips were spent, about 15 minutes. Then I transferred them to the oven rack and slow-roasted them until tender.

After days of ribs for lunch, dinner, and mid-afternoon snacks, I'd had more than my fill, but I'd succeeded in making my dream ribs in just a couple of hours. Maybe I wouldn't eat them every day, but now I could if I wanted.

The Best Smoked Oven-Roasted Ribs (Outdoor/Indoor Version)

These ribs are smoked on a gas grill for 15 minutes. If you can spare the extra few minutes for the smoking, you'll be rewarded with ribs that rival the best. Just keep in mind that for every slab, you'll need 2 tablespoons each brown sugar and paprika, 1 tablespoon each black pepper and garlic powder, and $1/2$ teaspoon salt. If you have a gas oven, you can double this recipe. Since the foil-lined pan can be placed directly on the oven floor, you can use both oven racks and cook up to 6 slabs of spareribs or 8 slabs of baby backs, but you'll need to do the smoking in two batches. Simply discard the foil under the second rack of ribs once the ribs have been smoked.

3 cups wood chips, such as hickory or mesquite
6 tablespoons light or dark brown sugar
6 tablespoons paprika
3 tablespoons freshly ground black pepper
3 tablespoons garlic powder
   Salt
3 slabs pork spareribs *or* 4 slabs baby back ribs
$1/2$ cup plus 1 tablespoon Dijon or yellow mustard

   Your favorite barbecue sauce, or one of the glazes on pages 156–57 (optional)

Place chips in a small bowl; fill bowl with water to cover completely, and let stand 15 to 20 minutes. Drain. Mix dry rub of brown sugar, paprika, pepper, garlic powder, and $1\frac{1}{2}$ teaspoons salt in another small bowl and set aside.

2 Adjust one oven rack to low position. Remove remaining oven rack and place on a large sheet of heavy-duty aluminum foil the same size as rack to facilitate cleanup; you'll use it later in oven. Lay ribs directly on removed oven rack and sprinkle very lightly with salt. Brush both sides of ribs with mustard, then sprinkle both sides with dry rub. Heat oven to 250 degrees.

Remove rack or racks from a gas grill. Lay a large sheet of heavy-duty foil the size of grill over burners. Carefully puncture foil all over with a fork. Scatter drained chips over foil. Set grill racks back in position and close grill lid. Turn all burners on high and heat grill until first wisps of smoke from smoldering chips appear. Transfer ribs to grill, meat side up. Close lid, reduce heat to medium-high, and smoke ribs until grill stops smoking, about 15 minutes.

4 Meanwhile, wipe sheet of foil clean of dry rub and place on a jelly-roll pan. Set foil-lined pan on bottom oven rack, making sure foil extends over pan sides to cover entire rack. When ribs are smoked, transfer them to removed oven rack and place rack in upper-middle position in oven. Roast ribs until fork-tender, 2 to 3 hours for spareribs and 1½ to 2 hours for baby back ribs.

5 If coating ribs with barbecue sauce or glaze, remove jelly-roll pan from oven and pour off excess fat. Transfer ribs to foil-lined pan, meat side down. Turn on broiler.

6 Brush ribs with half of sauce or glaze and broil until glaze bubbles vigorously. Turn ribs over, brush with remaining glaze, and broil until glaze bubbles vigorously. Let stand 5 to 10 minutes, then cut slabs into individual ribs and serve.

The Best Oven-Roasted Ribs (Indoor Version)

Serves 6 to 8

This recipe is similar to the previous one except that the ribs are not smoked on the grill. As with the smoked ribs, cooks who have gas ovens can double the quantity of ribs, placing the foil-lined pan directly on the oven floor.

6 tablespoons light or dark brown sugar
6 tablespoons paprika
3 tablespoons freshly ground black pepper
3 tablespoons garlic powder
  Salt
1/2 cup plus 1 tablespoon Dijon or yellow mustard
2 teaspoons liquid smoke (optional)
3 slabs pork spareribs *or* 4 slabs baby back ribs

Your favorite barbecue sauce, or one of the glazes that follow (optional)

1 Adjust one oven rack to low position, remove remaining oven rack, and heat oven to 250 degrees. Mix a dry rub of sugar, paprika, pepper, garlic powder, and 1 1/2 teaspoons salt in a small bowl. Mix mustard and liquid smoke, if using, in another small bowl. Lay ribs directly on removed oven rack and lightly sprinkle with salt. Brush both sides of each slab with mustard, then sprinkle both sides with dry rub.

2 Line a jelly-roll pan with a large sheet of heavy-duty foil, extending foil so it covers oven rack.

3 Slide rack with ribs into upper-middle position and place foil-lined pan on lower oven rack, making sure that foil covers rack. Roast ribs until fork-tender, 2 to 3 hours for spareribs and 1 1/2 to 2 hours for baby backs.

4   If coating ribs with barbecue sauce or one of the glazes, remove jelly-roll pan from oven and pour off excess fat. Transfer ribs to foil-lined pan, meat side down. Turn on broiler.

5   Brush ribs with half of sauce or glaze, and broil until glaze bubbles vigorously. Turn ribs over, brush with remaining glaze, and broil until glaze bubbles vigorously. Let stand 5 to 10 minutes, then cut slabs into individual ribs and serve.

Streamlined Glazes for Ribs

Makes enough for
3 slabs of spareribs
or 4 slabs of baby
back ribs

Tired of bottled barbecue sauce but don't have time to spend an hour simmering your own? Most of the ingredients for these simplified sauces and glazes are probably already in your refrigerator or pantry.

To prepare each of the following glazes, mix all ingredients in a small bowl and brush onto ribs as directed in preceding recipes.

Maple Cranberry Glaze

$^1/_2$ cup maple syrup
$^1/_2$ cup whole-berry cranberry sauce
4   teaspoons red wine vinegar
$^1/_4$ teaspoon ground cloves

Sweet and Sour Orange Glaze

1   cup orange marmalade
$^1/_4$ cup rice wine vinegar
1   teaspoon dried thyme

Apricot Sherry Glaze

1   cup apricot jam
$2^1/_2$ tablespoons sherry vinegar
2   teaspoons ground cumin

Molasses Ketchup with Lime and Cilantro

This recipe is adapted from Chris Schlesinger and John Willoughby's *How to Cook Meat* (Morrow, 2000).

$^1/_2$ cup ketchup

$^1/_4$ cup molasses

$^1/_4$ cup lime juice

  4 teaspoons ground cumin

$^1/_4$ cup chopped fresh cilantro

Honey Mustard

$^1/_2$ cup honey

$^1/_2$ cup Dijon mustard

  1 teaspoon Worcestershire sauce

Except on certain holidays, leg of lamb isn't often the entrée that first comes to mind when many of us entertain — which is precisely why it may be the right thing to serve. It's less ordinary than ham and turkey. And when it's butterflied (boned and split open so that it lies flat), it offers all the convenience of a beef or pork roast, but with more flavor.

I first put butterflied leg of lamb on the menu during my catering years, and it was always a hit. Because it cooked so quickly, I often broiled it during cocktail hour. Guests were lured to the kitchen by the fragrance, and I usually ended up with an audience as I finished cooking and carving it.

I wanted to develop a foolproof technique for butterflied leg of lamb, whether I was cooking it in the oven or outside on the grill.

Buying the right lamb is key. Up to this point, I'd never bothered to inquire where the lamb came from. But after side-by-side tastings of American and imported lamb from Australia and New Zealand, I'll never forget to ask again. Whether aged or packed in Kryovac, American leg of lamb is markedly more tender than its chewy outback kin and is meaty and flavorful without tasting gamey.

Unlike imported lamb, which is grazed on grass its entire life, resulting in a tougher texture and wilder flavor, American lamb is first grazed, then corn-fed the last few months before slaughter, producing richer, more tender meat. And while some imported lamb has never been frozen, the majority of it has.

Although American lamb is a little more expensive than the imported variety (the reason many food clubs and chains specializing in low prices carry imported), many grocery stores make a point of promoting the American product. In my area, both butchers and half the grocery store chains feature domestic, the other half, imported. Domestic lamb is readily available. You just have to remember to ask if the label doesn't say.

Even better than American lamb is aged American lamb, which becomes meltingly tender in the aging process. To age properly, the leg must be left on the bone, with the fat still on it. The aging is best done by a butcher, but unlike aged beef, which is practically an endangered species, aged lamb is fairly common. Regardless of whether the lamb has been aged or not, have your butcher butterfly it for you. Explain that you want the leg opened up flat and that you want a roast of more or less uniform thickness to ensure even cooking.

More important than getting a roast of an even thickness is making sure the excess fat and the fell, the thin rubbery membrane covering the fat, are removed. The fell acts like a girdle during cooking, causing the butterflied leg to tighten and bow. It's better to remove most, but not all, of the surface fat before cooking. Thin patches will lubricate and flavor the meat during cooking, while large pockets may cause flare-ups during searing and will ultimately have to be carved from the meat anyway.

RUB, DON'T MARINATE

Yogurt- and lemon juice–based marinades are traditional for lamb, and with that in mind, I made seven classic marinades: three milk-based (yogurt, buttermilk, and milk), two lemon, one soy, and one red wine. In addition to the marinades, I made an oil-based rub with rosemary and garlic and another of spices. Unlike marinades, these rubs contain no liquid to dilute the intensity of the herbs, spices, and aromatic garlic. I refrigerated the lamb for 48 hours, cutting off and cooking large portions at 4, 8, and 24 hours.

I much preferred the oil-based spice and herb rubs, which flavor the lamb without moistening it or compromising its integrity. I also discovered that minced garlic slathered on the lamb's surface is preferable to garlic slices tucked into slits. The caramelized flavor of the minced garlic better complements the bold flavors of the grill.

As for the marinades, I didn't like them very much. I found that:

- Except for those containing sugar, wet marinades make wet meat, and wet meat doesn't sear very well.

- Marinades tend to mask rather than enhance the flavor of the lamb.

- Soft fresh herbs like cilantro, basil, and mint get lost in cooking. It's better to sprinkle them on the lamb when you take it off the grill or out of the oven.

- Acids like lemon juice taste fresher and bolder when drizzled on the hot meat rather than added to the marinades.

On the subject of cooking the lamb, most recipes weren't very helpful. Except for a few, they said little more than "grill over a medium-hot fire until done." Since I wanted a good crust and since butterflied leg looks like a big, raggedy, thick steak, my instinct was to cook the lamb over as high a heat as possible and get it off the grill quickly.

Working on a gas grill, I seared the lamb over high heat on one side for 8 minutes, flipped it, then seared it on the other side for 8 minutes longer. About 5 minutes into searing the second side, however, the grill started to flame, so I turned off the heat, covered the grill, and let the residual heat finish the cooking. The meat was beautifully seared and, after a good rest, respectably pink.

In subsequent tests, though, the high heat caused excessive flare-ups, resulting in charred meat.

I was intrigued by Paula Wolfert's method in *Mostly Mediterranean* (Penguin, 1996), formerly titled *Paula Wolfert's World of Food*. Wolfert sears the meat over a charcoal fire for 1 minute per side, then pulls the leg off the grill and lets it rest for 20 minutes. The lamb is then returned to the fire, which also has had a chance to cool during that time. Depending on its thickness, the lamb is cooked closer to or farther from the low fire until done.

THE SMART THERMOMETER

If you haven't replaced your clumsy old meat thermometer, now may be the time to do so. Instant-read thermometers allow you to take the precise temperature of a cut of meat at any point during the cooking process in just seconds. Costing between ten and twenty dollars, instant-reads are more accurate than old-style meat thermometers, and you don't end up with a hole in the roast from a thick, oversize probe.

But instant-read thermometers have their disadvantages as well. For one thing, they're not oven-proof. I've ruined several because I forgot to remove them from the roast when I put the meat back in the oven. And to get an instant reading, you have to take the roast out of the oven, causing both the roast and the oven to lose precious heat.

You may want to spend just a bit more for what is considered the ultimate in meat thermometers: the Polder, which allows you to monitor the roast's temperature without ever having to open the grill lid or oven door. This gadget consists of a two-foot-long thin metal wire with a probe, which is inserted into the roast at one end and into a digital-read thermometer that sits outside the oven at the other end. The wire is so thin that the oven door or grill lid can remain closed, allowing you to monitor the temperature without interfering with the cooking. The Polder Electronic Remote Thermometer-Timer is available at cooking stores and kitchen departments across the country and retails for about thirty dollars. Since the thin metal wire is heat-resistant only up to 390 degrees, do not insert the probe into the leg of lamb until after the initial searing process, and do not use the thermometer for roasts that are cooked above 400 degrees.

This technique had a lot going for it. Although I wanted a good crust on the meat, a short sear meant less chance for a grill fire. There were other benefits to this method as well, starting with the ability to serve the meat hot. In *How to Cook Meat* (Morrow, 2000), Chris Schlesinger and John Willoughby point out that lamb fat has a higher melting point than that of beef or pork and solidifies faster, making it much less appetizing at room temperature.

Searing the lamb for 4 minutes per side produced a decent crust with no threat of fire. I pulled the meat from the grill and stuck a meat thermometer in its thickest portion, while leaving it to rest for the suggested 20 minutes. During that time, the grill's temperature dropped to 250 degrees, and I returned the roast to the grill, turned the burner to low, and cooked the lamb until it reached 135 degrees. It took three times as long as I'd expected. An hour and a half later, I cut into it. It was nicely crusted and evenly cooked, juicy, and tender, but the meat was more red than pink and warm, not hot.

I liked this roast's look, texture, and potential convenience, but the technique needed tweaking. Clearly, the grill's temperature needed increasing — enough to shorten the cooking time, but not so much as to cause the meat to lose its juicy, evenly cooked, tender quality. The initial resting period needed to be shortened as well. Finally, since the wide surface of the butterflied lamb didn't hold the heat like a thick roast once it came off the grill, I needed to cook it to the temperature I wanted.

All of these changes worked. Maintaining the grill temperature at 300 to 350 degrees and reducing the resting period to 10 minutes brought the cooking time down to just 50 minutes, and removing the lamb when it was 140 degrees inside gave me a true rosy pink medium-rare roast. Adapting the technique to the oven, I first broiled, then slow-roasted the lamb at 325 degrees.

This technique works perfectly for entertaining. Sear the roast and let it rest before guests arrive, and then let it slow-cook during the social hour. Check it occasionally. If the roast's internal temperature seems to be climbing too quickly, simply turn down the heat 25 or even 50 degrees. If the temperature is rising too slowly, increase the grill or oven temperature by 25 degrees. Then, when the lamb is ready, take it out and listen to them rave.

Carefree Grilled Butterflied Leg of Lamb (Gas-Grill Version)

Serves 12 to 16

You can grill the lamb on a gas grill or on a charcoal grill (see opposite page). If the roast is getting done too quickly, decrease the oven temperature by 25 to 50 degrees. On the other hand, if it's not cooking quickly enough, increase the oven temperature by 25 degrees or so.

1   **leg of lamb (about 7 pounds), fell and excess fat removed, leg boned and butterflied to more or less even thickness (ask your butcher to do this)**
Herb or spice paste of choice (pages 165–66)
Juice of 1 lemon (optional)
Minced fresh cilantro, parsley, or mint (optional)

1   Spread both sides of lamb with paste and let stand for 1 hour to give meat a chance to come to room temperature.

2   Preheat gas grill, igniting all burners on high for at least 10 minutes.

3   Place lamb, cut side down, on hot grill rack; grill, covered, until nicely brown, 4 to 5 minutes. Turn lamb and continue to grill, covered, until nicely brown on other side, 4 to 5 minutes longer.

4   Turn off grill, transfer lamb to a platter, and stick an oven-safe meat thermometer into thickest portion for future monitoring. Let meat rest for 10 minutes (temperature should increase by about 10 degrees). Heat grill again, this time igniting only one burner on high. Return lamb to grill, setting it over the burner that is not lit. Cook, maintaining grill temperature at 300 to 350 degrees, or between low and medium, adjusting burner to medium heat as soon as grill temperature rises above those ranges. Cook until meat thermometer registers 140 degrees, 50 minutes to 1 hour. (To slow cooking, simply turn burner to low heat.)

5   As soon as lamb is done, drizzle with lemon juice and sprinkle with herbs, if using. Cut lamb into thin slices, arrange on a platter, drizzle with accumulated juice, and serve immediately.

Carefree Grilled Butterflied Leg of Lamb (Charcoal-Grilled Version)

The technique and timing of this recipe are similar to those of the gas-grill method.

1 leg of lamb (about 7 pounds), fell and excess fat removed,
      leg boned and butterflied to more or less even
      thickness (ask your butcher to do this)
   Herb or spice paste of choice (pages 165–66)
   Juice of 1 lemon (optional)
   Minced fresh cilantro, parsley, or mint (optional)

1 Spread both sides of lamb with paste, and let stand for 1 hour to give meat a chance to come to room temperature. Heat 5 pounds of charcoal (a large chimney full of briquets) until they are covered with white ash. Remove grill rack and pour coals onto one half of grill. Replace grill rack and return lid to grill to heat rack.

2 Place butterflied leg of lamb, cut side down, on hot grill rack. Grill uncovered, until nicely browned, 4 to 5 minutes. (If flare-ups occur, move lamb briefly to unlit side of grill and extinguish flames.) Turn lamb and continue to grill until nicely browned on other side. Transfer lamb to a platter and let rest for 10 minutes. Insert an oven-safe meat thermometer into thickest portion for future monitoring. Cover grill, closing vents. Return lamb to charcoal-less side of grill. Cover and grill, vents partially open, until meat thermometer registers 140 degrees, 30 to 50 minutes, depending on grill temperature.

3 As soon as lamb is done, drizzle with lemon juice and sprinkle with herbs, if using. Cut lamb into thin slices, arrange on a platter, drizzle with accumulated juice, and serve immediately.

Carefree Slow-Roasted Butterflied Leg of Lamb (Indoor Version)

As with the grilled version, you can control how fast the lamb cooks. If you want to slow the process, reduce the oven temperature by 25 degrees. If you want to speed things up, increase the oven temperature by 25 degrees. That way, the lamb is done when you're ready to serve.

1 leg of lamb (about 7 pounds), fell and excess fat removed, leg boned and butterflied to more or less even thickness (ask your butcher to do this)

Herb or spice paste of choice (see opposite page)

Juice of 1 lemon (optional)

Minced fresh cilantro, parsley, or mint (optional)

1   Spread both sides of lamb with paste (see opposite page) and let stand for 1 hour to give meat a chance to come to room temperature.

2   Adjust oven rack to upper position (for thinner butterflied lamb) or upper-middle position (for thicker lamb), and preheat broiler on high for at least 10 minutes.

3   Place lamb, cut side up, on a large wire rack set over a foil-lined roasting pan. Broil, moving pan around to ensure that entire surface browns evenly, about 8 minutes. Turn lamb and continue to broil, moving pan around, until well browned on other side, about 8 minutes longer.

4   Remove lamb from oven, and let rest for 10 minutes. Turn off broiler and heat oven to 325 degrees. Insert an oven-safe meat thermometer into thickest portion for future monitoring. Return lamb to oven until meat thermometer registers 140 degrees, 50 minutes to 1 hour.

5   As soon as lamb is done, drizzle with lemon juice and sprinkle with herbs, if using. Cut lamb into thin slices, arrange on a platter, drizzle with accumulated juice, and serve immediately.

Cumin-Lemon Paste

If sprinkling the cooked lamb with an herb, choose either cilantro or parsley and drizzle with lemon juice.

- 1/4 cup olive oil
- 8 garlic cloves, minced (2 1/2–3 tablespoons)
- 2 teaspoons finely grated lemon zest
- 2 1/2 teaspoons salt
- 1 teaspoon freshly ground black pepper
- 1 tablespoon ground cumin
- 2 teaspoons dried oregano

Mix all ingredients in a small bowl and spread on lamb.

Rosemary-Garlic Paste

If sprinkling the cooked lamb with an herb, choose either parsley or mint. Sprinkling the meat with lemon juice will add piquancy.

- 1/4 cup olive oil
- 8 garlic cloves, minced (2 1/2–3 tablespoons)
- 2 1/2 teaspoons salt
- 1 teaspoon freshly ground black pepper
- 3 tablespoons minced fresh rosemary

Mix all ingredients in a small bowl and spread on lamb.

Tandoori Spice Paste

If sprinkling the cooked lamb with an herb, choose cilantro.

- 1/4 cup olive oil
- 8 garlic cloves, minced (2 1/2–3 tablespoons)
- 1 tablespoon minced fresh ginger
- 2 1/2 teaspoons salt
- 1 tablespoon paprika
- 1 tablespoon ground cumin
- 1/2 teaspoon cayenne pepper

Mix all ingredients in a small bowl and spread on lamb.

Curried Spice Paste

Makes enough for
one 7-pound leg of lamb

¹/₄	cup olive oil
8	garlic cloves, minced (2¹/₂–3 tablespoons)
2	tablespoons minced fresh ginger
2¹/₂	teaspoons salt
1	tablespoon curry powder
1	tablespoon ground cumin
1¹/₂	teaspoons ground allspice
¹/₂	teaspoon cayenne pepper

Mix all ingredients in a small bowl and spread on lamb.

Moroccan Spice Paste

¹/₄	cup olive oil
2	garlic cloves, minced (2–3 teaspoons)
1	medium onion, quartered
2	tablespoons minced fresh ginger
2¹/₂	teaspoons salt
1	teaspoon freshly ground black pepper
1	tablespoon paprika
1	teaspoon ground cinnamon
1	teaspoon ground cloves

Puree all ingredients in a food processor to form a paste and
spread on lamb.

I had always taken good ham for granted until last Christmas, when I went to the butcher to purchase one with the bone in for the holidays. The butcher proudly set it on the counter and said, "Isn't she a beauty — hardly an ounce of fat on her." It was a fine-looking ham.

Following a recipe I had recently come across, I covered my ham with foil and baked it in a 275-degree oven until warm — 120 degrees. It seemed like a good idea: the low, gentle heat would keep the ham moist and juicy, the foil would protect it, and the low internal temperature would keep it from drying out.

But when I pulled it from the oven, I don't think I've ever beheld a more disappointing result. Covered with foil, the ham had steamed rather than roasted and looked wretchedly pale and unattractive. Hardly any moisture had evaporated, and it was spongy and waterlogged. Without any surface fat or marbling, its texture was rubbery — okay for soups and salads, but hardly what I had in mind for holiday fare.

Since a very lean ham is more the rule than the exception these days, the problem is how to make it taste as good as it looks in the store. After baking many hams since that fateful Christmas dinner, I can report that what matters is not so much how you cook your holiday ham, but how you choose it.

Through genetic engineering, the pork industry has been very successful at eliminating both surface fat and marbling. Before World War II, hogs were raised as much for their fat as for their meat. After the war, however, vegetable fats became popular, and lard was viewed as a liability rather than an asset. That, coupled with the trend toward healthier diets, forced the industry to put the pig on a diet.

But this fat reduction comes at a price. Without surface fat, ham cannot be scored, and any glaze simply runs off the smooth, slick surface. And without marbling, there's no intermuscular fat to give the meat flavor and body.

Selecting a bone-in wet-cured ham can be confusing. Inspect the ham case and you're likely to find many different styles of wet-cured hams. All are injected with a brine: a mix of water, salt, sweetener, and sodium nitrite or nitrate for color. Depending on how much brine is injected, the hams are variously labeled. On hams ranging from dry to moist, the labels include: "ham with natural juices," "ham with water added," and "ham and water product." The driest, ham with natural juices, contains only the amount of liquid necessary to bring the ham back to its pre-cooked weight, usually 1% to 2%. Ham with water added contains 10% more brine than its pre-cooked weight, while the bone-in ham and water product contains up to 23% more liquid. After cooking each kind, I prefer ham with water added. This style contains just enough added moisture to keep the ham from drying out in the oven, while the ham and water product tastes a bit waterlogged. If you choose that kind, you'll want to cook the ham longer to evaporate more water. But the amount of brine pumped into the ham affects its quality less than does the fat content.

For that reason, look less at the labels and more at the appearance of the ham. If there's no fat around the edge, avoid it. As much as you may fear it, a modest amount of fat helps the ham's flavor and texture dramatically. Without fat, it's

COUNTRY HAM, CITY HAM

There are two kinds of ham: those that have been dry-cured, also known as country hams, and those that have been wet-cured (a.k.a. city hams). Up until World War II, nearly all hams were dry-cured. That is, a fresh leg of pork was coated in salt and maybe a little sugar, with a little nitrate thrown in for color, flavor, and additional preservation. Once the salt mixture had permeated the entire cut, the ham was usually smoked, then aged, both of which deepened flavor and dehydrated the ham, ensuring its preservation. Used initially as preservatives, the salt, nitrate, and smoke gave the ham its distinct flavor, texture, and color.

With the postwar advent of home refrigeration, hams no longer had to survive at room temperature, and production quickly shifted to wet curing. For meat companies, wet-cured hams were easier to produce. By the simple means of injecting the ham with a salt solution, curing was reduced from several months to several days.

This new-style ham was easier for the cook as well. The process of soaking a dry-cured ham for days and boiling it for hours to remove the salt was eliminated. City hams required nothing more than a shove into the oven. As a result, they've replaced their country cousin at the meat case.

Country hams must be sought out and mail-ordered, and the preparation and cooking process must begin at least four or five days before serving. The tedious process results in rich, salty, ripe-tasting ham, which is mild enough to slice thin and sandwich between light, fluffy biscuits and intense enough to mince fine and flavor vegetables, soups, pastas, and eggs.

impossible to score the ham, and a glaze or flavoring paste won't adhere during baking. (Percentages of fat are not noted on most labels for bone-in hams, which is why the visual test matters.)

If buying a half ham, you'll also be faced with whether to buy the shank or butt end. The pointed shank end looks like a classic ham. Slightly less expensive, it contains more bone per ounce of meat and its muscles are more firm-textured. The more rounded butt end is less attractive but more tender and easier to carve. I generally choose the shank end for its festive look and because I like having more bone for soup.

To cook a half ham, start by scoring the surface fat, cutting diagonal lines in each direction to form diamond shapes. Cover the cut surface with a sheet of foil to keep it from drying out. Then line a baking sheet with foil (to keep the pan clean), place the ham on a wire rack over the pan (to keep the bottom from overcooking), pop it in the oven, and let it bake for an hour or so until the scoring is more pronounced.

The ideal baking temperature is 250 degrees. At this low temperature, the ham roasts evenly, so its outer section won't overcook and dry out before the center heats through. This temperature is also warm enough to crisp up and brown the ham's surface, yet low enough to keep a glaze from burning. A half ham (weighing about 8 pounds) is done in 4 hours, or when it has cooked for about 30 minutes per pound.

Once the ham has baked for an hour or so and the diamond pattern is raised, it's time to brush on the glaze. The ones that I like are thick enough to cling to the ham's surface and don't require further basting. After glazing, you can forget about the ham for the next 2½ hours, at which point the foil on the cut surface should be removed. For the next half hour, brush the cut surface once or twice with the pan drippings to keep it moist and develop its color. The ham is done when a meat thermometer inserted into the center registers about 140 degrees. Unlike a turkey or a pork roast, which can dry out with the slightest overcooking, ham contains enough salt, sugar, smoke, and added liquid to keep it moist and flavorful regardless of how much it's tortured — provided that it has enough fat to begin with.

Now when my butcher declares his trim ham a beauty, I'll know better. A lean ham may look good at the market, but to be savored and remembered, she's got to have a little fat on her bones.

Ham for the Holidays

Serves 16 to 20

For the classic ham shape, choose the shank end. For more tender meat and fewer bones, select the butt end.

1 bone-in half ham (7–9 pounds), with as much surface fat as possible
Glaze (see following recipes)

Adjust oven rack to low position and heat oven to 250 degrees. Score ham fat to create a diamond pattern on surface. Cut a piece of foil the shape of ham's cut surface. Place foil on cut surface to keep it from drying out.

2 Cover a shallow roasting pan with a sheet of foil. Place ham on a wire rack set over foil-lined pan. Bake ham until scored fat is well pronounced, about 1 hour. Remove from oven and brush ham's surface with all glaze. Bake for $2^1/_2$ hours longer. Remove foil from cut surface and continue to roast, brushing cut surface with pan drippings once or twice, until a meat thermometer inserted deep into ham's center registers 140 degrees, approximately 30 minutes longer. Total roasting time is about 4 hours, or 30 minutes per pound. Serve hot, room temperature, or cold.

GOOD HAMS

I've found that nationally available Gwaltney brand water-added hams (which may be labeled as Smithfield or John Morrell) have enough surface fat for scoring, making it possible for a glaze to adhere. If these hams are not at your local grocery store, they can be ordered at (800) 926-8448 or online at www.smithfield-hams.com. Whole hams (16 to 18 pounds) sell for $59.95, while half hams (7 to 9 pounds) sell for $37.95, plus shipping and handling charges, which vary from state to state.

Mustard–Brown Sugar Glaze
with Garlic and Rosemary

Makes enough for one
7-to-9-pound ham

Dried rosemary is not a good substitute for the fresh called for here. If you can't find it, substitute 2 teaspoons dried thyme leaves.

- 1/2 cup dark brown sugar
- 1/4 cup Dijon mustard
- 8 garlic cloves, minced
- 2 tablespoons minced fresh rosemary
- 2 teaspoons freshly ground black pepper

Mix all ingredients in a small bowl. Set aside until ready to glaze ham.

Orange Marmalade Glaze
with Mustard and Sage

For a different flavor, apricot jam can be substituted for the orange marmalade and dried thyme for the rubbed sage.

- 1/2 cup orange marmalade
- 1/4 cup Dijon mustard
- 1 tablespoon rubbed sage
- 2 teaspoons freshly ground black pepper

Mix all ingredients in a small bowl. Set aside until ready to glaze ham.

Supporting
Sides

Imagine salad creator Caesar Cardini ordering a Wendy's Chicken Caesar Pita. He would doubtless be amused and amazed at his salad's ageless popularity. But I suspect he'd be perplexed as well. Was this the same dish he created at his Tijuana restaurant nearly eighty years ago?

It isn't, of course, but just to see how far the Caesar salad has evolved since its creation, I tested one of the original versions of the salad in *From Julia Child's Kitchen* (Knopf, 1975). In preparation for one of her 1960s TV segments featuring Caesar salad, she interviewed Caesar Cardini's daughter, who passed on her father's method in detail. The abbreviated version follows:

- For the croutons, bake bread cubes, brushing them with olive oil that has been steeped in garlic for days, until crisp. (Realizing that most cooks didn't think days ahead before making the salad, Julia permitted the garlic to be steeped in the oil for just a couple of minutes.)

- Separate the inner leaves of romaine lettuce, leaving them whole.

- Gently toss the romaine with the best olive oil available.

- Season the romaine with salt, pepper, and more olive oil; toss again.

- Add lemon juice, Worcestershire, and a coddled egg (one that has been dropped in boiling water for a minute or so); gently toss again.

- Sprinkle on Parmesan cheese; toss again.

- Add croutons; toss once more.

- Serve immediately, eating whole leaves with fingers.

After making this version of the original, I couldn't recall having eaten a better Caesar salad. Unlike today's typical creamy dressings that burden the lettuce, this one was light and fresh. The salad's flavors were pleasantly tart and clean; the garlic, Parmesan, and anchovy (an ingredient in Worcestershire sauce) refreshingly restrained. The small, crisp inner leaves were far superior to the wilted dark green outer leaves I'd often been served and used myself. Unlike boxed croutons, which reek of garlic and cheese powder, the fresh croutons in this salad were subtly perfumed with fresh garlic.

With this salad in mind, I began my testing. Eventually I hoped to develop a salad like this one, without the undercooked egg so many people fear today.

REAL GARLIC CROUTONS, REAL QUICK

To develop the best crouton, not only did I need to figure out how to toast the bread, but I had to determine the most effective way to infuse it with garlic.

Since the croutons in the original recipe were baked, I was partial to that method. But after baking, broiling, and sautéing bread, I opted for sautéing. Regardless of the oven temperature, the baked croutons were too brittle, shattering when pierced with a fork. Despite the broiled croutons' perfect texture — crisp on the outside with a little chewiness at the center — I found the method too tricky. Even when I set the timer and checked them after 1 minute, I nearly burned them. The sautéed ones were equally crisp yet tender, making them easy to fork. Unlike baking, the stovetop method was quick, and unlike broiling, it was foolproof.

Many cooks prefer baked croutons to sautéed ones because they're lower in fat. I found, however, that by drizzling and tossing the soft bread cubes with oil *before* sautéing (as opposed to adding them to hot oil), the croutons required no more fat than if I had baked them.

Figuring out how to infuse the croutons with garlic turned out to be more difficult than choosing a cooking method. Mixing minced garlic with oil, as suggested in the original recipe, worked, but I found that for the flavor to come through, the garlic and oil needed at least 12 hours together. Unless I found a quicker way, impromptu Caesar salad wasn't possible. Heating garlic with the oil sounded promising, but I soon discovered that regardless of how slowly or quickly I did it and regardless of how I prepared the garlic — slivered, sliced, smashed, or minced — the resulting oil lacked that garlic edge, and so did the croutons.

Croutons seasoned with garlic powder were garlicky enough but tasted more like my mother's garlic bread. One recipe suggested tossing sautéed garlic with sautéed bread cubes. Unfortunately, the garlic didn't stick to the croutons and sat at the bottom of the bowl like unpopped corn. Top-of-the-line commercial garlic oil smelled pungent, but its flavor was practically imperceptible on the croutons.

I ultimately found that the 12-hour infusion could be reduced to a few short minutes if I pureed the garlic with the oil. Dropping the garlic cloves into a running food processor, then adding the oil, released the pungent oils immediately. Since the garlic bits from the puree burned during cooking, I strained out the garlic before tossing the cubes with the flavored oil. With this technique, I could make home-made garlic croutons in less than 15 minutes.

After testing a variety of breads — everything from Wonder Bread to artisan sourdough — I preferred the straightforward flavor and firm texture of croutons made from a good-quality baguette or Italian loaf.

The fat in which I sautéed the bread, however, made more of a difference. Olive oil won the contest, delivering a full-flavored crouton that tasted neither too distinct nor "off." Croutons sautéed in extra-virgin olive oil had a bitter aftertaste. Croutons sautéed in butter browned beautifully, but their flavor was wrong for this salad. Croutons fried in vegetable oil tasted boring.

THE MIX-UP

Although there were many variations on a theme and a few offbeat techniques, I identified four basic methods for making the dressing. Besides the original method in which the ingredients are tossed one by one with the lettuce leaves, the dressing could be made in a food processor or a blender, shaken in a glass jar, or whisked right in the salad bowl before the lettuce was added. I tested the different mixing methods, starting with this composite dressing:

Mince (if making by hand), or process in food a processor or blender:
  1   garlic clove
  4   anchovy fillets

Mix in:
  2   tablespoons lemon juice
  1   coddled egg
  $1/4$ cup grated Parmesan cheese
  $1/2$ teaspoon Worcestershire sauce
  $1/4$ teaspoon salt
      A few grinds of black pepper

Gradually mix or, if using the jar method, add with the previous ingredients:
  $1/2$ cup olive oil

The shake-in-a-jar dressing never came together, the oil floating on top, the remaining ingredients settling below. The whisked dressing looked more like vinai-grette, and without the egg I had hoped to leave out, I questioned whether this method would deliver a full-bodied dressing. Ditto for the original Caesar method (without the egg). At this point, it seemed the blender or food processor was my best shot in creating a rich, yet eggless dressing. I began testing, switching back and forth between the two machines.

Since my main goal was to get rid of the undercooked egg, I started by testing alternative ways to thicken the dressing. Because of its thick, creamy texture and obvious flavor potential, roasted garlic seemed like a strong candidate. Unfortunately, the dressing turned an unappetizing taupe color and lacked the bright, fresh Caesar flavor I wanted.

Other eggless recipes recommended soft tofu to give the dressing body. Although it looked creamy and tasted acceptable, the tofu gave the dressing an unmistakably chalky mouth-feel. I tried substituting mayonnaise for the egg as well. Neither the food processor nor the blender dressings emulsified.

The American Egg Board had developed two techniques that I tried. The dressing recipe calls for 2 egg yolks to be cooked with a puckery 2 tablespoons each of lemon juice and vinegar, dry mustard, and Worcestershire until the eggs thicken. The mixture is transferred to a blender and, with the motor running, 1/2 cup oil is gradually added. The resulting dressing was an inedible, overly acidic, thick sauce, more akin to hollandaise.

Following a tip from the Egg Board's *Eggcyclopedia,* indicating that the risk of salmonella can be reduced if the egg yolks are first beaten with vinegar and lemon juice and allowed to stand while the other ingredients are readied, I prepared two more dressings. One was made with a coddled egg, the other with a raw egg. Both were silky and smooth, the one made with a coddled egg displaying slightly better body. Still, I was not happy with this gloppy dressing. Moreover, according to Elisa Maloberti, the Egg Board's Consumer Information Coordinator, this method "would eliminate some of the risk but is not a fail-safe measure."

Lemon juice is the only acid in most Caesar dressings, but some recipes call for a mix of lemon juice and vinegar. In this series of tests, I made dressings with equal parts lemon juice with each of the following: red wine vinegar, balsamic vinegar, rice wine vinegar, and sherry vinegar. I also made another dressing with all lime juice. Although most of the mixed acid dressings were fine, none of them tasted like Caesar. The lime juice dressing lacked the clean sharpness that lemon offered.

With so many other strong, competing tastes, extra-virgin olive oil was too prominent in the salad, while neutral vegetable oil created a flavor void in which the anchovy, lemon, and Worcestershire all became too pronounced. During the course of testing, it became clear that although Parmesan cheese may have a role in the salad, it didn't belong in the dressing. It gave it a chalky texture and muddied the flavors.

Garlic was the second to go. Up to this point, I had been using the strained garlic used to make the oil for the croutons, but it was too harsh. I tested anchovies by making dressings with the tinned kind, those packed in salt (rinsed and boned), as well as anchovy paste. I didn't like any of those dressings.

I took out a bowl and made Julia Child's version of Caesar Cardini's salad again. The method was fast and simple, the salad light and pleasantly tart. The only garlic was on the croutons and the only anchovies were invisible hints in the Worcestershire sauce. I enjoyed this salad and wanted to keep eating it. A good sign.

While the blender's forceful mixing had caused the mayonnaise-based dressings to separate, I decided to try mayonnaise again, using this gentler mixing method. I reduced the oil, tossing it, along with salt and pepper, with the salad greens. I mixed a couple tablespoons of mayonnaise with the lemon juice, Worcestershire, and half of the leftover minced garlic that I had used to make the oil for the croutons. Then I tossed the mixture with the oiled and seasoned greens. The resulting salad was light, tart, and almost identical in character to the original Cardini salad.

This Caesar salad is safe, simple, and scrumptious, and both my teenage daughters say they could eat it every night.

DOES CAESAR SALAD NEED PARMIGIANO-REGGIANO?

After discovering that the quality of Parmesan cheese for chicken Parmesan is not crucial, I decided to perform the same test with Caesar salad. Would pre-grated Parmesan cheese in a jar or can make as good a Caesar salad as the aged, imported Parmigiano-Reggiano?

I found that cheese quality, in fact, makes a big difference in this dish. Unlike the cheese in chicken Parmesan, which is broiled, the cheese in Caesar salad is not cooked, and its flavor and texture are more prominent. Pre-grated jarred and canned Parmesan cheese are dehydrated during processing to keep them from molding. Their sawdust texture and lack of flavor (or their off flavors) were distinctly noticeable in the salad.

Among the Parmesan cheeses that I bought and grated myself, Parmigiano-Reggiano was a clear winner. Its nutty tang made an obvious and valuable contribution to the salad's flavor. Parmesans that are aged for less time make far better salads than the pre-grated varieties but lack the complexity of the real McCoy. If you are unable to find Parmigiano-Reggiano, at least buy a wedge or block of Parmesan and take the time to grate it yourself.

Simple, Scrumptious Caesar Salad with Quick Garlic Croutons

Serves 4 to 6

The mayonnaise in this salad does not make the dressing gloppy. It's used as a stand-in for the coddled egg to ensure that the salad is salmonella-free.

Since washing and drying lettuce is time-consuming, try to buy packages of pre-washed romaine hearts. If the idea of serving a whole-leaf lettuce salad that guests eat with their fingers bothers you, simply tear the leaves into bite-size pieces. Slice the bread with a serrated knife. Use heavy-duty kitchen shears to cut the sliced bread into cubes.

Anchovy fans should feel free to garnish the salad with anchovy fillets or to mix in $1/2$ teaspoon anchovy paste along with the mayonnaise and lemon juice.

GARLIC CROUTONS

- 4 garlic cloves
- $1/4$ cup olive oil
- 2 heaping cups $3/4$-inch bread cubes, cut from a good-quality baguette or Italian loaf
- Large pinch salt

SALAD

- 3 romaine hearts (remove any dark green outer leaves and reserve for another use); about 10 generous cups
- 2 tablespoons lemon juice
- $2^1/2$ tablespoons mayonnaise
- $1/4$ teaspoon Worcestershire sauce
- 5 tablespoons olive oil
- $1/4$ teaspoon salt
- Freshly ground black pepper to taste
- $1/4$ cup freshly grated Parmesan cheese (preferably Parmigiano-Reggiano), plus extra for sprinkling

LEAF LOGISTICS

To measure whole romaine leaves, lightly pack them in a 2-quart Pyrex measuring cup or a 2-quart (8-cup) bowl. After dumping the 8 cups in the salad bowl, fill the cup or bowl halfway again, equaling the 10 generous cups you need for this salad. (If you make it in the same bowl each time, just remember what 10 cups looks like and you won't have to measure.)

1 **FOR CROUTONS:** Heat a large skillet over low heat. With motor running, drop garlic cloves through feeder tube of a food processor to mince. (A blender works as well.) Scrape down sides of bowl and add oil through feeder tube. Continue to process so that garlic releases its flavor into oil, about 30 seconds. Strain garlic from oil through a fine-mesh strainer; reserve half of garlic for dressing and set aside remaining half for another use. You should have about 3 tablespoons garlic oil.

2 Raise heat under skillet to medium. Place bread cubes in a medium bowl. Drizzle 2 tablespoons garlic oil evenly over bread, along with a big pinch of salt; toss to coat. Add remaining 1 tablespoon oil; toss again.

3 Add bread cubes to hot skillet and toast, turning cubes and shaking pan often, until crisp and golden brown, 5 to 7 minutes. Return croutons to bowl and set aside to cool while preparing salad.

4 **FOR SALAD:** Cut off bottom 1½ to 2 inches of core from bottom of each romaine heart. Separate heart into individual leaves. Put leaves in a large bowl.

5 Whisk lemon juice, mayonnaise, Worcestershire and reserved garlic in a small bowl.

6 Drizzle lettuce with oil, sprinkle with salt and pepper, and toss lightly, carefully, and thoroughly so that lettuce is evenly coated. (Clean hands work well.)

7 Drizzle lemon mixture over lettuce; toss again.

8 Sprinkle ¼ cup Parmesan over greens; toss again.

9 Sprinkle croutons over salad, toss, and serve, sprinkling each portion with a little more Parmesan cheese.

grew up eating green beans one way. My mother meticulously snapped them into 1-inch pieces, covered them with salted water, tossed in a big chunk of fatback, then simmered them for 2 to 3 hours. The long simmering resulted in a unified dish, with the pork and beans flavoring the broth, which in turn flavored the beans and pork. I loved green beans cooked this Southern way, especially when Mom added scrubbed new potatoes.

Neither the cooking method nor the style was right for me once I got married, however. For years, I struggled to find a new way to cook green beans. I came to adulthood during the nouvelle cuisine era, so it's not surprising that I started off barely cooking my green beans. Neither cooked nor raw, these beans were, at best, healthful and, at worst, bland.

Mother did not approve. To press the point, she served her green beans whenever I came to visit, secretly hoping to convert me back. And to "enlighten" her, I'd hardly cook them when she visited me. We both laugh about one of the first times I made green beans for her. Every time she walked past the stove, she'd turn the burner on. Every time I walked past, I'd turn it off. Neither one of us was happy with the beans that night.

Over the years, I've reclaimed a share of my heritage. I've come to like my beans fully cooked and well seasoned, but I haven't reverted to simmering them for 3 hours with a piece of pork. What is the best way to cook them so that the beans cook completely and quickly yet taste flavorful?

In my research, I saw countless flavoring combinations, but when I focused on just the cooking methods, I had seven basic choices: four moist-heat methods, two dry-heat methods, and a combination wet-dry technique that I call the steam-sauté.

Using moist-heat methods, I could cook the beans in a large quantity of boiling water, simmer them in water to cover, steam them until tender, or microwave them. Once drained, the hot beans could be tossed with fat and flavorings or sautéed in the fat, with the flavorings added during cooking.

The dry-heat methods include broiling and roasting, in which the beans are tossed with fat and seasonings, laid out in a single layer on a roasting pan, and either broiled or roasted in a very hot oven.

Finally, there is the combination steam-sauté technique, in which green beans are cooked, covered, in a small amount of salted water, along with a little butter, olive oil, or bacon renderings. By the time they cook through, the liquid has evaporated. Then the lid is removed, and with the fat as a buffer, the beans are briefly sautéed.

IS FRESH NECESSARILY BEST?

Green beans are traditionally harvested in the summer, but because of consumer demand and improved shipping, they've become available year-round. Availability, however, is only half the game. I've gone to the green bean bin off-season, only to find a shriveled, sad-looking lot. For these times, were canned or frozen green beans an option? Before testing the various cooking methods, I decided to taste these off-season offerings and find out.

I've never liked canned green beans, but with new technology, I thought they might have improved. I skipped over unsalted, snapped, frenched, and flavored varieties. I went straight to the best can I could find: Delmonte fresh whole green beans. After one taste, I'm here to report that the industry has done nothing to improve the look and flavor of canned green beans since the last time I tried them. Not only are they unsalvageable, they aren't much of a bargain either. At 78 cents a can, a pound costs $1.56. Most out-of-season green beans don't even cost that much.

Frozen green beans are a much better alternative. Following package directions, I brought 1 pound frozen beans to a boil in ³/₄ cup water and simmered them, covered, until tender, about 10 minutes. After draining the beans, I salted, peppered, and buttered them. Although somewhat tough and chewy and lacking the sweetness of fresh beans, they weren't bad. Still, at $1.69 per 1-pound package, frozen green beans may save a little preparation time, but they're still no bargain.

Just to see how much preparation time I might save, I timed myself stemming and snapping 1 pound of fresh green beans. From start to finish, the task took a mere 5 minutes. I make very few meals when I can't spare 5 minutes to stem fresh green beans (or find someone else to perform the task). Only if fresh beans looked inferior would I buy frozen.

It was time to start cooking.

Since the majority of recipes called for cooking green beans, or blanching them, in a large pot of boiling water, I started there. Cooks were divided on whether the water should be salted, and if so how much, so I tested different salt quantities in the water as well.

Starting out with unsalted water, I cooked a batch of beans for 5 minutes and seasoned them with a little butter, salt, and pepper once they were cooked. Beans prepared this way were acceptable, but like pasta cooked in unsalted water and seasoned after, the beans tasted seasoned from without, bland from within. After adding 1 teaspoon salt per quart of water, I cooked a second batch. These did not taste fully seasoned either.

Only in my third batch of beans, which cooked in 1 tablespoon salt for every quart of water, did I notice any difference. Although the salt flavor was not overt, it seemed to bring out the beans' sweetness. Surprisingly, beans blanched in 2 tablespoons salt for every quart of water didn't seem to taste much different from the beans that cooked in the lesser amount of salt, but the beans had lost their sweetness.

Following another popular method, I tried shallow-boiling the beans by placing them in a saucepan in salted water to cover. Then I drained them and tossed them with butter and pepper. Unlike those cooked in a large quantity of water, these had more bean flavor, but because they were brought to the boil in cold water, the gradual heating process caused them to look and taste overcooked, with a crunchy, undercooked texture. Of all the methods I tried, this one was my least favorite. Cooked this way, the beans reminded me of their canned cousins.

Steaming is another common technique for cooking green beans. As with blanching, there were different opinions about salting the beans: some recipes recommended doing it before steaming, some after.

I started by steaming unseasoned green beans, then seasoning them with salt, pepper, and butter. They were bright green and their flavor was strong, but after a few bites, I realized that I didn't enjoy eating them. They tasted more like an edible plant than a delicious vegetable. Salting them before cooking, however, helped immensely.

Following the method described in *Joy of Cooking,* I also tried microwaving a batch of beans. The recipe said to cook the beans in a very small amount of salted water (1/4 cup water for 1 pound of beans) in a covered microwave-safe container, stirring them a couple of times, until they were tender, 9 to 13 minutes. Cooking a half pound, I checked the beans at 5 minutes. Since they were still too crisp, I microwaved them a minute more. Unfortunately, in just a few short minutes, the beans had turned drab green and were leathery-textured and wrinkled. I moved on.

Although I had never tried roasting or broiling beans, I was eager. Cooked at such high heat and without additional liquid, they might taste fresh and flavorful. That turned out to be wishful thinking. Much like roasting a bell pepper, broiling caused the invisible paper-thin membrane over the skin to bubble and separate from the bean. In addition, the beans turned leathery after a few minutes of sitting. Roasting green beans in a hot oven produced very similar results.

TWO METHODS IN ONE

It was time to try the steam-sauté method. I put $1/3$ cup water, 1 tablespoon butter, and a scant $1/2$ teaspoon salt in a Dutch oven with 1 pound of green beans, covered it, and turned the heat on medium-high. Once I saw wisps of steam coming from the pot, I set the timer for 5 minutes, at which time the beans were bright green, flavorful, and fully cooked.

Ease and speed made this the winning technique. No bringing large quantities of water to a boil, no draining, no steaming apparatus to fuss with. In one short, seamless process and in one pan, I accomplished both cooking and seasoning the beans.

I did notice one small problem with this method. Added to the pan with the raw vegetables, the fat — butter and extra-virgin olive oil — seemed to lose some of the fresh flavor during the cooking. I increased the fat by a teaspoon and added part of it at the beginning of cooking and the remaining amount at the end. (Other fats like sour cream and heavy cream can stand in for the butter and olive oil and can be added at the end of cooking.)

Steam-sautéing is perfect for hot green bean dishes, but I wasn't sure it would be ideal for cold bean salads. After all, I didn't want a thin layer of congealed fat on my salad beans. If I left it out, would the beans burn?

To find out, I tried cooking a pound of beans without fat, increasing the salted water from $1/3$ to $1/2$ cup to ensure they would be done before the liquid completely evaporated. The beans were fully cooked in 5 minutes once they began steaming. As soon as they were done, I dropped them into ice water to stop the cooking, then laid them out on paper toweling to dry. I compared these beans with blanched beans and found them equally bright in color, more intensely flavored, and ready to stand up to any vinaigrette or cold dressing.

My mother and I have long since stopped trying to convert each other to our own styles of green beans. But the last time she was here, I decided to cook green beans following my new method. She skeptically observed the process during dinner preparation. But I noticed she ate a healthy portion of them for dinner. As we moved to the kitchen to clean up, she turned to me and said, "The green beans weren't bad tonight." That was the best compliment she could have paid me.

Simple Steam-Sautéed Green Beans

Try to cook the beans in just enough water so that it's almost evaporated by the time the vegetables are cooked through. If your pan is larger than the one I've suggested, you may need to add a tablespoon or so more water. If you're cooking in a large saucepan, you may need a little less. If the green beans are thin, you may want to leave them whole rather than snapping them in half.

This recipe and the ones that follow can be doubled, as long as you increase the pan surface by using a large, deep (11-to-12-inch) sauté pan and increase the water to $^1/_2$ cup.

A host of other vegetables can be cooked using this same technique: carrots, asparagus, snow peas, sugar snap peas, cabbage, turnips, rutabagas, and cauliflower and broccoli florets.

1 **pound green beans, stem ends trimmed, snapped in half**
4 **teaspoons butter**
   Scant $^1/_2$ teaspoon salt
   Freshly ground black pepper

Add green beans, $^1/_3$ cup water, 2 teaspoons butter, and salt to an 8-to-9-inch pot. Cover and cook over medium-high heat until steam escapes around lid. Set timer for 5 minutes and continue to steam until beans are brightly colored and just tender. Remove lid and continue to cook until water evaporates and green beans start to sauté, 1 to 2 minutes longer. Turn off heat and stir in remaining 2 teaspoons butter and pepper to taste. Serve immediately.

Steam-Sautéed Green Beans
with Almonds and Parsley

Serves 4

Hazelnuts are equally good in this easy preparation. Or you can leave the nuts out altogether and simply flavor the beans with lemon zest and parsley.

1/4 **cup slivered almonds**
1 **pound green beans, stem ends trimmed, snapped in half**
4 **teaspoons butter**
Scant 1/2 teaspoon salt
1/4 **teaspoon finely grated lemon zest**
2 **tablespoons chopped fresh parsley**
Freshly ground black pepper

1 Heat an 8-to-9-inch pot over medium-low heat. When it's hot, add almonds and toast, stirring frequently, until they are golden brown and fragrant, 2 to 3 minutes. Remove from skillet and set aside.

2 Add green beans, 1/3 cup water, 2 teaspoons butter, and salt. Increase heat to medium-high, cover, and cook until steam escapes around lid. Set timer for 5 minutes and continue to steam until beans are brightly colored and just tender. Remove lid and continue to cook until water evaporates and beans start to sauté, 1 to 2 minutes longer.

3 Turn off heat, and stir in toasted almonds, lemon zest, parsley, remaining 2 teaspoons butter, and pepper to taste. Serve immediately.

Steam-Sautéed Green Beans
with Walnuts and Dill

Serves 4

If serving a first course before the green beans, toast the nuts ahead of time. Set up the pot with the prepared beans, water, butter, and salt. As you move from the kitchen to serve the first course, turn on the burner. The beans will be perfectly done by the time you're ready to serve the main course.

¼ cup walnuts
1 pound green beans, stem ends trimmed, snapped in half
2 teaspoons butter
½ teaspoon salt
2 tablespoons minced fresh dill
4 teaspoons sour cream
Freshly ground black pepper

1 Heat an 8-to-9-inch pot over medium-low heat. When it's hot, add walnuts and toast, stirring frequently, until they are golden brown and fragrant, about 3 minutes. Remove, coarsely chop, and set aside.

2 Add green beans, ⅓ cup water, butter, and salt. Increase heat to medium-high, cover, and cook until steam escapes around lid. Set timer for 5 minutes, and continue to steam until green beans are brightly colored and just tender. Remove lid and continue to cook until water evaporates and beans start to sauté, 1 to 2 minutes longer.

3 Turn off heat, and stir in walnuts, dill, sour cream, and pepper to taste. Serve immediately.

Steam-Sautéed Green Beans
with Pecans and Blue Cheese

If the beans are done before you're ready to serve them, simply turn the heat to low and leave the pot lid off, giving the beans a stir every few minutes.

¹/₄ cup pecans
   1 pound green beans, stem ends trimmed, snapped in half
   2 teaspoons butter
¹/₂ teaspoon salt
¹/₄ cup crumbled blue cheese
      Freshly ground black pepper

Proceed as directed in Steam-Sautéed Green Beans with Walnuts and Dill, substituting pecans for walnuts and blue cheese for sour cream.

Steam-Sautéed Green Beans
with Pine Nuts, Garlic, and Basil

Adding the garlic at the end ensures the garlic flavor is bold but not bitter.

¹/₄ cup pine nuts
   1 pound green beans, stem ends trimmed, snapped in half
   4 teaspoons butter
¹/₂ teaspoon salt
   1 garlic clove, minced
   2 tablespoons chopped fresh basil leaves
      Freshly ground black pepper

Proceed as directed in Steam-Sautéed Green Beans with Walnuts and Dill, substituting pine nuts for walnuts and toasting for 2 minutes. Use 2 teaspoons butter in step 2. Substitute garlic and basil for dill and remaining 2 teaspoons butter for sour cream in step 3.

Steam-Sautéed Green Beans
with Bacon, Vinegar, and Thyme

Butter and olive oil aren't the only fats that can be added to the pot. Bacon drippings give the beans wonderful flavor.

2   slices thick-cut bacon, cut into 1-inch pieces
1   small onion, cut into small dice
1   pound green beans, stem ends trimmed, snapped in half
1   garlic clove, minced
1/2   teaspoon dried thyme or 1 1/2 teaspoons fresh
1/2   teaspoon salt
1   tablespoon balsamic vinegar
   Freshly ground black pepper

1   Fry bacon over medium heat in an 8-to-9-inch pot. Remove bacon from pot and set aside.

2   Add onion and sauté, stirring until caramelized and rich brown in color, about 5 minutes. Add green beans, 1/3 cup water, garlic, dried thyme, if using (reserve fresh for later), and salt. Increase heat to medium-high, cover, and cook until steam escapes around lid. Set timer for 5 minutes, and continue to steam until beans are brightly colored and just tender. Remove lid and continue to cook until water evaporates and beans start to sauté, 1 to 2 minutes longer. Stir in bacon, fresh thyme (if using), vinegar, and pepper to taste. Serve immediately.

Steam-Sautéed Green Beans with Tomatoes, Kalamatas, and Basil

With the addition of the tomatoes, these beans are more stewed than steam-sautéed.

1 pound green beans, stem ends trimmed, snapped in half
4 teaspoons extra-virgin olive oil
²/₃ cup crushed tomatoes
¹/₄ cup pitted and chopped kalamata olives
¹/₂ teaspoon dried basil or 2 tablespoons chopped fresh basil
    leaves
    Scant ¹/₂ teaspoon salt
1 garlic clove, minced
    Freshly ground black pepper

Add green beans, ¹/₃ cup water, 2 teaspoons oil, tomatoes, olives, dried basil, if using (reserve fresh for later), and salt to an 8-to-9-inch pot. Cover and cook over medium-high heat until steam escapes around lid. Set timer for 5 minutes, and continue to steam until green beans are brightly colored and just tender. Remove lid and continue to cook until liquid evaporates and green beans and tomatoes start to stew, 1 to 2 minutes longer. Stir in garlic, fresh basil (if using), remaining 2 teaspoons oil, and pepper to taste. Serve immediately.

Steam-Sautéed Green Beans with Mustard Cream

Serves 4

Coarse-grain mustard can be used in place of the Dijon, if you like.

1 **pound green beans, stem ends trimmed, snapped in half**
2 **teaspoons butter**
¹/₂ **teaspoon salt**
2 **tablespoons Dijon mustard**
¹/₄ **cup heavy cream**
    Freshly ground black pepper

1 Add green beans, ¹/₃ cup water, butter, and salt to an 8-to-9-inch pot. Cover and cook over medium-high heat until steam escapes around lid. Set timer for 5 minutes and continue to steam until beans are brightly colored and just tender. Remove lid and continue to cook until water evaporates and beans start to sauté.

2 Mix mustard and cream together and add to beans, cooking until mixture coats them, about 1 minute longer. Add pepper to taste and serve immediately.

Steam-Sautéed Green Beans with Mushrooms, Thyme, and Sour Cream

Serves 4

This is my answer to the holiday green bean casserole.

4 teaspoons butter

8 ounces white mushrooms, sliced

1 pound green beans, stem ends trimmed, snapped in half

$1/2$ teaspoon salt

$1/2$ teaspoon dried thyme leaves or $1^1/2$ teaspoons fresh

$1/4$ cup sour cream

Freshly ground black pepper

$1/2$ cup Shallot Crisps (recipe follows) or canned french-fried onions

Heat butter over medium-high heat in an 8-to-9-inch pot. Add mushrooms, and sauté until liquid evaporates and mushrooms start to brown, about 5 minutes. Add green beans, $1/3$ cup water, salt, and dried thyme, if using (reserve fresh for later). Cover and cook until steam escapes around lid. Set timer for 5 minutes, and continue to steam until beans are brightly colored and just tender. Remove lid and continue to cook until water evaporates and beans start to sauté, 1 to 2 minutes longer. Stir in sour cream, fresh thyme (if using), and pepper to taste. Serve immediately with shallot crisps or french-fried onions sprinkled on top.

Shallot Crisps

Makes about ½ cup

Not only are these little crisps ideal for topping green beans, they're wonderful on seared or grilled steak and pureed turnips or rutabagas.

2 **tablespoons butter**
1 **tablespoon olive oil**
2 **large shallots, thinly sliced**

Heat butter and oil in a small skillet over medium heat. Add shallots and cook, stirring frequently, until crisp and golden, 8 to 10 minutes. Transfer with a slotted spoon to paper toweling to drain. (Shallots can be made a day in advance, covered, and held at room temperature.)

Steam-Sautéed Green Beans
with Indian Spices

Serves 4

Toss the hot beans, if you like, with ¼ cup plain yogurt. Don't add the yogurt to the hot skillet, or it will curdle.

4 teaspoons vegetable oil
2 garlic cloves, minced
1 tablespoon peeled, minced fresh ginger
½ teaspoon hot red pepper flakes
½ teaspoon ground coriander
½ teaspoon ground cumin
1 pound green beans, stem ends trimmed, snapped in half
Scant ½ teaspoon salt
1 tablespoon minced fresh cilantro

1 Add oil, garlic, ginger, pepper flakes, coriander, and cumin to an 8-to-9-inch pot. Cook over medium heat, stirring, until garlic and ginger start to sizzle and spices are fragrant. Be careful not to scorch.

2 Add green beans, ⅓ cup water, and salt. Increase heat to medium-high, cover, and cook until steam escapes around lid. Set timer for 5 minutes, and continue to steam until beans are brightly colored and just tender. Remove lid and continue to cook until water evaporates and beans start to sauté, 1 to 2 minutes longer. Stir in cilantro. Serve immediately.

Simple Steamed Green Beans for Salad

Cooking green beans by this method is much faster than blanching, but you've got to keep your eyes on them. If all the liquid evaporates, they will scorch.

1 pound green beans, stem ends trimmed, snapped in half
Scant ¹/₂ teaspoon salt

Add green beans, ¹/₂ cup water, and salt to an 8-to-9-inch pot. Cover and cook over medium-high heat until steam escapes around lid. Set timer for 5 minutes, and continue to steam until beans are brightly colored and just tender. Immediately pour green beans onto layers of paper or cloth toweling in a single layer to dry, and continue with bean salad that follows.

Sesame–Green Bean Salad with Lemon Dressing

Serves 4

To toast sesame seeds, place them in a small skillet over medium heat and cook, stirring frequently, until fragrant and lightly colored, about 5 minutes.

Simple Steamed Green Beans for Salad (opposite page)
1 **garlic clove, minced**
2 **tablespoons olive oil**
   Salt and freshly ground black pepper
1 **tablespoon lemon juice**
1 **tablespoon sesame seeds, toasted (see note above)**

Place green beans in a medium bowl. Add garlic, oil, and a light sprinkling of salt and pepper and toss to coat. Add lemon juice; toss to coat again. Sprinkle with sesame seeds, taste, adjust seasonings, and serve.

I can't remember the last picnic or potluck I've attended that didn't include at least one pasta salad. Unfortunately, they often look better than they taste. At a large party, you snail down the buffet line and spy the smart-looking bow-tie salad with asparagus and chicken. You take a heaping scoop, sit down, quickly unwrap your fork, and spear a bite. What a disappointment! Now you're stuck with a pile of greasy, flavorless noodles with hard vegetables and bland white meat.

When I went looking for a good basic recipe, the pickings were pretty slim. A few cookbook authors are so embarrassed by the dish that they even apologize for starting the trend.

In *The Dean & DeLuca Cookbook* (Random House, 1996), the authors write, "Public confession and apology: Felipe Rojas-Lombardi, the first chef in our kitchen, was the chef who put pasta salad on the map. . . . Today, the monster has gotten out of control; bad pasta salad is everywhere, turning tons of good dried pasta into trays of gluey, soggy starch with very little flavor."

Italian culinary expert Marcella Hazan also expresses regret for her part in the trend. "If I had invented pasta salads, I would hide. As it is, I am uncomfortable in recalling that it was after a recipe for pasta salad appeared in my preceding book, nearly a decade ago, that the item became a fixture of delicatessens and take-home food shops everywhere."

Dean & DeLuca and Marcella Hazan may be guilty of expanding the theme, but people in this country have been making pasta salad for decades. We may have only had one pasta shape (macaroni) and one dressing in which to toss it (mayonnaise), but the tradition has been long established.

And for good reason. Unlike delicate lettuce salads that quickly wilt, pasta salads hold up well on picnic and buffet tables. Leftovers are good the next day, too. Besides being durable, pasta salads are colorful and complete. Chock-full of vegetables, meat, and other flavorful ingredients, they can be light and refreshing or hearty and substantial.

But pasta salad's strength is its weakness. Because pasta is so neutral, it can be paired with just about any salad ingredient. Unless cooked and flavored correctly, though, it will end up tasting bland, pickled, doughy, gummy, or soft. Green vegetables aren't a necessity in pasta salad, but they are an attractive addition. Yet when tossed with the acidic dressing that the salad desperately needs, vegetables like asparagus, broccoli, green beans, and snow peas can turn from kelly- to army-green in minutes, dragging the rest of the salad down with them.

I needed a pasta salad that tasted as good as it looked and would stay moist, bright, and fresh. I also wanted to see if I could develop a formula — not just a single recipe — that would work with whatever flavoring ingredients I had and with whatever style of dressing I chose.

In building my formula, I started by determining the best way to cook and cool the pasta. I cooked 1 pound of pasta in the following three ways:

In 1 gallon of water seasoned with 1 tablespoon salt
In ½ gallon of water seasoned with 1 tablespoon salt
In 1 quart each of water and chicken broth, seasoned with salt

Of the three methods, I preferred the firm yet al dente texture of the pasta cooked in the full gallon of water, but I liked the fully seasoned flavor of the pasta in the more heavily salted water. Pasta cooked in less than a gallon of water tasted a little gummy by comparison, and pasta cooked in part chicken broth tasted as though it had been fished from a pot of weak chicken noodle soup — not bad, just not right.

I had a cooking method — 1 pound of pasta cooked in 1 gallon of water seasoned with 2 tablespoons salt — but how should it be cooled? I tried four different methods:

I plunged the pasta into *cold* water to stop the cooking, then drained and tossed it with a light vinegar and oil dressing.
I tossed *hot* pasta with the dressing.
I drained the pasta and cooled it to *room temperature,* then tossed it with the dressing.
I drained the pasta and *immediately tossed it with oil* to keep it from sticking, *then cooled it to room temperature* and tossed it with dressing.

And finally, to get an idea of how green vegetables might respond to the cooking, cooling, and dressing process, I threw a handful of broccoli and asparagus into each pot of pasta during the last minute of cooking.

The most common method — cooling the pasta in cold water — was my least favorite. The salad made from these noodles tasted cold, waterlogged, and bland, reminding me of why pasta salads get a bad rap.

The hot pasta and vegetables absorbed the dressing and tasted flavorful, but within minutes, the broccoli turned khaki-colored and the pasta tasted slightly pickled.

Draining the pasta and vegetables, then spreading them in a shallow baking pan, allowed the two to cool to room temperature very quickly. Unlike the first two pastas that were dressed when wet, this one had a chance to dry before being tossed, causing the dressing to cling perfectly. Cooled to room temperature, the vegetables held their bright color. Since the cooled pasta didn't stick once dressed, I saw no reason to toss it with extra oil.

THE ACID TEST

Although I planned to develop buttermilk- and soy-based dressings, my most frequently used pasta salad dressing is vinaigrette. Since vinaigrette has a higher proportion of vinegar than the other two styles, I tested it first. What worked for vinaigrette, I reasoned, would work for the other two.

I tested a total of six acids: three mild ones (lemon juice, balsamic, and rice wine vinegar) and three more assertive ones (red wine, white wine, and sherry vinegar), using a ratio of 3 parts oil to 1 part vinegar. The vinaigrettes made with the more assertive vinegar tasted harsh, and the dressed vegetables dulled within 20 minutes.

All three lower-acidity vinegars — lemon juice, rice wine, and balsamic — tasted balanced and did not affect the green vegetables. Balsamic, however, stained the pasta pale brown. From my experience, I also knew that balsamic vinegars varied dramatically, with cheaper ones (which aren't true balsamics anyway) often tasting as strong as cider vinegar. Lemon juice and rice wine vinegar were the best of the lot. They tasted assertive but not harsh and didn't affect the vegetables.

While monitoring the vinaigrette's effects on the salad, I noticed that my thin dressing of vinegar, oil, salt, and pepper quickly separated, the vinegar being absorbed by the pasta, the oil clinging in droplets to the pasta's surface. To prevent this, the dressing needed to be thick and emulsified. Mayonnaise, Dijon mustard, and sour cream were all potential thickeners. Accordingly, I made three vinaigrettes. All three helped create a thicker dressing that clung to and lightly coated the pasta without being absorbed by it.

Of the three, I prefer mayonnaise for milder pasta salads and Dijon for those more assertively flavored. Sour cream thickened well and tasted fine, but its dressing lacked the sheen of the mayonnaise- and mustard-thickened dressings and the finished salads looked dull.

Regardless of style, pasta salads have six basic components: **pasta** (bite-size shapes are preferable); **major flavorings** (raw and cooked vegetables, meat, poultry, seafood, mild cheeses, and canned beans); **flavor enhancers** (olives, capers, strong cheeses, nuts); **herbs** (fresh or dried) and zests; **onion** (red onion and scallions are both good choices); and a **dressing**. After some experimentation, I found that a ratio of 2 pounds of major flavorings to 1 pound of pasta makes a substantial, interesting salad.

For your next potluck or picnic, make one of the pasta salads that follow, or use the formula on page 217 to create your own. The cooking and cooling technique guarantees flavorful pasta and bright vegetables every time, and the dressings are designed to coat the pasta lightly. Prepared this way, your salad will never be gluey, soggy, or flavorless, and you won't need to apologize for it. In fact, someone will probably ask you for the recipe.

Pasta Salad
with Antipasto Flavorings

Serves 12 to 16
as a side dish,
6 to 8 as a main course

Salami is another good meat choice here. Pepperoncini are mild Italian pickled peppers.

2 tablespoons salt

1 pound bite-size pasta (see page 217)

8 ounces pepperoni, thinly sliced

8 ounces mozzarella cheese, cut into $^1/_2$-inch cubes

$^1/_2$ pound (1 large) green bell pepper, stemmed, seeded, and cut into bite-size slices

$^1/_2$ pound (4 medium stalks) celery, cut into $^1/_4$-inch-thick slivers

$^1/_2$ cup small pimiento-stuffed olives

$^1/_2$ cup sliced pepperoncini

$^1/_2$ cup jarred roasted red peppers

$^1/_2$ medium red onion, cut into small dice

2 tablespoons minced fresh parsley

1 teaspoon dried oregano or 1 tablespoon minced fresh

Creamy Vinaigrette, made with lemon juice and Dijon mustard (page 207)

1. Bring 1 gallon water to a boil in a large pot.

2. Add salt and pasta to pot, and cook until just tender. Drain, spread out in a shallow baking pan, and let cool to room temperature.

3. Transfer pasta and remaining ingredients, except dressing, to a large bowl; do not mix. (Pasta salad can be covered and refrigerated for up to 2 hours.) When ready to serve, add dressing, toss to coat, let stand for 15 minutes, and serve.

Pasta Salad with Asparagus, Mushrooms, Artichoke Hearts, and Parmesan

A vegetable peeler is perfect for shaving cheese from a block of Parmesan. Grated Parmesan can be used as well, but preferably not the kind shaken from the can, which is dry and has little flavor.

2 tablespoons salt

1 pound bite-size pasta (see page 217)

1 pound (1 bunch) asparagus, trimmed and cut into 1-inch lengths

1 package (8 ounces) mushrooms, sliced

8 ounces drained artichoke hearts from a 14-ounce can, rinsed and cut into bite-size pieces

1/2 cup shaved or grated Parmesan cheese

3 large scallions, thinly sliced

3 tablespoons chopped fresh parsley

2 teaspoons finely grated lemon zest

Creamy Vinaigrette, made with mayonnaise and lemon juice (page 207)

1. Bring 1 gallon water to a boil in a large pot.

2. Add salt and pasta to pot, and cook until just tender, adding asparagus for last 1 minute of cooking. Drain, spread out in a shallow baking pan, and let cool to room temperature.

3. Transfer pasta, asparagus, and remaining ingredients, except dressing, to a large bowl; do not mix. (Pasta salad can be covered and refrigerated for up to 2 hours.) When ready to serve, add dressing, toss to coat, let stand for 15 minutes, and serve.

Pasta Salad
with Grilled Eggplant and Pepper

Serves 12 to 16
as a side dish,
6 to 8 as a main
course

If you don't feel like heating up the grill, you can broil the eggplant and peppers.

---

1 pound (1 large) eggplant, cut into $1/2$-inch-thick rounds, brushed with oil, and sprinkled with salt and pepper

$1/2$ pound (1 large) red or yellow bell pepper, stemmed, seeded, and quartered, brushed with oil and sprinkled with salt and pepper

2 tablespoons salt

1 pound bite-size pasta (see page 217)

$1/2$ pound (2 medium) tomatoes, seeded and cut into $1/2$-inch dice, lightly sprinkled with salt

$1/2$ small red onion, cut into small dice (about $1/2$ cup)

3 tablespoons torn fresh basil leaves

$1/4$ cup capers, drained

Creamy Vinaigrette, made with mustard and rice wine vinegar (page 207)

1 Bring 1 gallon water to a boil in a large pot. Preheat gas grill on high for 10 minutes.

2 Grill eggplant and pepper until well browned, about 4 minutes on one side and 3 minutes on the other. When they are cool enough to handle, cut into bite-size pieces. Set aside.

3 Add salt and pasta to pot and cook until just tender. Drain, spread out in a shallow baking pan, and let cool to room temperature, about 10 minutes.

4 Transfer pasta, vegetables, and remaining ingredients, except dressing, to a large bowl; do not mix. (Pasta salad can be covered and refrigerated for up to 2 hours.) When ready to serve, add dressing, toss to coat, let stand for 15 minutes, and serve.

Greek-Style Pasta Salad

Serves 12 to 16 as a side dish, 6 to 8 as a main course

One teaspoon dried oregano and 2 tablespoons minced fresh parsley leaves can stand in for the fresh mint.

1 pound (1 small) seedless cucumber, cut into bite-size pieces
Salt
1 pound bite-size pasta (see page 217)
1 pound (about 1¹/₂ dry pints) cherry tomatoes, halved and lightly sprinkled with salt
¹/₂ cup crumbled feta cheese
¹/₂ cup pitted kalamata olives, coarsely chopped
¹/₂ medium red onion, cut into small dice
3 tablespoons minced fresh mint
Creamy Vinaigrette, made with rice wine vinegar and mayonnaise (page 207)

1 Bring 1 gallon water to a boil in a large pot.

2 Meanwhile, sprinkle cucumber lightly with salt, and place in a colander set over a bowl to drain.

3 Add 2 tablespoons salt and pasta to pot and cook until just tender. Drain, spread out in a shallow baking pan, and let cool to room temperature.

4 Pat cucumbers dry, and transfer them with pasta and remaining ingredients, except dressing, to a large bowl; do not mix. (Pasta salad can be covered and refrigerated for up to 2 hours.) When ready to serve, add dressing, toss to coat, let stand for 15 minutes, and serve.

Niçoise-Style Pasta Salad

Because I prefer tuna chunks rather than flakes in this salad, I recommend solid white albacore tuna. Fresh tuna, grilled, cooled, and broken into chunks, would also be excellent.

8 ounces (³/₄ dry pint) cherry tomatoes
    Salt
1 pound bite-size pasta (see page 217)
1 pound green beans, ends trimmed, cut into bite-size pieces
8 ounces drained tuna from 2 cans (6 ounces each)
¹/₂ cup pitted kalamata olives, coarsely chopped
¹/₂ medium red onion, cut into small dice
2 tablespoons minced fresh parsley leaves
1 tablespoon minced fresh thyme leaves
2 teaspoons finely grated lemon zest
    Creamy Vinaigrette, made with lemon juice and mayonnaise (page 207)

1   Bring 1 gallon water to a boil in a large pot.

2   Meanwhile, halve tomatoes, lightly sprinkle with salt, and set aside.

3   Add 2 tablespoons salt and pasta to pot, and cook until just tender, adding green beans for last 1 minute of cooking. Drain, spread out in a shallow baking pan, and let cool to room temperature.

4   Transfer tomatoes, pasta, beans, and remaining ingredients, except dressing, to a large bowl; do not mix. (Pasta salad can be covered and refrigerated for up to 2 hours.) When ready to serve, add dressing, toss to coat, let stand for 15 minutes, and serve.

Pasta Salad with Grilled Shrimp, Tomatoes, Feta, and Olives

Serves 12 to 16
as a side dish,
8 to 8 as a main
course

If you'd rather have the shrimp more evenly distributed throughout the salad, simply halve them, lengthwise or crosswise, before
tossing them with the remaining ingredients.

1	pound medium shrimp
	Olive oil
	Salt and freshly ground black pepper
1/2	cup pine nuts
1	pound bite-size pasta (see page 217)
1	pound (3 medium) tomatoes, seeded, cut into medium dice, and lightly sprinkled with salt
1/2	cup pitted kalamata olives, coarsely chopped
1/2	cup crumbled feta cheese
1/2	medium red onion, cut into small dice or thin slivers
2	tablespoons minced fresh parsley
1	tablespoon minced fresh rosemary
	Creamy Vinaigrette, made with lemon juice and Dijon mustard (page 207)

1. Bring 1 gallon water to a boil. Preheat grill on high for 10 minutes.

2. Meanwhile, thread shrimp on metal or water-soaked bamboo
skewers, brush with oil, and sprinkle with salt and pepper. Grill
over high heat until pink, about 2 minutes per side. Remove
from skewers and set aside.

3. Toast pine nuts in a small skillet over medium-low heat, shaking pan, until fragrant, about 5 minutes. Set aside.

4. Add 2 tablespoons salt and pasta to pot and cook until just tender. Drain, spread out in a shallow baking pan, and let cool to
room temperature.

5. Transfer shrimp, nuts, pasta, and remaining ingredients, except
dressing, to a large bowl; do not mix. (Pasta salad can be covered and refrigerated for up to 2 hours.) When ready to serve,
add dressing, toss to coat, let stand for 15 minutes, and serve.

Pasta Salad with Sausage, Chickpeas, Red Pepper, and Black Olives

Serves 12 to 16 as a side dish, 6 to 8 as a main course

Fully cooked sausages, such as kielbasa, may be substituted for the Italian sausage. Simply fry them in a film of oil until brown, then cool, slice, and toss with the remaining salad ingredients.

1   pound Italian sausages
1   tablespoon vegetable oil
1   large red bell pepper, cut into bite-size pieces
    Salt and freshly ground black pepper
1   pound bite-size pasta (see page 217)
8   ounces drained and rinsed chickpeas (from a 15-ounce can)
1/2 cup pitted oil-cured olives, coarsely chopped
1/2 medium red onion, cut into small dice
2   tablespoons minced fresh parsley
1   tablespoon minced fresh rosemary
    Creamy Vinaigrette, made with vinegar and Dijon mustard (page 207)

1. Bring 1 gallon water to a boil in a large pot.

2. Meanwhile, bring sausages, 1/3 cup water, and oil to a boil in a covered medium skillet. Steam until sausages are cooked through and water has almost evaporated, about 5 minutes. Remove lid and continue to cook until water evaporates and sausages brown. Remove from skillet and slice into bite-size rounds when cool. Set aside. Meanwhile, add red pepper to the hot skillet and sauté, seasoning with salt and pepper, until crisp-tender, 3 to 4 minutes. Set aside.

3. Add 2 tablespoons salt and pasta to pot and cook until just tender. Drain, spread out in a shallow baking pan, and let cool to room temperature.

4. Transfer sausages, red pepper, pasta, and remaining ingredients, except dressing, to a large bowl; do not mix. (Pasta salad can be covered and refrigerated for up to 2 hours.) When ready to serve, add dressing, toss to coat, let stand for 15 minutes, and serve.

Creamy Vinaigrette

Makes about 1 cup, enough for 1 pasta salad

If you don't have a small whisk, you'll need to mix the dressing in a heavy bowl rather than the suggested Pyrex measuring cup.

¹/₄ cup rice wine vinegar or fresh lemon juice
 2 tablespoons Dijon mustard or mayonnaise
 1 large garlic clove, minced
    Salt and freshly ground black pepper
²/₃ cup olive oil

Put vinegar or lemon juice and mustard or mayonnaise in a 2-cup Pyrex measuring cup. With a small whisk, stir in garlic, a big pinch of salt, and a couple of grinds of pepper. Slowly whisk in oil, first in droplets, then in a slow, steady stream, to make an emulsified vinaigrette. (Vinaigrette can be made and refrigerated 1 day in advance.)

Creamy Pasta Salad
with Grilled Chicken, Avocados, and Tomatoes

If you're not a cilantro fan, simply substitute 3 tablespoons minced fresh parsley leaves.

1 **pound boneless, skinless chicken breasts, brushed with vegetable oil and sprinkled with salt and pepper**

2 **tablespoons salt**

1 **pound bite-size pasta (see page 217)**

6 **ounces (about ½ dry pint) cherry tomatoes, halved and lightly sprinkled with salt**

4 **ounces (about 6 medium) radishes, thinly sliced**

3 **large scallions, cut into bite-size pieces**

3 **tablespoons chopped fresh cilantro**

6 **ounces (1 medium) avocado, halved, pitted, skinned, and cut into bite-size chunks**

Creamy Buttermilk Dressing (page 212)

1 Bring 1 gallon water to a boil. Preheat grill on high for 10 minutes.

2 Grill chicken over high heat until opaque throughout and fully cooked, about 3 to 4 minutes per side, depending on size. Let cool, cut crosswise into thin slices, and set aside.

Add salt and pasta to pot and cook until just tender. Drain, spread out in a shallow baking pan, and let cool to room temperature.

4 Transfer chicken, pasta, and remaining ingredients, except avocado and dressing, to a large bowl; do not mix. (Pasta salad can be covered and refrigerated for up to 2 hours.) When ready to serve, add avocado and dressing, toss to coat, let stand for 15 minutes, and serve.

Pasta Salad with Smoked Salmon and Asparagus

Serves 12 to 16 as a side dish, 6 to 8 as a main course

Smoked trout can be substituted for the salmon in this recipe.

2 tablespoons salt

1 pound bite-size pasta (see page 217)

1 pound asparagus, cut into 1-inch lengths

8 ounces smoked salmon, cut into bite-size pieces

8 ounces radishes, trimmed and thinly sliced

1/4 cup capers, drained

1/2 medium red onion, cut into small dice

3 tablespoons minced fresh dill

2 teaspoons finely grated lemon zest

Creamy Buttermilk Dressing (page 212)

1 Bring 1 gallon water to a boil in a large pot.

2 Add salt and pasta and cook until just tender, adding asparagus for last 1 minute of cooking. Drain, spread out in a shallow baking pan, and let cool to room temperature.

3 Transfer pasta, asparagus, and remaining ingredients, except dressing, to a large bowl, but do not mix. (Pasta salad can be covered and refrigerated for up to 2 hours.) When ready to serve, add dressing, toss to coat, let stand for 15 minutes, and serve.

Creamy Pasta Salad
with Green Vegetables and Tarragon

Serves 12 to 16
as a side dish,
6 to 8 as a main
course

A pound of ham, sliced or diced into bite-size pieces, can be substituted for two of the vegetables called for in this recipe.

2 tablespoons salt

1 pound bite-size pasta (see page 217)

1/2 pound asparagus, cut into 1-inch lengths

1/2 pound snow peas, halved crosswise

1/2 pound (1/2 medium) zucchini, halved lengthwise if small, quartered lengthwise if large, then thinly sliced

8 ounces (2 cups) frozen green peas

1/2 cup shaved Parmesan cheese

2 tablespoons minced fresh tarragon

1 tablespoon minced fresh parsley

2 teaspoons finely grated lemon zest

3 large scallions, cut into bite-size pieces

Creamy Buttermilk Dressing (page 212)

1. Bring 1 gallon water to a boil in a large pot.

2. Add salt and pasta and cook until just tender, adding asparagus, snow peas, and zucchini for last 1 minute of cooking. Drain, spread out in a shallow baking pan with peas, and let cool to room temperature.

3. Transfer pasta, asparagus, snow peas, zucchini, peas, and remaining ingredients, except dressing, into a large bowl, but do not mix. (Pasta salad can be covered and refrigerated for up to 2 hours.) When ready to serve, add dressing, toss to coat, let stand for 15 minutes, and serve.

Pasta Salad with Broccoli, Carrots, and Pepperjack Cheese

Serves 12 to 16
as a side dish,
6 to 8 as a main
course

I've suggested pepperjack for its pleasant bite. For a more kid-friendly salad, substitute Cheddar, Monterey Jack, or Swiss.

2 tablespoons salt

1 pound bite-size pasta (see page 217)

1 pound broccoli, cut into bite-size florets, stems peeled and cut into $1/4$-inch-thick coins

8 ounces carrots (3–4 medium), peeled and cut into $1/4$-inch-thick coins

8 ounces pepperjack cheese, cut into small cubes

$1/4$ cup sunflower seeds

$1/2$ medium red onion, cut into small dice

3 tablespoons minced fresh parsley

Creamy Buttermilk Dressing (page 212)

Proceed as directed in Creamy Pasta Salad with Green Vegetables and Tarragon (opposite page), substituting broccoli and carrots for asparagus and omitting snow peas, zucchini, and peas.

Creamy Buttermilk Dressing

Makes about 1 cup,
enough for 1 pasta
salad

Use this dressing for tossed salads as well.

        1   large garlic clove, minced
      $^1/_3$ cup mayonnaise
      $^1/_3$ cup sour cream
      $^1/_3$ cup buttermilk
        3   tablespoons lemon juice or rice wine vinegar
            Salt and freshly ground black pepper

Mix all ingredients in a small bowl; set aside or refrigerate until ready to toss with salad. (Dressing can be made and refrigerated up to 3 days in advance.)

Asian-Style Pasta Salad with Broccoli, Zucchini, and Red Pepper

Unlike bell peppers in the vinaigrette-based salads, those in Asian-style salads taste best cooked, which is why I stir-fry them until crisp-tender.

8 ounces (1 large) red bell pepper, cut into bite-size pieces, drizzled lightly with oil
Salt and freshly ground black pepper
1/4 cup sesame seeds
1 pound bite-size pasta (see page 217)
1 pound broccoli, cut into bite-size florets, stems peeled and cut into 1/4-inch-thick coins
8 ounces (1 small) zucchini, quartered lengthwise and sliced 1/4 inch thick
3 tablespoons minced fresh cilantro or parsley
3 large scallions, cut into bite-size pieces
Soy-Sesame Dressing (page 216)

Bring 1 gallon water to a boil in a large pot. Heat a medium skillet over medium-high heat. Add red pepper and sauté, seasoning with salt and pepper, until crisp-tender, 3 to 4 minutes. Remove from skillet and set aside.

2 Reduce heat to low. Add sesame seeds to skillet, and toast until lightly colored and fragrant, 2 to 3 minutes, shaking pan and stirring to ensure even cooking. Remove from skillet and set aside.

Add 2 tablespoons salt and pasta to pot, cook until just tender, adding broccoli and zucchini for last 1 minute of cooking. Drain, then spread out in a shallow baking pan, and let cool to room temperature.

4 Transfer red pepper, sesame seeds, pasta, broccoli, zucchini, and remaining ingredients, except dressing, to a large bowl. (Pasta salad can be covered and refrigerated for up to 2 hours.) When ready to serve, add dressing, toss to coat, let stand for 15 minutes, and serve.

Asian-Style Pasta Salad with Shrimp, Pepper, and Roasted Peanuts

Serves 12 to 16
as a side dish,
6 to 8 as a main
course.

Simple steamed shrimp taste bland when tossed with an Asian-style dressing. To solve the problem, I let them sit in a soy-sherry marinade for just a few minutes before steaming them.

1 pound large shrimp, peeled
1 tablespoon each soy sauce and sweet sherry
2 tablespoons salt
1 pound bite-size pasta (see page 217)
8 ounces (4 medium stalks) celery, sliced $^1/_4$ inch thick
8 ounces (1 large) bell pepper, cut into bite-size pieces
$^1/_2$ cup honey-roasted peanuts, coarsely chopped
3 large scallions, cut into bite-size pieces
3 tablespoons minced fresh cilantro or parsley
Soy-Sesame Dressing (page 216)

1 Marinate shrimp in a small bowl in soy sauce and sherry while preparing other ingredients.

2 Bring 1 gallon water to a boil in a large pot. Heat 1 inch water in a large, deep skillet or large soup kettle.

3 Arrange shrimp in a single layer on a steamer basket. Set basket over boiling water in skillet or soup kettle, cover, reduce heat to low, and steam, without lifting lid, until shrimp are opaque, checking at 5 minutes. Remove basket and set aside to cool to room temperature. Cut shrimp into bite-size pieces.

4 Add salt and pasta to the pot; cook until just tender. Drain, spread out in a shallow baking pan, and let cool to room temperature.

5 Transfer shrimp, pasta, and remaining ingredients, except dressing, to a large bowl; do not mix. (Pasta salad can be covered and refrigerated for up to 2 hours.) When ready to serve, add dressing, toss to coat, let stand for 15 minutes, and serve.

Asian-Style Pasta Salad
with Chicken and Snow Peas

Serves 12 to 16
as a side dish,
6 to 8 as a main
course

Asparagus, cut into bite-size pieces, is a fine stand-in for the snow peas in this recipe.

1 **pound boneless, skinless chicken breast**
1 **tablespoon each soy sauce and sweet sherry**
2 **tablespoons salt**
1 **pound bite-size pasta (see page 217)**
8 **ounces snow peas, halved crosswise**
8 **ounces fresh bean sprouts**
1/2 **cup roasted cashews, coarsely chopped**
3 **large scallions, cut into bite-size pieces**
3 **tablespoons minced cilantro or parsley**
   Soy-Sesame Dressing (page 216)

1. Marinate chicken in soy sauce and sherry in a small bowl while preparing other ingredients.

2. Bring 1 gallon water to a boil in a large pot. Bring 1 inch of water to a boil in a separate large, deep skillet or large soup kettle.

3. Place chicken in a steamer basket. Set basket over boiling water in skillet or soup kettle, cover, reduce heat to low, and steam, without lifting lid, until chicken is cooked through, about 10 minutes. Remove basket, cool chicken to room temperature, shred into bite-size pieces, and set aside.

4. Add salt and pasta to pot; cook until just tender, adding snow peas for last 1 minute of cooking. Drain, spread out in a shallow baking pan, and let cool to room temperature.

5. Transfer chicken, pasta, snow peas, and remaining ingredients, except dressing, to a large bowl. (Pasta salad can be covered and refrigerated for up to 2 hours.) When ready to serve, add dressing, toss to coat, let stand for 15 minutes, and serve.

Soy-Sesame Dressing

Makes about 1 cup, enough for 1 pasta salad

This dressing is sweet, salty, sour, hot, and aromatic. If you don't have a small whisk, you'll need to mix the dressing in a heavy bowl.

1 tablespoon minced garlic
1 tablespoon minced, peeled ginger
6 tablespoons soy sauce
1 tablespoon rice wine vinegar
1 tablespoon sugar
1 tablespoon sesame oil
³/₄ teaspoon hot red pepper flakes
2 tablespoons mayonnaise
¹/₄ cup vegetable oil

Mix garlic, ginger, soy sauce, vinegar, sugar, sesame oil, and red pepper flakes in a 2-cup Pyrex measuring cup. Using a small whisk, vigorously whisk in mayonnaise. Slowly whisk in oil, first in droplets, then in a slow, steady stream, to make an emulsified dressing. (Dressing can be made and refrigerated a day in advance.)

The Formula for Your Own Perfect Pasta Salad

Serves 12 to 16
as a side dish,
6 to 8 as a main
course

Using this formula, you can create your own pasta salad, drawing from the following choices. Under ideal circumstances, it tastes best when made, dressed, and served with little delay. If that's not possible (and it's usually not), prepare the individual salad ingredients up to the point of dressing them and refrigerate for up to 2 hours. Although not at its peak of perfection, leftover pasta salad is good for at least a couple of days.

2   tablespoons salt

1   pound bite-size pasta, such as farfalle (bow-ties), fusilli (corkscrews), penne, ziti, rotelle (wagon wheels), macaroni, *or* shells

2   pounds major flavorings (page 217–18)

    Flavor enhancers (page 219)

    Herbs and/or zests of choice (page 19)

¹/₂ small red onion, cut into small dice, or 3 large scallions, thinly sliced

1   cup choice of dressing (page 207, 212, or 216)

1. Bring 1 gallon water to a boil in a large pot.

2. Add salt and pasta and cook until just tender, adding any vegetables that need to be cooked during last 1 minute of cooking. Drain, spread out in a shallow baking pan, and let cool to room temperature.

3. Transfer pasta, vegetables, and remaining ingredients, except dressing, to a large bowl. (Pasta salad can be covered and refrigerated for up to 2 hours.) When ready to serve, add dressing, toss to coat, let stand for 15 minutes, and serve.

Major Flavorings

VEGETABLES THAT DON'T HAVE TO BE COOKED

Artichoke hearts (canned), drained and cut into bite-size pieces

Avocados, halved, pitted, peeled, and cut into bite-size pieces

Bean sprouts, rinsed and dried

Bell peppers, trimmed, cored, and cut into bite-size pieces

Celery, trimmed and sliced ¼ inch thick

Cherry tomatoes, halved and sprinkled with salt

Cucumbers, preferably seedless, quartered lengthwise, cut into bite-size pieces, and sprinkled with salt

Fennel, trimmed, halved, cored, and thinly sliced

Green peas (frozen), thawed

Mushrooms, thinly sliced

Tomatoes, seeded, cut into medium dice, and sprinkled with salt

Zucchini, halved lengthwise if small, quartered lengthwise if large, then thinly sliced

VEGETABLES ADDED TO BOILING PASTA DURING THE LAST MINUTE OF COOKING

Asparagus, trimmed and cut into bite-size pieces

Broccoli florets, cut into bite-size pieces; stems peeled and cut into ¼-inch-thick coins

Carrots, peeled and cut into ¼-inch coins

Cauliflower florets, cut into bite-size pieces

Green beans, trimmed and cut into bite-size lengths

Snow peas, strings removed

Sugar snap peas, strings removed

Zucchini, halved lengthwise if small, quartered lengthwise if large, and sliced ¼ inch thick

VEGETABLES THAT CAN BE GRILLED OR BROILED

Brush these vegetables with olive oil and sprinkle with salt and pepper before grilling or broiling.

Bell peppers, stemmed, seeded, and quartered

Eggplant, cut into ½-inch-thick rounds, then cut into bite-size pieces after grilling

Fennel, trimmed, halved, core left intact, and cut into wedges (remove core after grilling)

Mushrooms, large, left whole; sliced or quartered after grilling

Zucchini, cut on the diagonal into ½-inch-thick slices

VEGETABLES THAT CAN BE SAUTÉED

Bell peppers, trimmed, cored, then cut into bite-size strips after grilling

Celery, trimmed and sliced ¼ inch thick

Other Major Flavorings

Chicken breasts, grilled, sautéed, or steamed, cut crosswise into thin bite-size strips

Chickpeas and kidney beans (canned), drained and rinsed (most white beans are too mushy)

Crabmeat (pasteurized lump)

Ham, sliced ¼ inch thick and cut into bite-size strips

Italian sausage, steam-sautéed and sliced thinly on a slight bias

Lobster, cooked and cut into bite-size pieces

Mozzarella and other mild cheeses, cut into ½-inch cubes

Shrimp, peeled, then steamed or grilled

Tuna (canned, drained, or grilled fresh)

Flavor Enhancers

CANNED/JARRED

Capers, drained

Olives, pitted and coarsely chopped

Pepperoncini, drained and thinly sliced

Roasted peppers, cut into strips

Sun-dried tomatoes, packed in oil and cut into small dice

MEATS

Bacon, fried and crumbled

Prosciutto, thinly sliced and cut into small dice

Smoked salmon, thinly sliced and cut into thin strips

CHEESES

Feta, crumbled

Goat cheese, crumbled

Parmesan, shaved with a vegetable peeler

NUTS AND SEEDS

Cashews, roasted, coarsely chopped

Peanuts, roasted, coarsely chopped

Pine nuts, toasted

Sesame seeds, toasted

Sunflower seeds

Herbs and Zests

Basil, stemmed and torn into pieces

Cilantro, stemmed and coarsely chopped

Dill, stemmed and coarsely chopped

Mint, stemmed and coarsely chopped

Parsley, stemmed and coarsely chopped

Rosemary, stemmed and minced

Tarragon, stemmed and coarsely chopped

Lemon zest, finely grated

Orange zest, finely grated

Although I invariably order french fries at restaurants, several things used to conspire to keep me from making them at home. First there was all the hassle and mess of the frying itself, not to mention the problem of what to do with the leftover oil. I also knew that good french fries are supposed to be fried twice, so they crisp up outside but still cook all the way through. Frying them once was hard enough!

For weeknight suppers, I usually opted for baked or roasted potatoes or an occasional potato pancake. I was certain these potato dishes contained less fat than a plateful of fries. Was it possible, I wondered, to make crisp fries with creamy insides without all the fat and fuss?

WHITES ARE RIGHT

I started by frying the four most widely available potato varieties: Yukon Golds, russets (also called Idahos), red boiling potatoes, and white all-purpose. For lack of a better method, I heated a full gallon of oil (which measured only 2½ inches deep in my large soup kettle) and fried each batch of potatoes twice, the first time at 300 degrees until a blistery pale shell had formed and a quick final time at 375 degrees until crisp and golden brown.

Although shapely with an attractive golden hue, the Yukon Golds were too sweet and too dense for the light french fry I wanted. Low-starch boiling potatoes tasted more like fried roasted potatoes than french fries, and their surfaces were leathery and tough. I was betting on the russets, but they fried up relatively limp and tasted a little too earthy. White all-purpose potatoes triumphed. Their potato flavor was clear and clean, and their crisp exteriors protected a light, creamy interior.

Before starting to test, I had wondered if there might be a way to consolidate the first and second frying into a single, seamless process. Luckily for me, the answer was yes, and someone else had already figured out how to do it. The unconventional technique comes from a recipe in Jeffrey Steingarten's *The Man Who Ate Everything* (Knopf, 1997). Called Easy Frites, which Steingarten attributes to famed French chef Joël Robuchon, it starts with 1½ pounds of raw potato sticks placed in a cold skillet and covered with a mere 2 cups of *cold* oil. The pan is placed over the highest heat and cooked until the oil reaches 350 degrees, at which point the potatoes are "deep golden brown and ready to eat." I couldn't understand how such a large quantity of potatoes could cook in such a small amount of oil — especially cold oil — without absorbing most of it. But I owed this method a try.

In less than half an hour, I was converted from a skeptic to an enthusiastic believer. The fries cooked the Robuchon way had a crisp surface and a soft interior. And great taste was only one of the benefits. These fries absorbed hardly any oil at all. Measuring before and after frying, I discovered that the potatoes never absorbed more than 1 tablespoon per serving — less than most people use on a baked potato.

The dreaded task of cooling, straining, and storing a gallon of used frying oil had also been solved. The 2 cups cooled down in a flash and were simple to strain and store, and I didn't feel guilty about throwing such a small amount away if I felt like it. Unlike deep-frying, this method was clean and safe.

After retesting several times, I made a few refinements. Success, I learned, depends on the right ratio of oil to potatoes and the right heat level. If cooked over very high heat or in too much oil, the potatoes don't "blanch" properly, brown too quickly, and are soggy. On the other hand, if they cook too slowly, they become leathery and dry. Medium heat works best. I also found that the shorter potato sticks cut from medium potatoes are much easier to work with than those cut from jumbos.

There were still a few unanswered questions. Did the potatoes need soaking or rinsing before frying? Not in my experience. Besides adding a time-consuming extra step to the recipe, soaking and hand-drying large quantities of wet potato sticks didn't seem to help. The all-purpose white potatoes that had soaked overnight were no more crisp and seemed to stick more than those that had not been soaked at all. After frying the potatoes in safflower, vegetable, corn, peanut, and olive oil, as well as shortening, I preferred those cooked in the peanut oil.

The resulting method is simple, clean, and efficient, and the fries light, crisp, and downright healthy.

French Fries for the Home Cook

This frying method is attributed to Joël Robuchon by Jeffrey Steingarten in *The Man Who Ate Everything* (Knopf, 1997).

Don't bother the potatoes while they cook. Simply add them to the cold oil, turn the heat on medium, and find something else to do. To fry potatoes for two, halve the recipe, use a medium skillet, and reduce temperature to low.

2¹⁄₂ **cups peanut oil**

2 **pounds medium white all-purpose potatoes (about 6), peeled and cut into approximately ³⁄₈-inch-thick sticks**

Coarse salt, such as kosher or sea salt

1. Pour oil into a 12-inch skillet. Add potatoes to *cold* oil. They should be packed in a single layer with several sitting on top and with oil almost covering them. As potatoes fry and their moisture evaporates, they will eventually fit in pan in a single layer. Turn heat to medium, and fry until potatoes just start to turn pale golden, occasionally jiggling pan, 25 to 30 minutes. (You can move potatoes around for first 10 to 12 minutes if you like, but do not disturb them for the next 10 to 15 minutes, because they are too fragile.)

2. Once potatoes have developed a pale gold shell, increase heat to medium-high and fry, continuously moving them around to ensure even browning. When they are golden brown, transfer them (I use spring-action tongs) to a wire rack set over a cookie sheet or jelly-roll pan. Sprinkle with salt and serve immediately.

Before I even started testing, I was pretty sure I'd found the ultimate onion ring. Of the many good dishes at Havana Restaurant in New Hope, Pennsylvania, the onion rings are perhaps the biggest draw. Crisp and colossal, they are cut from onions the size of grapefruits. The sesame-studded coating is substantial but not greasy, enhancing the sweet, flavorful onion ring. Fortunately, they can be prepared ahead; otherwise, the kitchen staff could never keep up with the orders.

Before frying them, the owners of Havana, Jane and Jim Faraco, slice them 1 inch thick and soak them in water, dredge them in flour, dip them again into a thinned pancake batter, and then press them into a mix of bread crumbs and sesame seeds. With such a substantial coating, the rings are sturdy enough to be stacked on lipped cookie sheets for up to 24 hours before frying.

With this onion ring as my gold standard, I began my research to see if I could top it.

DIP AND DREDGE

The simplest onion ring recipe I found called for a flour-only dredge, but getting flour to stick to a dry onion ring is like pressing sand onto glass. With nothing for the flour to cling to, the resulting rings were naked and limp. Perhaps suitable as a garnish on top of a steak, these were fried onion rings in name only.

Most cookbook authors recognized the necessity of dunking the onions before dredging them but were divided on the liquid. Suggestions ranged from straight water to a combination of egg and milk. I tested them all. Although some liquid dip–flour dredged fried onion rings tasted better than others, none from this series of tests was stellar. Soaking the rings in plain water before dipping them in flour was better than no water at all, but the flour clung mostly to the textured cut surfaces, leaving the two slick sides of the onion exposed. An all-milk dip added a noticeably sweet flavor that complemented the cooked onion. Still, the rings were limp, the coating fragile. More viscous than milk, buttermilk did a better job of attracting flour to the ring, but its sour flavor was an immediate turnoff. The egg-water and egg-milk dips were the most substantial of the lot, but both crusts were wimpy at best. I was already starting to see that the Faracos' water dip and flour dredge was important, but only when used as a first step to create a neutral culinary glue to which another batter or crumb could adhere.

Some recipes went a step further, calling for a milk or an egg dip and a flour dredge, then repeating the dipping and dredging steps once more before frying. Although not ideal, the egg-dipped onion ring created the most substantial coating, while the milk-dipped ring was the most crisp.

Taking the opposite approach, some recipes recommended dredging the rings first in dry ingredients, then in wet, and finally in dry again. Following that method, I dusted the onion rings in bread crumbs, dunked them in egg, and then gave them a final bread crumb dredge. As good as they looked going in the fryer, the coating crumbled into the hot fat, resulting in an unevenly coated onion. Once drained, the dry, limp coating quickly deteriorated and cracked.

Many recipes called for a batter dip. Most consisted of flour, salt, and liquid, and some included egg. Since there was variety in batter flours, I started with a simple flour, salt, and milk formula, testing it with all-purpose flour, rice flour, instant flour, cake flour, and self-rising flour, as well as potato starch and a cornstarch/all-purpose flour combination. Finally, to test the Faraco method, I made a batter from boxed pancake mix. Unlike the other batches, the pancake batter and the one made with self-rising flour worked equally well, puffing during frying and clinging to the ring, creating an impressive coating.

Since egg is a leavener as well, I also made egg batters based on recipes I had seen. For one, I simply stirred a whole egg into the batter, while for the other, I separated the egg, whipped the egg white, and folded it into the yolk-enriched batter. Eggs certainly helped leaven, but they hindered crispness. Beer was a common batter liquid, and though beer-batter onion rings sounded good, after making a few batches, I realized I didn't like the lingering smell or flavor.

By now, I knew that:

➤ The bigger the onions and the thicker the rings, the simpler the process. Thick onion rings are easier to slice than thin ones, and since the ratio of onion to coating is high, the onion flavor really comes through.

- It's important to remove the papery thin membrane covering the inside of each ring. Otherwise, the coating adheres to the membrane rather than the ring and tends to fall off during frying.

- Soaking the onions for several hours as some recipes suggest does remove their bite — but too much so. I prefer the more assertive flavor of onions that are dipped rather than soaked.

- Since it's virtually impossible to get any batter or coating to cling to the onion's slick surface, the water dip and flour dredge help create a rough pastelike texture, to which the next coating can adhere.

- A batter is important. Skipping the batter step and performing only the water, flour, and bread crumb steps result in lackluster, relatively flavorless rings.

- Leavened batters adhere better during frying, but making one from scratch overly complicates the recipe. Using a commercial pancake batter, which requires nothing more than stirring in water, is easiest and best.

- A thin batter is better than a thick one. A thick batter forms an impressive but messy spongelike coating, which absorbs grease during frying. A thin batter is less greasy but insubstantial; a thin batter in combination with a bread crumb coating, however, is impressive.

- The bread crumb coating is important. Coated with thick or thin batter, onion rings are messy and have to be fried immediately. The bread crumbs create a thick, durable, impressive shell, resulting in exceptionally crisp rings. Coated in this way, the rings can be prepared ahead, making it possible for the cook to clean up before starting to fry. The bread crumb coating also helps the rings brown more quickly, keeping the onions from overcooking and collapsing.

Having verified that each step of the Faraco onion ring was important, I wondered if any flavoring beyond the sesame seeds could improve them. Chili powder, dry mustard, garlic powder, cayenne, and paprika are all common additions to the bread crumbs, while hot red pepper sauce is sometimes added to the batter. Most flavorings were lost in the frying process, and none was as good as the sesame seeds.

I've also discovered that the onion rings not only can be made in advance but, because of their substantial crisp coating, can be fried ahead as well. They are drained on a wire rack set over a cookie sheet and can be held in a 200-degree oven for about 30 minutes before serving.

Jumbo Onion Rings
with Sesame Bread Coating

Size is more important than variety in choosing an onion to make these rings. The bigger the onion, the fewer rings you have to coat and fry. Give yourself time between the coating and frying process, if possible. (The onion rings can be prepared up to 24 hours before frying.) Separating these tasks gives you a chance to clean the kitchen before you start to fry. Since the onion rings hold well in a 200-degree oven, they can also be fried before guests arrive.

1   very large yellow or white onion (about 1 pound, or the
      size of a grapefruit), trimmed, peeled, sliced, and
      separated into rings as shown
1   cup all-purpose flour
1   cup store-bought pancake mix
      Salt
4   cups plain dry bread crumbs
1/4   cup sesame seeds
6   cups peanut oil or vegetable oil

To cut the onion into 1-inch-thick slices, place a chef's knife 1 inch from the onion's end. Use the knife to roll the onion across the work surface and heavily score the onion where you plan to cut.

Using the scoring line as a guide, slice the onion. Depending on the size of the onion, repeat 2 or 3 more times.

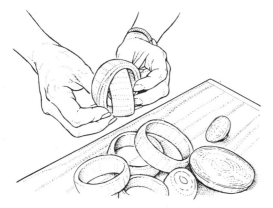

Pushing the rings through the wider end, separate the onion into rings.

Remove the papery thin membrane from each onion ring.

1. Place a sheet of newspaper over work surface. Place onion rings in a large bowl of cold water.

2. Put flour in a medium bowl. Set aside.

3. In a separate medium bowl, combine pancake mix and $1/2$ teaspoon salt. Stir in 1 cup water to form a smooth batter about the thickness of house paint.

4. In a third medium bowl, mix bread crumbs and sesame seeds.

Use the tip of a knife to cut out the root end.

Stack the coated onion rings in alternating layers so that the edges are touching as little as possible.

Remove an onion ring from water. (It's best to use one hand for dipping into wet ingredients and the other for dipping into dry ones.) Coat onion in flour, then knock on side of bowl to remove excess flour. Transfer ring to other hand and completely coat in pancake batter, allowing excess to drip off. Make a well in bread crumbs. Transfer onion to other hand, drop in crumbs, bury, and use palm to press crumbs onto onion. Place rings in a large, shallow pan, such as a jelly-roll pan, so that edges touch as little as possible. Continue stacking rings in layers as shown. As you work, thin pancake batter with additional water as it thickens and occasionally use a slotted spoon to remove any clumps that form in bread crumbs. Refrigerate onion rings until ready to use. (They can be refrigerated, uncovered, for up to 24 hours.)

6   Heat oven to 200 degrees. Heat oil in an 8-quart soup kettle to 350 degrees. Set a cooling rack over a baking sheet for stacking and draining onion rings. Carefully drop onion rings (spring-action tongs work well) one at a time into hot oil, fitting 4 or 5 in pot. (Do not crowd!) Cook for about 2 minutes, turning each ring halfway through, until they are a rich brown. Drain and keep warm in oven while you fry remaining rings. (Onion rings can be held for up to 30 minutes before serving.) Sprinkle with salt and serve immediately.

Holiday cooks can be divided into three groups. There are those who make baked casseroles of sweet potatoes mashed with butter and milk and topped with marshmallows (or brown sugar and nuts). There's the "candied yam" contingent, who slice the sweets and cook them in a syrupy liquid. Then there are the cooks who find both these dishes too sweet or want a savory, silky-textured puree for other occasions.

Rather than focus on just one of these dishes, I decided to try to make each one the best it could be. I cooked nearly eighty pounds of sweet potatoes before I got what I wanted.

BUY FRESH AND BAKE

You might think it doesn't matter how you cook your sweet potatoes, since they're going to be flavored with so many other ingredients. But after making each dish with differently cooked potatoes, I found that it matters very much.

Most recipes tell you to boil, then peel and cut (or mash) the potatoes, or do the opposite: first peel and cut, then boil them. A few other recipes suggest baking the potatoes or steaming them. And of course, there's the microwave possibility.

Neither boiling nor steaming produced sweet potatoes that could compete with the deep, rich, sweet flavor of baked. The steamed or boiled potatoes absorbed water and were heavier cooked than when they were raw, whereas the baked sweet potatoes shrank from their skins, losing a full ounce of water. This dehydration results in two positives. First, the more liquid that evaporates, the more intense the flavor. Second, the potato liquid that evaporates can be replaced with a richer, more flavorful liquid, such as milk or orange juice.

Although the microwave cooked the potatoes quickly — in just 10 minutes for medium-size ones — and although their color was the most vibrant of the lot, they tasted utterly bland. The quick cooking allows no time for the natural sugars and flavors to develop.

I also discovered that taking a shortcut by using canned sweet potatoes is a bad idea. Even the best brand I could find — one that was vacuum-packed with no additives or flavorings — looked and tasted washed out. Thinking that a little butter, sugar, milk, and eggs could improve things, I made the canned sweet potatoes into a casserole. No luck: it was still flavorless. Not even a big bag of marshmallows could save this casserole.

HOW MUCH SWEETENER DOES A SWEET POTATO NEED?

Since I wanted to keep the sweet potato puree savory, I didn't need to sweeten it at all. For both sweet potato casserole and candied yams, mild sweeteners such as granulated sugar were too bland. Assertive sweeteners like molasses were too overpowering, but middle-of-the-road sweeteners were just right.

For the casserole, I tested eight different sweeteners. I tried white, light, and dark brown sugars, as well as a mix of dark and white. And I made casseroles with maple syrup, condensed milk, molasses, and honey. Granulated sugar offered nothing but a cheap sweet hit. The condensed milk made the casserole taste like dessert. At the other extreme, honey was too distinct and out of step, and molasses too assertive. The more moderate taste of maple syrup had appeal, but brown sugar was my ultimate choice. It underscored the potatoes' earthy sweetness without overpowering it and added a pleasant caramel dimension to the dish. Because dark brown sugar dulled the potatoes' vibrant orange color, I settled on light.

For candied yams, I tested the same sweeteners as for the casserole (though not the condensed milk). I also tried light and dark corn syrup and golden syrup, orange marmalade, and many dry sweetener-syrup combinations. The results were almost identical to those of the casserole test. Light sweeteners, such as granulated sugar and light corn syrup, made the candied yams taste one-dimensional, while the darker syrups and marmalade vied for attention. Other than brown sugar, maple syrup was the only sweetener that held any appeal. Since the more flavorful dark brown sugar glazed the potatoes nicely, I chose it over light.

I experimented with various sweetener amounts, too, ranging from zero for the casserole (or a modest 2½ tablespoons for the candied yams) up to ¾ cup per pound of potatoes. I ultimately settled on 2 tablespoons of brown sugar per pound for the casserole.

The candied yams are not called candied for nothing. In order to make a thick enough glaze, either I needed a healthy dose of sugar or else I had to figure out another way to thicken the syrup. I had observed that some cooks compensate with cornstarch, and after a couple of tries, I made a not-too-sweet syrupy glaze using brown sugar and cornstarch that looks just like a sugar-thickened one.

Besides making a casserole with no additional liquid — just potatoes mixed with sugar, eggs, and butter — I made eleven others with different liquids. Starting with dairy, I tried milk, buttermilk, evaporated milk, half-and-half, heavy cream, and even eggnog. In addition, I tried pineapple, orange, and peach juice as well as chicken broth and water.

Sweet potato casseroles need some liquid, or they end up heavy and dry. The rich ingredients — eggnog, half-and-half, cream, evaporated milk — muted the sweet potato flavor. Plain milk was better, adding richness without masking the flavor. Peach juice and pineapple juice were a little too distinct. Chicken broth was not the answer, either, and the casserole made with water was acceptable, but something was missing.

Buttermilk and orange juice — both mildly acidic — dramatically lightened and freshened the casserole. Though each was too pronounced on its own, when mixed with regular milk, they worked well. Orange juice and water were the winning combination for candied yams, and milk and buttermilk were best for sweet potato puree.

There's a strong temptation to tart up sweet potatoes. But after trying an astounding number of herbs, spices, flavorings, zests, nuts, extracts, and booze, I found that I preferred these earthy beauties minimally adorned.

Baked Sweet Potatoes

Serves 6 to 8 or
enough to make any
of the recipes that follow

Pricking the sweet potatoes keeps them from bursting during baking, and lining the pan with foil eliminates cleanup.

3   **pounds sweet potatoes, small, medium, or large, washed**

Adjust oven rack to upper-middle position and heat oven to 400 degrees. Prick each potato all over with a fork, place on a foil-lined shallow baking pan, and bake until fork-tender, about 30 minutes for small potatoes, 45 minutes for medium, and 1 hour for large. Let stand until cool enough to handle, then peel, and proceed with one of the following recipes.

Sweet Potato Casserole
with Pecan Crumble

Serves 8 to 10

Without eggs, a sweet potato casserole is just a sweetened puree. Separating the eggs and whipping the whites pleasantly lightens the dish.

You can substitute 1 cup miniature marshmallows for the nut crumble. Bake the untopped casserole as directed below, then add the marshmallows and broil for about 2 minutes, until light brown and puffy, watching carefully.

CASSEROLE

Baked Sweet Potatoes (opposite page), mashed (about 4 cups)

- 6 tablespoons light brown sugar
- 1/4 teaspoon salt
- 1/4 teaspoon ground nutmeg
- 2 large eggs, separated
- 1/2 cup milk, whole or 2%
- 1/2 cup buttermilk or orange juice
- 6 tablespoons butter, melted
- 2 tablespoons sugar

PECAN CRUMBLE

- 1/2 cup chopped pecans or walnuts
- 6 tablespoons light brown sugar
- 1/4 cup all-purpose flour
  Pinch salt
- 2 tablespoons butter, melted

1 FOR CASSEROLE: Adjust oven rack to upper-middle position and heat oven to 350 degrees. Grease a 9-inch square or similar-size baking pan.

2 Process sweet potatoes to a puree in a food processor; add brown sugar, salt, nutmeg, egg yolks, milk, buttermilk or orange juice, and butter and continue to process until smooth. Transfer to a medium bowl; set aside.

3   Meanwhile, beat egg whites in a medium bowl until foamy. Continue beating, gradually adding the white sugar, until egg whites are stiff and glossy. Fold egg whites into potato mixture and pour mixture into prepared pan.

4   FOR CRUMBLE: Mix nuts, brown sugar, flour, salt, and butter in a small bowl until clumps form. Sprinkle evenly over sweet potato mixture. Bake until casserole puffs slightly and topping is golden brown and crunchy, 45 to 50 minutes. Let cool for 5 minutes and serve.

Sweet Potato Pineapple Casserole with Pecan-Coconut Crumble

Serves 8 to 10

Because of the crushed pineapple in this casserole, I opted for buttermilk rather than orange juice as the flavoring liquid. If you find yourself with no buttermilk on Thanksgiving morning, however, feel free to substitute orange juice.

CASSEROLE

Baked Sweet Potatoes (page 232), mashed (about 4 cups)

6 tablespoons light brown sugar

$1/4$ teaspoon salt

$3/4$ teaspoon ground ginger

2 large eggs, separated

$1/2$ cup milk, whole or 2%

$1/2$ cup buttermilk

6 tablespoons butter, melted

$1/2$ cup drained crushed pineapple

2 tablespoons sugar

PECAN CRUMBLE

6 tablespoons chopped pecans or walnuts

$1/4$ cup flaked sweetened coconut

6 tablespoons light brown sugar

$1/4$ cup all-purpose flour

Pinch salt

2 tablespoons butter, melted

1 FOR CASSEROLE: Proceed as directed in steps 1, 2, and 3 of Sweet Potato Casserole with Pecan Crumble (page 233), adding ginger instead of nutmeg and stirring in pineapple after mixture has been transferred to bowl. Continue as directed.

2 FOR CRUMBLE: Proceed as directed, adding coconut with other ingredients.

Candied Yams
with Pecan-Orange Glaze

Excessive quantities of sugar are essential in forming the classic glaze in candied yams, making most recipes too sweet for my taste. To solve this problem, I've substituted a very small quantity of cornstarch for some of the sugar. When cooked with orange juice and sugar and poured over the potatoes, it thickens enough during baking to glaze the potatoes — without all the sugar.

Baked Sweet Potatoes (page 232), sliced as shown
6 **tablespoons dark brown sugar**
$^1/_4$ **teaspoon salt**
6 **tablespoons butter**
$1^1/_2$ **teaspoons cornstarch**
$^1/_4$ **cup orange juice**
$^1/_2$ **cup coarsely chopped pecans**

Heat oven to 350 degrees. Spray a 9-inch square or similar-size pan with vegetable-oil cooking spray. Arrange sweet potatoes in slightly overlapping rows, using stubby end pieces to prop up the first slice in each row and to fill in gaps between potatoes.

2 Meanwhile, bring brown sugar, salt, $^3/_4$ cup water, and butter to a boil in a medium saucepan, stirring. Dissolve cornstarch in orange juice in a small bowl and gradually whisk it into boiling syrup. Cook, whisking constantly, until syrup thickens to consistency of heavy cream. Pour syrup over potatoes, sprinkle with nuts, and bake, spooning glaze over potatoes once after about 30 minutes, until glaze thickens enough to coat potatoes, about 45 minutes total. Let cool for 5 minutes and serve.

Slice long, thin sweet potatoes on an extreme bias. Slice short, fat sweet potatoes on a slight bias.

Silky Sweet Potato Puree

Serves 8

This puree and any of the following purees are even better when topped with Shallot Crisps (page 192) and are excellent with poultry and pork roast.

Baked Sweet Potatoes (page 232), mashed (about 4 cups)
and reheated in a microwave or in a large saucepan
over low heat
$^1/_4$ teaspoon salt
Freshly ground black pepper to taste
$^1/_2$ cup buttermilk
$^1/_2$ cup milk, whole or 2%
6 tablespoons butter

Process sweet potatoes and salt and pepper in a food processor until smooth. With motor running, gradually add both milks through feeder tube. Stop machine, add butter, then process until potatoes are silky smooth. Reheat, if necessary, and serve. (Puree can be made up to 2 days in advance, stored in an airtight container, and reheated before serving.)

Sweet Potato Puree
with Rosemary and Lemon

Serves 8

A little flavoring in these potatoes goes a long way, so don't be heavy-handed when measuring the rosemary and lemon zest. They will continue to permeate the dish as it heats and sits.

6 **tablespoons butter**

$1/4$ **teaspoon minced fresh rosemary**

$1/4$ **teaspoon finely grated lemon zest**

**Baked Sweet Potatoes (page 232), mashed (about 4 cups)
and reheated in a microwave or in a large saucepan
over low heat**

$1/4$ **teaspoon salt**

Freshly ground black pepper to taste

$1/2$ **cup buttermilk**

$1/2$ **cup milk, whole or 2%**

1. Heat butter in a small skillet over medium-low heat. Add rosemary and lemon zest and continue to heat for 1 to 2 seconds, just until flavorings are fragrant.

2. Proceed as directed in Silky Sweet Potato Puree (page 237), substituting flavored butter for ordinary butter.

Sweet Potato Puree
with Nutmeg and Orange

Serves 8

Sweet potatoes and nutmeg are a classic pairing. When in doubt about guests' tastes, serve this sweet potato dish or Silky Sweet Potato Puree (page 237).

6 tablespoons butter

¹/₄ teaspoon nutmeg

¹/₂ teaspoon finely grated orange zest

Baked Sweet Potatoes (page 232), mashed (about 4 cups) and reheated in a microwave or in a large saucepan over low heat

¹/₄ teaspoon salt

Freshly ground black pepper to taste

¹/₂ cup buttermilk

¹/₂ cup whole milk

1 Heat butter in a small skillet over medium-low heat. Add nutmeg and orange zest and continue to heat for 1 to 2 seconds, just until flavorings are fragrant.

2 Proceed as directed in Silky Sweet Potato Puree (page 237), substituting flavored butter for ordinary butter.

Sweet Potato Puree
with Cumin and Cayenne

Slowly toasting the spices in the butter brings out their flavor, but don't let them cook too long. Toasting takes just seconds when the spices are ground.

6   tablespoons butter
    Scant 1/2 teaspoon ground cumin
1/4 teaspoon cayenne pepper
    Baked Sweet Potatoes (page 232), mashed (about 4 cups)
        and reheated in a microwave or in a large saucepan
        over low heat
1/4 teaspoon salt
    Freshly ground black pepper to taste
1/2 cup buttermilk
1/2 cup milk, whole or 2%

1   Heat butter in a small skillet over medium-low heat. Add cumin and cayenne and continue to heat for 1 to 2 seconds, just until flavorings are fragrant.

2   Proceed as directed in Silky Sweet Potato Puree (page 237), substituting flavored butter for ordinary butter.

Thyme-Flavored Sweet Potato Puree

Serves 8

I'm particularly fond of this puree as an accompaniment to a simple pork roast.

6   tablespoons butter

1/4   teaspoon dried thyme leaves

Baked Sweet Potatoes (page 232), mashed (about 4 cups)
        and reheated in a microwave or in a large saucepan
        over low heat

1/4   teaspoon salt

Freshly ground black pepper to taste

1/2   cup buttermilk

1/2   cup milk, whole or 2%

1   Heat butter in a small skillet over medium-low heat. Add thyme and continue to heat for 1 to 2 seconds, just until flavorings are fragrant.

2   Proceed as directed in Silky Sweet Potato Puree (page 237), substituting flavored butter for ordinary butter.

Proper Iced Tea in Under 15 Minutes

Sweet tea is to a Southerner what wine is to a Frenchman. Winter or summer, we drank it at supper almost every night when I was a child. And since I despised milk, my mother even put it in my thermos for lunch. I have helped make or have made thousands of gallons of my mom's iced tea.

Her original method for a gallon of tea is branded in my brain. Add 8 tea bags to an enameled teapot of boiling water, boil for 3 minutes, then let bags steep for 15 minutes. Remove bags and add sugar (or saccharin tablets, when we were trying to cut calories). Pour the undiluted hot tea into a gallon milk jug (they were thicker back then) and return the tea bags to the teapot, running cold water over them to extract as much flavor as possible. Add this weak tea water to the jug until it's full. Refrigerate if there's time. There usually wasn't, and for that very reason, Mom always kept a set of glasses filled with ice on the freezer door.

With the invention of the drip coffeemaker, Mom developed a new method of making iced tea. And when she got her first microwave, she figured out an even simpler way to duplicate her original stovetop method.

In addition to my mom's tea, I have drunk hundreds of glasses in homes and restaurants over the years — some that merely quenched thirst or washed down a meal; others that put an Ahhhh in my voice and a smile on my face. For me, great tea is strong but not bitter; richly colored, not cloudy and dark; and pleasantly, but not toothachingly, sweet. Is it the brewing method, steeping time, brand of tea, type of water, or ratio of ingredients that consistently ensures the perfect glass of iced tea?

BREWING LESSONS

I was certain the brewing method was key. The overwhelming number of iced tea recipes were a variation of the back-of-the-box method. Pour X quarts of boiling water over X number of tea bags and let steep for X minutes or hours. The number of bags ranged from 1 bag per cup to 1 bag per quart, while steeping times ranged from 3 minutes to overnight.

In addition to the usual method, I wanted to test two standard kitchen appliances that could double as a tea brewer: the microwave and the drip coffeemaker. Then there was sun tea, a sort of solar method of slowly extracting flavor from a tea bag through the sun's heat and light. And although I had never tried it, I had seen recipes for "refrigerator tea" — tea bags steeped in a pitcher of water in the refrigerator overnight.

I started with the time-honored method: pouring boiling water over tea bags and letting them steep for 5 minutes. After testing this method again and again with different numbers of bags and varying brands, I found that all the teas made by this method were bitter and downright unpleasant to drink, especially without sugar and lemon.

Not quite willing to give up on this method yet, I tested various steeping times, ranging from 1 minute to 1 hour, with even less success. The 1-minute steeped tea wasn't bitter, but it didn't have any flavor, either. At 3 minutes, the tea was starting to taste a little bitter but still had very little flavor. At 5 minutes, the bitterness was noticeable, and at 10 minutes, it was overwhelming. At 15 minutes and beyond, the tea was more medicine-like than beverage. I tried boiling the tea bags, too. This method resulted in a dark caramel-colored liquid, lacking a distinctive tea flavor and tasting bitter as well.

MR. AND MRS. TEA

In addition to using standard brewing techniques, I tested two specialty tea machines: Details, the 3-Quart Iced Tea Pot made by Mr. Coffee (formerly known as Mrs. Tea), and TeaMate Electric Tea Maker by Chef's Choice International.

I was particularly skeptical of the iced tea pot (which retails for about $22.99), a culinary white elephant in my mind. Much as with a drip coffeemaker, water heats up and flows into a steeping basket filled with tea bags. The hot tea drips into a pitcher of ice, resulting in cold tea. The method was quick and simple, and the tea was very good. If I hadn't found a better way, this appliance might have gotten a strong endorsement.

A more elaborate and expensive unit (about one hundred dollars retail), TeaMate Electric Tea Maker by Chef's Choice International is specially designed for brewing hot tea, although it works for iced tea, too. The operating principle is similar to the Mr. Coffee Tea Pot, except that while the water is heating, the glass carafe is warming and tea leaves (or bags) steam. A portion of the sub-boiling water steeps the leaves to make a concentrate that combines with the remaining hot water and flows into the carafe. The machine makes a flawless cup of hot tea and a perfect glass of iced tea. If you're a steady tea drinker, it may be worth a look.

Though perfectly acceptable, the low-tech teas — both sun and refrigerator — required a higher number of tea bags, were relatively light in color and tasted a bit one-dimensional. The refrigerator tea had the added disadvantage of turning cloudy overnight. Given a choice, however, I much preferred them to bitter tea.

Success was closer than I thought. As it turns out, the microwave makes an exceptional pitcher of iced tea. In my first attempt, I microwaved 4 tea bags in 4 cups of water in a 2-quart measuring cup, covered, until it was very hot, about 8 minutes. I immediately removed the tea bags and stirred in a quart of ice. The resulting tea was on the weak side, but it was not bitter. A little stronger, I thought, and this method would have a lot going for it. The equipment was simple, the technique was simple and fast, and the tea was not astringent.

In an attempt to extract more flavor from the tea bags without picking up the bitterness, I upped the microwave time and tacked on some steeping. It worked. With 9 to 10 minutes of microwaving and 3 minutes of steeping, I had great iced tea in about 15 minutes, from start to finish. To strengthen the tea a bit, I fiddled with number of bags and steeping times. If a 3-minute steep was good, would longer be better? Not so. I found that longer steeping resulted in acrid tea. For stronger tea, some recipes suggested increasing the bags, not the steeping time. If 4 tea bags were good, would 5 or 6 be better? Five bags for a scant 2 quarts water turned out to be the right number. Even with reduced steeping times (including no steeping), 6-bag tea was too strong.

As long as I gave it a good rinse, my coffeemaker was happy to do double duty as a tea maker, too. In the past, I had always put the tea bags in the coffee basket and let the hot water simply flow over the bags. With no steeping time, the tea was weak. But as with the microwave method, it wasn't bitter. Moving the tea bags from the basket to the carafe made all the difference. With this arrangement, the bags spent some time in hot (not boiling) water, and the resulting tea was strong, smooth, and clear. If making tea this way, however, do not rely on the cup markings on the carafe for accuracy. Measure the water in a measuring cup before pouring it into the water reservoir, and measure the ice before pouring it into the carafe of tea.

For those without a microwave or drip coffeemaker, this method can be duplicated on the stovetop. I prefer the microwave and coffeemaker methods, however, since if you're using the microwave or the coffee carafe, a 2-quart Pyrex measuring cup acts as brewer, steeper, and pitcher all in one.

Why do these methods work when traditional steeping doesn't? The experts I interviewed all agreed that many of the bitter tannins contained in tea are not extracted until the boiling point. All the methods I deemed successful relied on slow, steady heat (or steam, as with the Chef's Choice TeaMate) and hot but not boiling water.

For consistent results, I had performed all of the tests thus far with spring water. But was it necessary? After tasting teas made with running tap water, filtered tap water, and spring water, I think so. The tea made with spring water was the favorite, giving the tea the freshest, cleanest, clearest look and taste. If the quality of your tap water is good, with no off flavors, however, feel free to use it.

Should you sweeten iced tea? Unless you can't because of health reasons, I think you should. Sugar rounds out the flavor and brings the tea alive. Even for "unsweetened" tea, I recommend adding 1 tablespoon of sugar per quart. For lightly sweetened tea, figure 2 tablespoons per quart, and for sweet tea, allow 3 tablespoons per quart (and many Southerners, I know, will not be satisfied with anything less than 1/4 cup per quart).

In addition to sweetening the tea with sugar, I tried regular honey, dry honey (Honey Sweet, a mix of dry honey, fructose, and maltodextrin), and natural cane sugar. Honey was too distracting, taking away from the great tea flavor I had worked so hard to get. Like regular honey, dry honey tasted too distinct, more of fruit than of honey.

The tea sweetened with regular sugar tasted okay, with a quick sweet hit. The surprise was the natural cane sugar. Before tasting it, I would have bet using it wouldn't matter. But the tea made with it had a pure sweet flavor that enveloped my mouth and lingered.

I used to like to add lemon and sweeteners. Now I know why: to mask the bitterness. With my new brewing methods, however, I found these flavors very easily overwhelmed the tea. To incorporate other flavors when I want them, I simply bruise a small number of mint leaves (or strips of lemon zest or coins of fresh ginger) against the ice with a wooden spoon. This action releases natural oils, which, when stirred into the tea along with the ice, add fresh, yet subtle flavor.

Iced Tea, Simply and Quickly
(Stovetop Method)

Makes 1½ to 2 quarts, serving 6 to 8

Since ice is added to the hot tea to cool it down quickly, the quality of ice you use also matters. Particularly during the summer months, keep a bag of crushed ice in the freezer.

5 tea bags, preferably Red Rose

1 quart water, bottled spring water if your tap water tastes off

2–6 tablespoons sugar, preferably natural cane sugar (to taste)

3 cups ice, plus additional cubes for glasses

Place tea bags and water in a medium nonreactive saucepan. Heat mixture over medium-low heat until very steamy and dark-colored and bubbles form on bottom and sides of the pan, about 190 degrees, or 8 to 10 minutes. Remove from heat and let steep for 3 minutes, no longer. Remove and discard tea bags without squeezing them, which makes the tea bitter. Pour into a small pitcher. Add desired amount of sugar, and stir until dissolved. Add ice; stir until melted. Fill desired number of glasses with ice. Stir tea, pour over ice, and serve immediately.

TEA TEST

Is one tea bag better than the next? I performed a blind tasting of iced tea to find the answer. After tasting fifteen different teas, imported and domestic, loose and in bags, Red Rose tea bags were my first choice, followed by Twinings Orange Pekoe bags. Jackson's Orange Pekoe bags came in third.

To find out if there was a reason for Red Rose's superior flavor, I consulted with the National Tea Association. Representatives said it is generally accepted in the industry that Red Rose uses superior tea (it's all hand-plucked, not machine-picked). Red Rose leaves are rich, dark, and clean and have the least amount of "stem," the light, weedy-looking stuff that's a result of machine-picking.

Microwave Tea

Makes 1½ to 2 quarts,
serving 6 to 8

Using a 2-quart Pyrex measuring cup makes this tea a one-pot drink — from brewing to pouring.

5 tea bags, preferably Red Rose
1 quart water, bottled spring water if your tap water tastes
   off
2–6 tablespoons sugar, preferably natural cane sugar (to taste)
3 cups ice, plus additional cubes for glasses

Place tea bags and water in a 2-quart Pyrex measuring cup. Cover with a small plate. Put in microwave and heat mixture on high power until very steamy and dark-colored and water starts to move but not boil, about 190 degrees, or 8 to 10 minutes, depending on starting water temperature and power of microwave. Remove cup from microwave and let steep for 3 minutes, no longer. Remove and discard tea bags without squeezing them. Add desired amount of sugar and stir until dissolved. Add ice; stir until melted. Fill desired number of glasses with ice. Stir tea, pour over ice, and serve immediately.

Iced Tea Made in a Drip Coffeemaker

The coffee carafe makes this iced tea a one-pot drink. Since coffee cups are not true cups, do not rely on the carafe markings for accuracy. Measure the water and ice in a separate measuring cup. My coffee carafe is at least 2 quarts. If yours is not, however, simply pour steeped and sweetened tea into a large pitcher before adding ice.

5 tea bags, preferably Red Rose

1 quart water, bottled spring water if your tap water tastes off

2–6 tablespoons sugar, preferably natural cane sugar (to taste)

3 cups ice, plus additional cubes for glasses

Rinse coffee carafe and basket thoroughly to remove coffee odor. Put tea bags in carafe; pour measured water into reservoir. Turn machine on until all water has dripped into carafe. Turn machine off and let tea bags steep for 3 minutes, no longer. Remove and discard tea bags. Add desired amount of sugar, and stir until dissolved. Add ice; stir until melted. Fill desired number of glasses with ice. Stir tea, pour over ice, and serve immediately.

Minted Iced Tea

Follow any of the recipes for iced tea (pages 246–48), adding 2 tablespoons fresh mint leaves to ice. Using a wooden spoon, bruise leaves against ice to release oils. Add mint and ice to tea, straining leaves or not, as desired, before serving.

Iced Tea with Lemon

Follow any of the recipes for iced tea (pages 246–48), adding three or four 2-inch-long strips of lemon zest to ice. Using a wooden spoon, bruise zest against ice to release oils. Add zest and ice to tea, along with $^1/_2$ teaspoon lemon juice, removing zest or not, as desired, before serving.

Gingered Iced Tea

Follow any of the recipes for iced tea (pages 246–48), adding 3 or 4 coins of fresh ginger, $^1/_4$ inch thick, to ice. Using a wooden spoon, bruise ginger against ice to release oils. Add ginger and ice to tea, removing ginger pieces or not, as desired, before serving.

Bread
Lines

Watching my grandmother make biscuits is one of my earliest food memories. I was too young at the time to be impressed by the fact that she made them just by sight and feel, but I look back now in amazement. Had she gone blind, I'm certain she could have done the job by touch alone.

She stored her self-rising flour in a large, open bowl below the counter. What better place for an ingredient she used every single day? To make biscuits, she lifted the bowl onto the counter, slung in a couple large spoonfuls of shortening, and worked it in with her fingers until she had a mixture that looked like tiny bits of tattered cloth. With her shortening- and flour-coated hands, she'd pull open the refrigerator, reach for the buttermilk, and pour in just enough to make a soft, sticky dough. She'd remove the hunk of dough to the counter, wipe her hands, dust them with flour, and knead the dough, never incorporating a fleck more flour than was required.

Then she pinched off golf ball–size pieces of dough, gingerly rolled them into balls and arranged them snugly in a pie plate. When finished, she'd return her bowl of flour, dry as a bone, back under the counter. Once the biscuits were in the pan, my grandmother would let me press my floured knuckles into the soft dough balls to flatten and dimple them. I could hardly wait for them to come out of the oven so that I could smear those soft, tender breads with honey mixed with butter.

Could I develop a biscuit as soft, light, and tender as my grandmother's and as layered, flaky, and crisp as the kind that comes from a can?

BISCUIT BAKE-OFF

All biscuit recipes start with some type of flour. In addition, they call for salt and leavener: baking powder, baking soda, or yeast (and sometimes two or even all three of these). Whether lard, butter, shortening, oil, or liquid-fat combinations like cream and sour cream, all biscuits need fat. And finally there's the liquid. Biscuit dough can be moistened with anything from plain water to heavy cream.

Despite the consistency in ingredients, there are many biscuit styles — buttermilk, baking powder, yeasted, beaten, cream, sour cream — with different flavors and textures. I knew immediately that "beaten" biscuits were a dead end. These dry, hard biscuits were barely related to the tender, flaky ones I was looking for. "Angel" or "feather" biscuits' yeasted flavor and texture disqualified them as well. And I wasn't interested in developing biscuit dough that needed to rest from 2 to 24 hours before baking.

Beyond that, I was open to whatever style could help me achieve my goal of a tender, light, flaky biscuit with a crisp crust. To get my bearings, I made four distinct styles: buttermilk biscuits, baking powder biscuits, cream biscuits, and sour cream biscuits. I also made a second batch of baking powder biscuits, substituting an egg for part of the milk.

From this series of tests, one theme emerged, affirming what I'd always known. First, biscuits are easy to make. And second, it's hard to make a bad one. Although there were distinct differences among these five biscuits and I wasn't close to finding what I was looking for, they all tasted pretty darn good.

The cream and sour cream biscuits rose taller than the baking powder and buttermilk ones, but their texture was cakelike and tender, lacking even a modicum of flakiness. Since flakiness results from fat cut into flour, there was little chance for these biscuits. The egg-enriched biscuit also seemed more cakey than flaky.

While on the squatty side, both buttermilk and baking powder biscuits were tender and a little flaky. Though far from the flaky kind of biscuit I was shooting for, this seemed like the right path. Since baking powder biscuits are more straightforward to make (no acidic buttermilk that can neutralize the baking powder), I focused on them, knowing that if I could develop a good one, a good buttermilk biscuit would probably not be far behind. Working from a composite recipe, I mixed:

2   cups flour
1   tablespoon baking powder
1   teaspoon salt
6   tablespoons shortening
3/4   cup milk

I began to work through the ingredients list, testing the biscuit with a variety of flours, milks, and fats, as well as with different quantities of milk, fat, baking powder, and salt.

I made six batches of biscuits with different "sweet" milks — nonfat dry milk, 2%, whole milk, evaporated milk, half-and-half, heavy cream — plus one with plain water. All were decent. Even the biscuit made with water, though a little anemic in color and a little flat in flavor, tasted fine. Other than its slightly funky pale peach color, the evaporated milk biscuit wasn't bad, either. The half-and-half biscuit was a little heavy, and the one with heavy cream was predictably heavy and rich.

If given a choice, I'd make biscuits with whole milk — they were full-flavored, light, and fluffy. But if I were out of whole milk, I wouldn't hesitate to make them with just about any sweet milk — even water and cream — and increasing or reducing the added fat. Over the course of testing, I made biscuits with varying amounts of liquid. I found that the more liquid the dough, the softer the biscuits and the more they rose up, not out. Determining the quantity of liquid would have to wait.

It isn't just the type of fat that matters, but the amount and its temperature as well. To start, I made biscuits with shortening, both chilled and at room temperature. I also made batches with melted and cooled butter as well as with butter that had been refrigerated and frozen. Since some experts say the best biscuits are made with a combination of butter and shortening — butter promotes flakiness; and shortening, tenderness — I tried that, too. Though they were a long shot, I tested biscuits made with butter-flavored shortening, lard, and oil.

The biscuits made with chilled shortening were the most tender, crisp, and fluffy of the lot. Although later testing would prove otherwise, biscuits made with frozen or refrigerated butter weren't dramatically more flaky or flavorful than those made with shortening.

Biscuits made with liquid fats like melted butter and oil were far from ideal. When these soft fats mixed with the dry ingredients, they formed hard impenetrable flour balls. Coated with fat, the dry ingredients had trouble absorbing the liquid and did not dissolve. Biscuits made with lard had similar problems. As for the butter-flavored Crisco, I preferred the neutral flavor of the regular variety.

I had been using a fairly common ratio of 6 tablespoons of fat for every 2 cups of flour. To see if that ratio was correct, I made four batches of biscuits: one with 2 tablespoons shortening, one with 4, one with 6, and a final one with 8 tablespoons. As it turned out, the quantity I had been using was just right.

From previous experience, I knew that lower-protein flours deliver a more tender biscuit, while higher-protein ones produce a more sturdy, chewy result. I tested seven different flours or flour combinations from lowest to highest protein:

Cake flour
Equal parts cake flour and bleached all-purpose flour
2 parts all-purpose flour to 1 part instant (Wondra) flour
4 parts all-purpose flour to 1 part cornstarch
Bleached all-purpose flour
Unbleached all-purpose flour
Bread flour

Bleached all-purpose flour produced biscuits with a light, tender crumb and a decently crisp crust. The flour-cornstarch combination was the worst of the lot, with a pasty, starchy texture and an unappealing corn flavor. The biscuits made with all cake flour lacked shape and had a chemical flavor and a gummy, yet crumbly texture. The biscuits made with part instant flour weren't much better. Even the all-purpose flour–cake flour blend tasted a little off. The biscuits made with high-protein bread flour and the unbleached flour looked beautiful. They rose tall and did not spread. Their crusts were as crisp as crackers, their flavor was good, but their crumb was just a little too tough and chewy to meet the soft, tender standard.

To determine if sugar was an important biscuit ingredient, I made two batches of biscuits: one with 1 teaspoon, another with 1 tablespoon. A Southerner at heart, accustomed to unsweetened breads, I didn't care for either, and I observed that the bottoms of both, especially the high-sugar biscuits, tended to overbrown.

I also tested biscuits with varying amounts of baking powder and found that 1 teaspoon of baking powder per cup of flour is sufficient. Much more than that, and the chemical flavor of the leavener starts to come through. I had reduced the baking powder a little, had decreased the salt by a pinch, and had taken the milk down a hair, but the formula was almost identical to the one I had started with two days before. The slight flakiness I had achieved thus far had resulted from cutting solid fat into the dry ingredients. If I wanted more, it wasn't going to come from tinkering with the ingredients list. Flakiness was a result of something that happened once the ingredients were combined.

In my research, I had come across two rolling and folding techniques that I thought might improve my biscuits' flakiness. To make "The Ultimate Extra-Flaky Biscuit," Camille Glenn in *The Heritage of Southern Cooking* (Workman, 1986) starts by making a rich buttermilk biscuit. Before cutting her biscuit rounds, however, she dots the rolled-out dough with 6 generous tablespoons of chilled butter, folds the dough into thirds, then rolls it out again. Although Glenn's biscuits were indeed flaky — layered, no less — they were too rich and heavy for my tender, light specifications, and such a large quantity of butter cubes actually left little indentations in the baked biscuit.

Mark Sohn in *Mountain Country Cooking* (St. Martin's, 1996) has a technique similar to Glenn's with a couple of changes. He starts with a less buttery biscuit dough, rolling it out and folding it in half twice, making four, rather than three, layers. Unlike Glenn, he does not sprinkle any fat between the layers. His double rolling and folding technique produced a taller, flaky, impressive-looking biscuit that lacked the peel-off layers of Glenn's.

I combined the best of the two techniques and added a little trick of my own. Starting with a leaner biscuit dough like Sohn's, I rolled out and folded my dough twice before cutting out the biscuits. Reducing the quantity of butter and grating it rather than cutting it into cubes, I sprinkled a little butter in between each layer. It worked. I got light, tender biscuits, with layers so thin, I could peel them off in sheets — the biscuit of my dreams.

Light, Flaky Biscuits

Makes eight 2½-inch biscuits, plus 3 or 4 extra biscuits rolled from the scraps

For grating the frozen butter, I use a small box grater with grating holes measuring about ³/₈ inch. Be sure to keep the grated butter frozen until you're ready to use it and return the unused portion to the freezer when it's not being used. If you decide to make larger or smaller biscuits, just remember to roll the dough to a dimension that will get you as many cuts as possible from the first rolling. Though biscuits made from re-rolled dough taste fine, they look a little scrappy. You don't need to buy self-rising flour for this recipe, but if you use it regularly, feel free to substitute 3 cups self-rising flour for the all-purpose flour, baking powder, and salt in this recipe.

8   tablespoons (1 stick) unsalted butter, frozen
3   cups bleached all-purpose flour
4   teaspoons baking powder
1½ teaspoons salt
3   tablespoons vegetable shortening, frozen
1   cup cold milk, plus extra for moistening and brushing

Grate about one third of the butter onto a paper towel, then sprinkle shreds with a big pinch of flour; toss to coat to prevent sticking. Transfer to a small bowl. Repeat process twice more, then place bowl in freezer.

2 Mix flour, baking powder, and salt with a rubber spatula in a medium bowl. Cut shortening into dry ingredients with a pastry cutter or two forks until it looks like coarse meal. Add a heaping ½ cup of the grated frozen butter; toss to coat, then cut butter into flour 4 or 5 times to blend. Return remaining butter to freezer.

Stir in milk with a rubber spatula. Once dough starts to clump, bring it into a coherent ball with your hands, pressing it into bottom of bowl to pick up remaining scraps. If dough does not readily come together, sprinkle in a drop or two more of milk and continue pressing on dough scraps until they incorporate.

4 On a lightly floured surface, press dough into a rough square, then roll out into a 10½-by-6-inch rectangle, about ¾ inch thick. Following illustration, sprinkle one third of remaining grated butter over half of dough and brush edges with milk.

Fold as shown in second illustration, and roll out again as shown in third illustration. Repeat, sprinkling half of dough with one third of butter, brushing border with milk, folding in half, and pinching seam. Freeze remaining grated butter to keep it chilled. Place folded dough square on a baking sheet and freeze for about 10 minutes to firm up and let gluten relax.

Roll dough out again as before, sprinkle with remaining butter, and fold in half for a third time. Roll out dough a final time into a 10¹/₂-by-6-inch rectangle. Freeze again for 10 to 15 minutes to let dough firm up and relax.

6. Meanwhile, adjust oven rack to middle position and heat oven to 450 degrees. Use a 2¹/₂-inch biscuit or cookie cutter to cut dough into 8 rounds and place them about 1 inch apart on a baking sheet. Pinch dough scraps together and cut 3 or 4 more dough rounds. Bake until biscuits are golden brown, 13 to 15 minutes. Serve immediately.

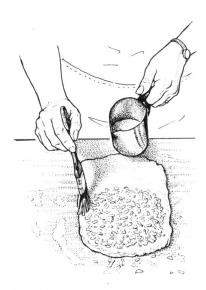

Sprinkle grated butter over half of the rectangle of dough, leaving a ¹/₂-inch border. Lightly brush the border of the dough with milk.

Roll the dough out again into an approximately 10-by-6-inch rectangle.

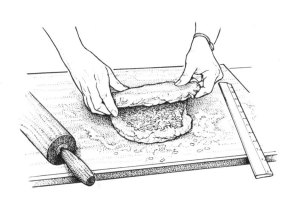

Fold the dough in half like a book. Pinch the seams to seal and lightly pat in the center to eliminate air pockets.

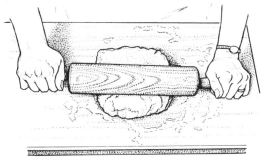

Although I've owned a waffle iron for years and use it often, I like the *idea* of waffles better than the actual experience of eating them. They are supposed to be light, airy, and most of all, crisp. But by the time they get to the plate, they're usually damp and limp.

Trying to serve them to company is worse. Either you serve everyone a decent waffle, one at a time, or you hold the waffles in the oven and let everyone eat bad waffles together. My goal was to develop a waffle that was light and crisp to the last bite, even when syrup-coated.

I'd always been led to believe that if you had a good pancake recipe, you could make a good waffle just by throwing in a few extra tablespoons of melted butter for crispness. I already had a perfect pancake recipe:

1	cup bleached all-purpose flour
2	teaspoons sugar
$^1/_2$	teaspoon salt
$^1/_2$	teaspoon baking powder
$^1/_4$	teaspoon baking soda
1	egg
$^3/_4$	cup buttermilk
$^1/_4$	cup milk
2	tablespoons melted butter

By doubling the butter to 4 tablespoons, I made waffles that were okay, but they weren't all that light, and they didn't stay crisp for much more than five seconds after they came off the waffle iron. With that composite recipe, I began my tests.

Many waffle recipes call for all-purpose flour, but others ask for some pretty off-beat choices as well. So in addition to making waffles with bleached and unbleached flours, I also made them with cake flour, rice flour, potato starch flour, and soy flour.

The soy flour waffle tasted like a bad bean cake. Because rice flour contains no gluten, the rice flour waffle was lacy-textured and gritty. Its floral flavor was equally off-putting. The high-protein unbleached flour made the toughest, most leaden of all the waffles. The bleached all-purpose flour delivered a slightly better waffle, but not by much.

The performances of two other flours gave me some insight. The waffle batter made with cake flour was thin, but the resulting waffle was relatively crisp and light, with a creamy, flavorful crumb. And although the waffle made with potato starch flour had the gluey texture of potatoes mashed in the food processor, the crust was incredibly crisp. Better yet, the crispness didn't fade immediately. Even though the texture and flavor of the potato starch was completely unacceptable, it gave me an idea. Might cornstarch offer an equally crisp waffle without the potato starch's liabilities?

THE TIES THAT BIND

Why does cornstarch make such crisp, light waffles? According to Don MacElmur-ray, food technologist at Best Foods, makers of Argo Cornstarch, "When you combine cornstarch with liquid and apply heat, the starch molecules trap water, creating a gel." This gel binds the water in a matrix and keeps it there, even as the waffle cools.

In fact, cornstarch turned out to be key. Testing waffles made with a combination of cornstarch and flour against those made with cake flour and cake flour–all-purpose flour, I determined that the cornstarch waffles were crisp on the outside and tender, yet toothsome inside. Though I hadn't developed the perfect waffle yet, using ³/₄ cup bleached all-purpose flour and ¹/₄ cup cornstarch pointed me in the right direction.

SUGAR AND WHIPPED WHITE MAKE EVERYTHING LIGHT

Some cooks said it didn't matter whether you separated the egg and whipped the white before folding it into the batter, but it seemed logical that this extra step would reinforce the light texture. It's true: waffles made with whipped egg white were lighter and more airy, and they were also taller and more tender. And they browned better.

I moved on to sugar. Having tested the batter with 2 teaspoons, I made two additional batters: one with 1 tablespoon of sugar, and another with 2 tablespoons. I preferred the waffle made with 1 tablespoon.

Since I had observed that egg whites beaten with sugar are much more stable than plain egg whites, I decided to see what would happen if I beat the 1 tablespoon of sugar into the whites rather than mixing it in with the dry ingredients, as most recipes instruct. Following a tip from my father, I also added a touch of vanilla extract to the mix. The "meringue" dramatically improved the batter's staying power and was easier to fold into the batter than plain egg white.

Although this waffle was certainly crisp, it was losing its crispness more quickly than I wanted. Perhaps it was true that more fat equaled more crispness. Increasing the fat to 4 tablespoons, I tested the current recipe with shortening, bacon fat, butter, and vegetable oil. After this test, it became clear that up to a point, the thinner the batter, the crisper the waffle. None of the solid fats performed as well as the liquid vegetable oil. The waffle with 6 tablespoons of oil was the best.

Knowing now that waffle batter needed to be thin, I suspected the thicker ingredients like cream and sour cream would not produce the light, crisp waffle I was looking for. Indeed, they did not. Making the proper adjustments in leavening and oil, I tested five different liquids: sour cream, heavy cream, a mixture of buttermilk and milk, straight milk, and even seltzer water. As I pried bits of waffle off my iron with a knife, I cursed the person who suggested seltzer. Waffles made with all milk weren't as flavorful as those made with buttermilk. Buttermilk and milk was the winning combination — buttermilk for flavor, milk for thinning.

I turned on the oven to 200 degrees. As the waffles came off the iron, I set them directly on the oven rack to keep them crisp. The low heat maintains the waffles' crispness so beautifully that regardless of whether I'm preparing two waffles or twenty, I now make the oven rack part of the process.

Light, Crisp Waffles

Depending on how many people you're serving, this recipe can be doubled, tripled, or even quadrupled. Don't stack the waffles, or they will turn moist and limp within seconds. If you forget, just separate them and place them in a single layer on the oven rack to crisp them up again.

$3/4$ cup all-purpose flour
$1/4$ cup cornstarch
$1/2$ teaspoon salt
$1/2$ teaspoon baking powder
$1/4$ teaspoon baking soda
$3/4$ cup buttermilk
$1/4$ cup milk
  6   tablespoons vegetable oil
  1   large egg, separated
  1   tablespoon sugar
$1/2$ teaspoon vanilla extract

Maple syrup or Brown Sugar Syrup with Walnuts (page 263)

1   Heat oven to 200 degrees. Mix flour, cornstarch, salt, baking powder, and baking soda in a medium bowl. Put buttermilk, milk, and vegetable oil in a 2-cup Pyrex measuring cup, mix in yolk, and set aside.

2   Beat egg white almost to soft peaks. Sprinkle in sugar and continue to beat until whites are firm and glossy. Beat in vanilla.

3   Pour wet ingredients into dry ingredients and whisk until just mixed. Add egg white to batter in dollops and fold in with a spatula until just incorporated.

4   Add batter to hot waffle iron (mine takes about $2/3$ cup) and cook until crisp and nutty brown. Set waffle on oven rack for at least 5 minutes and up to 20 minutes to keep it warm and crisp. Repeat with remaining batter. Serve immediately with syrup.

Whole Grain Waffles

Proceed as for Light, Crisp Waffles, adding 1/4 cup wheat germ to dry ingredients.

Buckwheat Waffles

Proceed as for Light, Crisp Waffles, reducing flour to 1/2 cup and adding 1/2 cup buckwheat flour.

Chocolate Chip Waffles

Proceed as for Light, Crisp Waffles, stirring 1/2 cup coarsely chopped chocolate chips (or 1/2 cup mini chocolate chips) into batter before folding in egg white in step 3.

Cornmeal Waffles

Proceed as for Light, Crisp Waffles, reducing flour to 1/2 cup and adding 1/2 cup cornmeal.

Cranberry Orange Waffles

Proceed as for Light, Crisp Waffles, stirring 2 teaspoons finely grated orange zest and 1/2 cup coarsely chopped dried cranberries into batter before folding in egg white in step 3.

Brown Sugar Syrup
with Walnuts

Makes a scant 2 cups

If you have a little extra time — just a few minutes — you can make a delightfully thick pancake syrup. I've adapted this recipe from one in Camille Glenn's *The Heritage of Southern Cooking* (Workman, 1986).

1 cup dark brown sugar

1 cup sugar

$1/4$ cup light corn syrup

3 tablespoons butter

$1/4$ cup chopped walnuts, toasted (Toast the nuts in a
      325-degree oven until fragrant, about 10 minutes —
      or omit them if you like.)

Bring sugars, corn syrup, and 2 cups water to a boil in a medium saucepan. Reduce heat to low and simmer until mixture thickens to a syrup consistency, 10 to 12 minutes. Stir in butter and nuts, if using. Cool slightly and serve. (Syrup can be refrigerated for up to 1 month.)

If you think the check-in line at most airports is too long, then take a look at the Starbucks and Cinnabon queues. Starbucks I understand. Early-morning travelers desperately need a caffeine jolt. Cinnabon is another story. What is it about cinnamon buns that lures innocent airline passengers?

Part of it, of course, is the sweet, yeasty aroma. But another reason these buns are so popular is that fresh cinnamon rolls are a rare treat. We crave what we can't have, and how many of us regularly bake these days?

I knew I had never made cinnamon buns that compared with the huge, soft, warm gooey rolls they serve at Cinnabon. Mine tended to be small, overly brown, and dry around the edges. Was it possible for me to produce irresistible buns, and could I figure out a way to do so regularly?

THE HUNT FOR GOOD BUNS

Based on research, I cobbled together a standard formula. It wasn't brilliant. On the other hand, I didn't think it would fail. The ratios follow:

- 2 cups flour
- $1/4$ teaspoon salt
- $1/2$ cup milk
- 3 tablespoons butter
- 3 tablespoons sugar
- 1 teaspoon yeast
- 1 egg

When testing baked goods, I nearly always start with flour. Using the above formula, I made buns with two national brands of bleached all-purpose flour: Gold Medal and Pillsbury. I also made buns with bread flour, cake flour, a mixture of bleached all-purpose and whole wheat, a mixture of bread and all-purpose, and finally, a mixture of all-purpose and cake flour.

I thought whole wheat flour might add a pleasant nutty flavor to the buns. It didn't. Even a small amount made them taste too "healthy" and gave them a dense, hard texture. The rolls made with the bread flour looked beautiful but lacked the softness I wanted. At the other extreme, cake flour rolls were too soft. The differences between the rolls made with the two brands of bleached all-purpose flour and those made with a mixture of all-purpose and cake flour were subtle, so I went with bleached all-purpose flour. (The brand did not seem to make a difference.)

During these tests, I found that the 2-cup flour formula made a perfect six buns. I'd ultimately double it to make an even dozen. It was also heartening to realize how really simple these rolls were to make.

Next, I made doughs with 2 yolks, 4 yolks, 1 egg, 2 eggs, 2 eggs plus 2 yolks, and finally, 3 eggs. Even when I compensated by adding extra milk, the buns made with 2 yolks were gummy and leaden. The 4 yolks improved the buns a little. Made with a whole egg and a little extra milk, the buns lacked the richness and tasted more like white bread, while the dough enriched with 2 eggs displayed a respectably tender texture but didn't rise impressively.

The 3-egg dough, in contrast, produced rolls that baked up impressively tall and soft. But these pillowy rolls eventually lost to the ones made with 2 whole eggs and 2 extra yolks. With equally impressive height, these buns were slightly more substantial, and they kept their seductive texture as they sat, rather than drying out as the rest did.

I liked the dough's sweetness at this point — at least I knew I didn't want it any less sweet. Larger quantities of sugar proved unsuccessful, thinning the dough to a batter-like consistency. The doughs with extra sugar also wouldn't rise. According to Shirley Corriher in *CookWise* (Morrow, 1997), this makes perfect sense. "When dough contains a lot of sugar," she writes, "the gluten proteins link with the sugar instead of with each other," resulting in "dough soup" instead of a dough ball. She also warns, "Too much sugar is damaging to yeast. It draws water from the yeast and inhibits its growth."

Substituting brown sugar made no difference in the dough, but honey was different. Without contributing any obvious flavor overtones, it made the buns noticeably softer and moister. In addition, the honey-sweetened buns stayed softer for longer than those made with other sweeteners.

For comparison, I made a fresh batch with a little ground cinnamon. Knowing that cinnamon retards yeast development, I added just $1/2$ teaspoon. With that quantity, the dough rose fine, but as I tasted the buns, I realized that with so much else going on in them, the cinnamon was barely detectable.

WATER AND OIL DON'T MIX

With bleached all-purpose flour, 2 eggs plus 2 yolks, and honey, the buns were rising high and relatively soft. Would the liquid matter? After making buns with whole, evaporated, and powdered milks, a combination of milk and water, buttermilk, cream, and water only, I discovered that it did. The choice fell between buns made with dry milk and those made with straight water. Both rose tall and had a pleasantly soft texture. The water-moistened buns were a little softer, the dry milk–moistened buns a touch more flavorful. The glaze and filling would give me all the flavor I needed. I chose water.

With the liquid and sweetener tests, I had made my decision based on texture. But with fat, it came down to flavor. Rolls made with shortening and oil smelled empty and tasted hollow compared with the rich flavor of those made with butter. Butter gave better-flavored rolls, and it made a more baker-friendly dough. The water-honey-oil combination produced a very soft, almost lava-like dough that was difficult to work with. Butter, however, solidified the dough, making it much easier to handle.

FAST RISE FAILS

Up to this point, I had been using active dry yeast. On average, my doughs were doubling in about 2 hours for their first rise and in 30 to 45 minutes for their final rise. It was time to see if fast-rise yeast, also known as rapid-rise, instant, or bread-machine yeast, could speed up the process or improve the rolls.

My first batch didn't turn out right. Even though I followed the directions on the package, undissolved yeast remained on the dough's surface. I reasoned that the butter and eggs were preventing the yeast from dissolving. I prepared a second batch, this time making sure the yeast had dissolved. Throughout the rising, forming, and second rising, this dough seemed right. The resulting rolls, however, had an odd texture. Unlike the yeast rolls made with regular yeast, whose crumb pulled off in thin, beautiful sheets, the rapid-rise rolls were drier and could only be broken off, not pulled from the roll.

Most recipes called for a cinnamon-sugar filling, but there were great differences in the sugar quantity and kind. After making fillings with cinnamon-flavored granulated sugar, light and dark brown sugar, alone and in combination with each other, I decided the cinnamon flavor was best complemented by dark brown sugar. After trying different cinnamon quantities, I came up with a respectable 4 teaspoons. Cinnamon lovers may prefer a little more, but much more and the rolls will start to taste too spicy.

Before the cinnamon sugar is sprinkled on, the dough is usually brushed with something to make it adhere. Options range from soft or melted butter to egg whites, milk, or water. Since I had leftover egg white from the dough, I was hoping it would work. Nothing, however, was superior to corn syrup in making the filling adhere. It added sweetness and sheen and seeped down during the baking, creating a pleasant sticky-bun bottom to the cinnamon rolls.

Once they are baked, cinnamon buns are topped with anything from a simple water–confectioners' sugar glaze to a cream cheese frosting. I preferred cream cheese frosting, in the Cinnabon tradition. Using a high ratio of cream cheese to sugar keeps the buns from being overly sweet, and it means they can sit for hours without developing a gritty sugar crust. A small amount of butter gives the frosting a melting quality, helping it to flow into the nooks and crannies.

I serve cinnamon buns for breakfast regularly now, making, baking, and freezing them at my convenience. I can savor them one at a time, for they warm in just 30 seconds in the microwave. Or, I can get up at nine o'clock, pop the whole pan in the oven, and wake my houseguests with the aroma.

Big, Beautiful Cinnamon Buns
with Cream Cheese Frosting

Makes a dozen
large buns

My food processor, with its 12-cup-capacity work bowl, can handle this dough, made with 4¼ cups of flour. Smaller food processors, however, cannot knead this large quantity at one time. If making the dough in a small food processor, measure half portions of the wet and dry ingredients in separate bowls at the same time, then make the two batches of dough back to back. Remember that it takes only 30 seconds for the dough to knead, and you don't have to clean the bowl between mixings. If making the dough in two batches, continue to keep them separate. Letting them rise in separate bowls will speed things along, too.

DOUGH

- 1 package (2¼ teaspoons) active dry yeast
- 6 tablespoons honey
- 2 large eggs, plus 2 large yolks, at room temperature (soak eggs in warm water if cold)
- 6 tablespoons unsalted butter, melted
- 4¼ cups bleached all-purpose flour, plus more if needed
- 1½ teaspoons salt

CINNAMON NUT FILLING

- 6 tablespoons light corn syrup
- ¾ cup packed dark brown sugar
- 4 teaspoons ground cinnamon
- ¾ cup pecan or walnut pieces (optional), toasted and finely chopped

CREAM CHEESE FROSTING

- 3 ounces cream cheese (6 tablespoons), softened
- 1½ tablespoons unsalted butter, softened
- ¾ cup confectioners' sugar
- ¼ teaspoon vanilla extract

FOR DOUGH — FOOD PROCESSOR METHOD: Pour yeast into ¾ cup warm water in a medium bowl and let stand until dissolved. Stir in honey, eggs, yolks, and butter.

2 Place flour and salt in a food processor; pulse to combine. Add yeast mixture, then process until a soft, sticky dough mass starts to form, adding additional flour, 1 tablespoon at a time, if dough doesn't come together. Continue to process until dough is soft and well kneaded, about 30 seconds.

STANDING MIXER METHOD: Mix yeast and ³/₄ cup warm water in mixer bowl and let stand until dissolved. Mix honey, eggs, yolks, and butter together in a medium bowl. Add to yeast mixture and mix using paddle attachment. Mix flour and salt in a medium bowl, then stir 3 cups of flour mixture into yeast mixture, beating on low speed until fully blended. Switch to dough hook and gradually blend in 1 cup of remaining flour over low speed. Add remaining ¹/₄ cup flour if dough is sticking to bowl's sides. Mix at medium speed for 8 to 10 minutes. Dough should be smooth and not stick to bowl's sides.

Scrape dough onto a lightly floured work surface and knead into a smooth ball. Place dough in a lightly oiled bowl (I use vegetable-oil cooking spray; if you used a standing mixer, you can use the washed and dried mixing bowl), cover with plastic wrap, and let stand at room temperature until doubled in size, 1¹/₂ to 3 hours, depending on dough and room temperature.

4 FOR FILLING: Measure corn syrup in a small bowl. In another bowl, mix together brown sugar, cinnamon, and nuts, if using.

Line a 13-by-9-inch metal baking pan (or the bottoms of two 8-inch cake rounds) with parchment paper so that it extends over two long sides. Without punching down dough, turn it onto a lightly floured surface. Halve dough, setting one portion aside. Stretch dough into an 18-to-20-inch-by-6-inch strip, making sure that you are standing in front of a short end. Drizzle dough evenly with half of corn syrup, then use a pastry brush to spread it, spreading all the way to dough's far end to ensure a good seal when rolled. Sprinkle dough with half the brown sugar mixture, leaving a ¹/₂-inch border at dough's far end. Roll dough up into a log, making sure it is thoroughly sealed. Make 5 even crosswise cuts to mark the dough, then cut dough (dental floss or fishing wire works best) into 6 rounds. Place in pan and form a plastic-wrap dome over rolls. Repeat with remaining dough half. (If using a 13-by-9-inch pan, put dough rounds in 4 rows of 3.) Let dough rounds rise until puffy and almost doubled in size, 30 minutes to 1 hour.

6 Adjust oven rack to lower-middle position and heat oven to 375 degrees. Remove plastic and bake rolls until puffy and golden brown, 25 to 30 minutes. (Buns can be cooled completely, double-wrapped in plastic, and frozen for up to 1 month. Reheat in a 300-degree oven until warm, 10 to 15 minutes.)

7 FOR FROSTING: While buns bake (or reheat), beat cream cheese and butter in a medium bowl with an electric mixer until light and fluffy. Beat in confectioners' sugar, then 1 teaspoon water and vanilla. Let buns cool for 5 minutes, spread a portion of frosting over each warm bun, and serve.

Perfect Endings

For all their simplicity, there's something about chocolate chip cookies that turns otherwise sensible bakers into obsessive gamblers willing to try anything in their quest for perfection. I was no different.

My dream chocolate chip cookie is as chewy inside and as crisp around the edges as one that's fresh-baked — I mean just out of the oven. It's big and puffy, with a wrinkled, rugged surface. Unlike a classic chocolate chip cookie, which quickly turns crisp as it cools, my ideal cookie stays soft, pliable, and fresh.

My mission, if I chose to accept it, felt impossible. My experience with cookies is that you get either one or the other: flat, chewy, and crisp, or soft, puffy, and cakey. It didn't seem likely that I could have my cookie and eat it, too.

When you're looking for the impossible, you have to be willing to try anything. A few days before starting my tests, I saw a glossy picture of a knockout cookie in a magazine ad. Dubbed "Death by Chocolate Cookie," it appeared to have a crackly crisp exterior with a chewy interior. The brownie-like ingredients list — lots of melted semisweet chocolate and very little flour — appeared to produce a gorgeous cookie. And, of course, a good brownie has a nice, crisp crust and a chewy crumb. Why not try it? Since I didn't want a chocolate-colored cookie like the one in the picture, I thought perhaps white chocolate could stand in for dark with similar results. In just a few unsuccessful minutes, those cookies melted flatter than pancakes.

Believing that a brownie-style dough might give me a cookie with a crisp exterior and chewy interior, I wasn't quite ready to give up. I found a recipe for "Classic White Blondies" on the white chocolate wrapper. Similar in proportions but with more flour than the first recipe, these cookies did rise more but still looked like smooth-textured pancakes that quickly lost their chew. I was going to have to do what I was hoping to avoid: start testing every known recipe for chocolate chip cookies.

I knew that the way in which the fat and sugar were mixed made a big difference in the cookie, so I decided to perform a mixing test before working my way down the ingredients list. Minus the chocolate chips, my dough was made from the classic Nestlé's Original Toll House Cookies formula:

2¼	cups flour
1	teaspoon baking soda
1	teaspoon salt
¾	cup granulated sugar
¾	cup brown sugar
1	teaspoon vanilla extract
16	tablespoons (2 sticks) butter
2	large eggs

I made three batches of cookies: one by creaming the butter and sugar with a mixer before adding the egg and dry ingredients and another by melting the butter, then stirring it into the sugar. Following a tip I found on the Internet, I made a final batch by heating the butter and sugar together before mixing in the remaining ingredients. Though none of the cookies was ideal, adding melted butter to sugar was the simplest of the methods and produced cookies with the best texture.

Since flour is the foundation of most baked goods, I started there to get my bearings. Testing combinations I had seen from published recipes, I made seven batches of cookies from the following flours:

Cake flour
Part cake flour and part bleached all-purpose flour
Bleached all-purpose flour
Bleached all-purpose flour with a little cornstarch
Part bleached all-purpose and part whole wheat
Instant flour (Wondra)
Unbleached all-purpose flour

I was amazed at the differences. The cake flour cookies were flat, yet the crispest and most chewy of the bunch. The remaining cookies got progressively thicker. The cake flour–all-purpose flour cookies and the all-purpose flour cookies lacked the crispness and chewiness of the all cake flour cookies. The all-purpose flour–cornstarch combination produced pasty cookies with "off" flavors. Although the Wondra-flour box displayed a gorgeous chocolate chip cookie, the real life version was quite dry. Unbleached flour made good-looking but hard, dry cookies. Ditto for the one made with part whole wheat.

If I could just figure out how to get the cake flour cookies a little thicker, this flour might be key. Perhaps a little baking powder, in combination with the baking soda, might give the cookies a lift. I made three half batches of Toll House dough with cake flour, each with different amounts of baking powder and soda. None of them had enough power to raise these flat cake flour cookies. Stubbornly, I kept coming back to cake flour throughout the testing, but I ultimately concluded that regardless of the formula, the low-protein flour was too weak to support this kind of cookie. The chewiness that I liked had come from the toffee-like union of butter and sugar. I'd go with bleached all-purpose flour.

After making chocolate chip cookies with varying proportions and quantities of brown and granulated sugar, I decided to stick with the original proportions and quantities of equal parts of each. Cookies made with all granulated sugar looked and tasted like sugar cookies. And since granulated sugar doesn't contain an acid for the baking soda to neutralize (as does the molasses that's contained in brown sugar), the leavener's soapy flavor was clear. On the other hand, cookies made with all brown sugar started to look like gingerbread. Although I had made cookies with higher and lower proportions of granulated and brown sugar, I saw no reason that either one should dominate. Less sugar resulted in a drier, less chewy cookie. Did dark or light brown sugar make a difference? I opted for the more robust dark variety.

I tested six different fats: butter, shortening, margarine, butter-flavored shortening, butter-shortening, and butter-oil. No single-fat cookie was ideal. The all-shortening cookies were the real lookers. They held their shape beautifully and developed folds and wrinkles. But one bite and I realized this tasteless, cakey cookie's beauty was only crust deep. The butter-flavored shortening cookies were even worse — better no flavor than fake flavor.

But cookies made with all butter weren't perfect, either. They had great flavor, but compared with the shortening cookies, they were flat and unattractive. Margarine cookies were as unattractive as the butter ones, with none of the flavor. The butter-oil combination, however, had potential. Displaying a subtle sheen, these cookies tasted just as buttery but spread slightly less than those made with all butter. Unlike the cakey shortening cookies, these were pleasantly crisp around the edges. Shortening, butter, and oil each had something to offer. As much as I might have preferred the simplicity of a single fat, my ideal cookie seemed to need all three: shortening for wrinkles and shape, butter for flavor, and oil for sheen and crispness.

To determine whether I needed three fats or not, I made several batches of cookies with varying proportions of butter, shortening, and oil. My goal was to use as much butter and as little shortening and oil as possible to achieve the best flavor, shape, and texture. After much trial and error, I determined that I could use as much as 12 tablespoons of butter and as little as 2 tablespoons each of shortening and oil. Cookies made with these fat proportions were puffy, chewy in the middle, and crisp around the edges. And they didn't get either too crisp or too hard after just a few hours. It bothered me, however, that my cookie seemed to need all three fats. And because the shortening had to be creamed, I had to pull out the hand mixer, too. Luckily, though, some simplification was just around the bend.

Tasting batch after batch, I had noticed the cookies were salty. Chocolate chip cookie dough contains very little moisture, and since salt was one of the last ingredients to get stirred in, it never dissolved. I decreased the salt and dissolved it in the egg and vanilla.

Leavener proved important to puffy, beautiful cookies. I could taste the 1 teaspoon baking soda in the original recipe. By halving the baking soda and using part baking powder, I accomplished two things. The cookie lost its unpleasant flavor, and it puffed beautifully during baking and fell slightly after cooling, enhancing the crinkled, wrinkled look I wanted.

I had worked my way through the ingredients list, but there were still some odd-ball ingredients to test. Would vanilla pudding, nonfat dry milk, corn syrup, or an extra egg yolk prove key? Adding dry instant pudding and milk powder along with the dry ingredients resulted in cookies with an unattractive store-bought flavor. Moist pudding — and any moist ingredient for that matter — made the cookies too soft and cakey. Corn syrup produced a chewy cookie but at the cost of crispness. An extra egg yolk resulted in a drier, slightly crumbly cookie.

I had tweaked the salt and leavener and called for three fats instead of all butter, but my current cookie wasn't much different from the original recipe.

Once I started testing different cooking times and temperatures, however, a few changes were in order. To achieve a beautiful, puffed cookie, I found that oven and dough temperatures were as critical as the formula itself. Since I was using melted butter, I had been refrigerating the cookie dough to firm it up a bit before forming the dough rounds and baking them in a 375-degree oven. At this point, the cookies were still spreading more than I wanted, and the cookie bottoms were darker than ideal.

Two things helped. Forming the dough into balls and freezing them solid before baking kept them from spreading. Getting the oven temperature right also improved things. After much time and temperature testing, I finally determined the cookies were at their best when baked at a relatively high 400 degrees until set, 8 to 10 minutes, then finished at a lower 350 degrees for another 10 minutes. The higher temperature caused the starch to set before the fat melted, resulting in a cookie that puffed rather than spread. The lower temperature allowed the cookies to crisp up and turn golden brown without burning. Since the cookies were spreading less with this new baking method, I found that I was able to eliminate the shortening from the recipe, using only butter for flavor and oil for crispness and preservation.

After baking several batches in which cookies on the bottom rack spread more than those on the top, I finally realized they had to be baked one sheet at a time. Freezing the cookie dough balls in a pan that fit in the freezer, then transferring them to room-temperature cookie sheets also helped.

This cookie dough base works for practically any nut, chip, or candy. Having made these cookies with different quantities and brands of chocolate, I prefer chopped chocolate bars to chips. When cut, the bar naturally breaks unevenly into small shards as well as big chunks. Both work together to color and flavor the cookie. Although not everyone does, I like toasted nuts in my chocolate chip cookies. Making the dough couldn't be simpler, but the baking step requires a little thought and care. These few extra steps are well worth it for a cookie that delivers the seemingly impossible: puffiness, crispness, and chewiness all in one bite.

Puffy, Crisp Chocolate Chip Cookies

Makes 16 large cookies If you have a $^3/_4$-cup measuring cup, it's the only one you need for this recipe. The sugars measure $^3/_4$ cup each, the chocolate chip quantity is $1^1/_2$ cups (or $^3/_4$ cup times 2), and the flour is $2^1/_4$ cups (or $^3/_4$ cup times 3). I prefer Ghirardelli bittersweet chocolate bars, cut into small chunks, for these cookies, but $1^1/_2$ cups of chocolate chips can be used as well. When adding nuts, I usually reduce the chocolate from $1^1/_2$ cups to 1 cup. Toasted nuts taste great in these cookies. Bake the nuts in a 325-degree oven until fragrant, about 10 minutes.

$2^1/_4$ **cups bleached all-purpose flour**
1 **teaspoon baking powder**
$^1/_2$ **teaspoon baking soda**
2 **large eggs**
1 **teaspoon vanilla extract**
$^3/_4$ **teaspoon salt**
14 **tablespoons ($1^3/_4$ sticks) unsalted butter**
$^3/_4$ **cup sugar**
$^3/_4$ **cup dark brown sugar**
2 **tablespoons flavorless oil, such as vegetable or canola**
8 **ounces good-quality bittersweet or semisweet chocolate bar, chopped into $^1/_4$-inch chunks (about $1^1/_2$ cups chopped), *or* 1 cup chocolate chunks and 1 cup toasted nuts (pecans, walnuts, macadamias, *or* unsalted peanuts; see note above)**

1   Mix flour, baking powder, and baking soda in a medium bowl; set aside. Mix eggs, vanilla, and salt in a small bowl; set aside. Microwave butter on high power until just melted but not hot, 30 to 45 seconds (or in a saucepan over low heat); set aside.

2   Mix sugars in a large bowl. Add butter and oil, and stir until smooth. Add egg mixture; stir until smooth and creamy. Add dry ingredients, and stir to form a smooth dough. Stir in chocolate and nuts, if using.

3   Using a $1^1/_2$-ounce (3-tablespoon) spring-action ice-cream scoop, spoon 16 dough balls onto a pan that will fit in your freezer. (Don't worry if balls are too crowded. They pull apart

when frozen.) Freeze until dough is hard, about 30 minutes. (Once balls are frozen, they can be stored in freezer bags for up to 3 months and baked as desired.)

4   Meanwhile, adjust oven rack to upper-middle position and heat oven to 400 degrees. Line two cookie sheets with parchment paper. Working with half batches, place 8 frozen dough balls on a cookie sheet (don't press them down). Bake until set but not brown, 8 to 10 minutes. Reduce oven temperature to 350 degrees. Continue to bake until cookies are golden brown around edges and lightly brown on top, about 10 minutes longer. Let cookies cool completely on cookie sheet. Repeat with remaining dough balls. (Cookies can be stored in an air-tight tin or container for up to 5 days.)

eat peanut butter and honey on toast for breakfast at least a couple of mornings a week, and I can hardly enjoy a bracing cocktail without a dish of roasted salted peanuts, but I've never been a peanut butter cookie fan. I just don't like what peanut butter does to cookie dough.

Unlike good chocolate chip cookie dough, which morphs into a crisp cookie, peanut butter cookie dough just sits on the baking sheet like a ball of modeling clay. Unless pressed down with a fork, the dough will not budge during baking. And the cookie is often hard and crumbly. I wanted to make a crisp, chewy peanut butter cookie if I could. To try to give it these uncharacteristic qualities smelled like trouble.

MAKING THAT COOKIE CRUMBLE

After checking several sources, I realized that if I added a cup of peanut butter, my chocolate chip cookie formula would be pretty close to the average peanut butter cookie recipe. So I made a batch of peanut butter cookies by mixing:

14	tablespoons (1¾ sticks) melted butter
2	tablespoons vegetable oil
1	cup creamy peanut butter

with

¾	cup sugar
¾	cup dark brown sugar

until smooth, then beating in

2	large eggs
¾	teaspoon salt
1	teaspoon vanilla extract

until smooth, then beating in

2¹/₄ cups flour
  1   teaspoon baking powder
 ¹/₂   teaspoon baking soda

Even during the mixing phase, I could tell that peanut butter was not a simple addition. Unlike chocolate chips or nuts that merely flecked the dough, peanut butter became part of it, stiffening its texture. With such large quantities of flour and peanut butter, the dough was stiff and heavy. For the dough balls to melt into pleasantly puffy mounds, some of one or the other (or a little of each) would have to go.

Interestingly, I found several peanut butter cookie recipes that contained absolutely no flour. Although some added a pinch of salt, others a touch of vanilla, the basic recipe consisted of just four ingredients:

  2   cups sugar
  2   cups peanut butter
  2   teaspoons baking soda
  2   eggs

Some of the creators of recipes like these swore they were the best peanut butter cookies ever. They were not. Except for a few cracks that developed from the baking soda, the cookies looked the same coming out of the oven as they did going in. Their texture was dense and crumbly, as though they had been made with whole wheat flour.

My instinct was to introduce some flour and butter back into the dough. So I made it again, adding a little butter and flour. To remedy the one-dimensional flavor, I substituted brown sugar for part of the granulated. The changed recipe follows:

  2   cups sugar (1 cup each brown and granulated)
  2   cups peanut butter
  2   eggs
  2   teaspoons baking soda
  1   cup flour
  8   tablespoons butter

Although the cookies made from this mix of ingredients weren't perfect, it was clear I was heading in the right direction. Though still sandy-textured and dense, these cookies actually spread a little during baking and looked quite attractive — a major improvement over the flourless, butterless variety.

Peanut butter was the next ingredient up for scrutiny. Responsible for the cookie's pleasantly potent flavor as well as its overly sandy texture, peanut butter was both its strength and its weakness. My hope was to reduce the amount, compensating for the loss with chopped roasted peanuts. So that the cookies would spread better and be more crisp, I would add more butter. To determine the right ratios of butter and peanut butter, I made two batches, decreasing the peanut butter from 2 cups to 1$\frac{1}{2}$ cups and increasing the butter from 8 to 12 tablespoons in the first one. In batch two, I decreased the peanut butter by half, to 1 cup, and doubled the butter from 8 to 16 tablespoons.

The cookies in batch one spread into a lovely oversize thick cookie with an appealing crackly (as opposed to cracked) top and an exceptional texture. Freezing the dough balls helped the cookies spread into a perfect slightly rounded mound. The dramatic increase in butter in batch two caused the cookies to spread as flat as a tuile.

With my new formula, I

WHAT ABOUT THE PEANUT BUTTER?

To see if it matters which brand of peanut butter you use, I made five batches of cookies from the most popular nationally available brands: Jif, Skippy, Peter Pan, Reese's, and Smucker's Natural.

Natural peanut butter (which contains no sugar or hydrogenated vegetable oils) may be healthier, but it certainly didn't make the best cookies. Cookies made with Smucker's Natural Peanut Butter did not spread nearly as much as the others, and they were also drier and more sandy-textured.

Those made with the remaining four brands of peanut butter all spread beautifully and offered the chewy-crisp texture I wanted. I detected slight flavor differences among the cookies, but they were not significant enough to cause me to prefer one brand over another. If forced to pick, however, I'd vote for Skippy, which gave the cookie a slightly more pronounced peanut flavor.

found that the cookies needed heat slightly higher than 350 degrees. A temperature of 375 degrees worked best. Fresh from the oven, the cookies were quite fragile. They looked but didn't feel done. The temptation was to bake them for another couple of minutes, but I was always sorry when I did, because they lost their chewiness and became completely crisp. If pulled from the oven at the right time and left on the cookie sheet for 5 minutes, they firmed up enough to be transferred to a wire rack. When cool, they were perfectly chewy and crisp, with just a hint of sandiness.

BROWN IS BEST

To find out if all brown sugar would be a better match for the peanut butter, I made two batches of cookies: one with all light brown sugar, another with all dark. Light brown sugar was the clear winner, making the cookies taste pleasant and flavorful. Decreasing the quantity of sugar prevented the cookies from spreading and made them crumbly and less chewy.

To see if I could reduce the baking soda, which left the cookies with a subtle metallic aftertaste, I made a batch with 1 1/2 teaspoons of baking soda rather than the original 2. The cookies made with the reduced baking soda looked as attractive as those made with the full 2 teaspoons, without the metallic undertones.

I had developed the best peanut butter cookie I had ever eaten: chewy-crisp, pleasantly crunchy with nuts, and just sweet enough, with a big, big peanutty flavor.

Not-Your-Average
Peanut Butter Cookies

Makes 18 large cookies

These peanut butter dough balls do not need to be flattened with a fork. The ratio of butter, flour, sugar, and peanut butter causes them to spread naturally as they bake.

1	cup all-purpose bleached flour
1¹/₂	teaspoons baking soda
12	tablespoons (1¹/₂ sticks) unsalted butter, melted just until warm, not hot
1¹/₂	cups creamy peanut butter
2	cups packed light brown sugar
2	large eggs
1	teaspoon vanilla extract
1	cup roasted peanuts, coarsely chopped

1. Adjust oven racks to upper-middle and lower-middle positions and heat oven to 375 degrees. Line two cookie sheets with parchment paper. Mix flour and baking soda in a small bowl; set aside.

2. Mix butter, peanut butter, and brown sugar in a medium bowl until smooth. Mix eggs and vanilla in a small bowl. Add to peanut butter mixture, and beat with a rubber spatula until smooth. Add flour mixture and peanuts; stir until well combined.

3. Line a 13-by-9-inch or similar-size pan with plastic wrap. Use a 2-ounce (¹/₄-cup) spring-action ice-cream scoop to form dough balls and scoop into pan. (About 14 balls will fit in first layer.) Lay a sheet of plastic wrap on top and make another layer, scooping balls from remaining dough. Freeze until solid, about 30 minutes.

4. Place 9 cookies on each of the cookie sheets. Bake, switching and turning cookie sheets from front to back after 15 minutes. Continue to bake until cookies are golden but not dark brown, 3 to 5 minutes longer. Remove from oven and let stand on cookie sheet for 5 minutes. (Cookies are relatively fragile at this point.) Transfer to a wire rack and let cool completely. (Cookies can be stored in an airtight tin or container.)

Clean-Cut Peach Pie (Blueberry, Blackberry, and Cherry, Too!)

When I make fruit pies, I get mad if I serve up a slice that looks like it fell on the floor before it landed on the plate. For that reason, I'd almost given up making fruit pies and converted to cobblers instead. This strategy worked for a while, but eventually, I tired of playing my cobbler hand when I really just wanted a beautiful pie.

My ideal pie would hold its shape when cut, and its top and bottom crust would bake to golden brown perfection. I wanted a filling with clear, soft, lightly thickened juices that just barely held the fruit in suspension. A pretty tall order, since most of the fruit pies I had made displayed none of those qualities.

Since peaches are plentiful in season and reasonably priced, I decided to learn what I could from testing with them. After that, I'd see if the same rules applied to other summer fruits: blueberries, blackberries, and cherries.

THE PICK OF THE THICKENERS

I ran thirty-one thickener tests alone. Because there were so many possibilities, I divided them into three categories. I started with the most straightforward methods, simply tossing the peaches with the thickener and sugar, dotting them with butter, and baking them in the pie. I tested the following thickeners:

Flour

Cornstarch

Arrowroot

Potato starch (available in the baking or the kosher aisle of most grocery stores)

Minute tapioca

Instant tapioca, pulverized in a coffee grinder

ClearJel (available at specialty food shops)

Egg

Grated apple

Egg and grated apple were easy to cross off the list. The egg-thickened filling was curdled, while the apple bits took away from the clear peach flavor. Flour was the pie thickener I had grown up with, so it's not surprising that despite the filling's cloudy look and loud starchy flavor, I found it familiar and comforting. Stronger and clearer than flour, cornstarch was usually among my favorite thickeners, but because of the large amount that I'd needed to thicken the juicy pie, it tasted a little off. ClearJel thickened nicely, but since it wasn't noticeably superior or widely available, I marked it off the list. Tapioca cooked up clear and glossy, and it had incredible thickening power, but the texture was distracting. Pulverizing the tapioca helped take care of the fish-egg texture but did nothing for the sliminess. Nor did letting the tapioca sit with the sugared peaches for 15 minutes. The filling was full of little softened tapioca balls.

Arrowroot and potato starch, on the other hand, thickened the peaches beautifully and cooked up smooth and clear. With so many techniques left to test, it was too early to declare a winner, but these two had certainly caught my attention.

To test the notion that two thickeners are better than one, I followed the same procedure as in the first round of tests and tried the following:

Flour/cornstarch

Cornstarch/tapioca

Cornstarch/arrowroot

Cornstarch/sugar/water/butter, cooked to a paste and tossed with the fruit

I saw no serious benefits to using two starches, except for the cornstarch-tapioca combination: in small quantity, the tapioca's texture was barely noticeable, and the cornstarch contributed softness. If nothing better had come along, this might have been it.

Although it ended up working for other fruit pies, the starch paste was not successful, making the peaches look and taste anemic.

THE PLOT THICKENS

It wasn't until I tried cooking the fruit and sugar together in the hopes of eliminating the thickener entirely that I understood the real role starch plays in pie. It doesn't just thicken; it also serves to mellow the taste of the fruit. Without starch, the juices were too thin and intense, the peaches too sweet. Cooking a small portion of the peaches on the stovetop with the sugar and starch (or cooking the sugared peach juice with the starch and stirring it into the peaches) compromised the fresh flavor and added extra time to the recipe. Sprinkling the peaches with sugar, however, seemed to give them a brighter, fruitier flavor, and using the drained fruit juice rather than water to make the starch paste was a technique with potential.

After making another round of pies using this method, I was finally able to declare potato starch the winner because of the way it powerfully thickened the pie, while allowing the peach juices to remain soft and clear.

SUGAR AND SPICE

Having endured many tedious thickening tests, I was pleased to move on to sweeteners and flavorings. Up to this point, my fillings had been sweetened with 3 tablespoons of sugar per cup of fruit. To determine whether granulated sugar was the right sweetener, I made fillings with dark brown sugar, light brown sugar, a mixture of light brown and granulated sugar, and a mixture of granulated sugar and corn syrup. Even small amounts of brown sugar overpowered the delicate peaches and stained them tobacco-brown. The sugar–corn syrup alliance only made the peaches juicier — a problem I didn't need.

My ratio of 3 tablespoons sugar per 1 cup of fruit gave me peaches that were neither overly sweet nor tart. Eaten alone, the peaches sweetened with 2 tablespoons sugar tasted a little spare, but with a rich crust and a scoop of ice cream, this quantity might be just right. I would withhold my final judgment on the amount of sugar until I'd made a pie.

To test flavorings, I made fillings with vanilla extract, almond extract, cinnamon, nutmeg, ginger, cloves, mace, lemon zest, and orange extract. Only the almond extract complemented the pure fresh peach flavor.

Once I made the pie, a few adjustments were needed. Sprinkling the peaches with a couple extra tablespoons of sugar and draining off the resulting juice not only helped to sweeten and intensify the flavor of the peaches but rid the pie of nearly half a cup of excess juice, resulting in a firm, yet luscious pie. By sacrificing some of the juice rather than increasing the thickener, I could fill the pie with peaches and not have to worry about oozing liquid.

CRISPY CRUST

Since a limp, gummy crust is as much responsible for a messy wedge as an overly juicy fruit filling, a fully cooked bottom crust is also crucial. Baking the pie on the lowest rack of the oven wasn't enough to brown the bottom. Following the suggestion of a few cookbook authors, I tried baking the pie directly on the oven floor, but the browning was uneven and part of the pie almost burned.

In *The Pie and Pastry Bible* (Simon & Schuster, 1998), the noted baking expert Rose Levy Beranbaum suggests baking pies on a pizza stone to improve the crust. Since I don't own a pizza stone, I tried baking a pie on four of my 9-inch unglazed quarry tiles (available at Home Depot for about 55 cents apiece) that had been pre-heated on the bottom rack for about 30 minutes before baking. It worked. The bottom pie crust browned beautifully.

Having drained $1/2$ cup of juice from the pie, I didn't have trouble with overflow, but I still liked setting the pie on a sheet of heavy-duty foil placed over the tiles. Not only does the foil catch any drips, it also keeps the fluted edge from overbrowning. Rather than trying to make and fit a foil ring to shield the pie edge from the oven's heat, I simply lift the foil up and around the pie edges during the last 20 minutes of baking. Brushing the fluted crust with egg white and sprinkling it with sugar 20 minutes into the baking process help the pastry hold its shape.

NOT ALL FRUITS COOK ALIKE

With my peach pie filling perfected, I was ready to move on to blueberries and blackberries. I knew these fruits were even more juicy than peaches. To determine if they should be treated the same way, I made two different pies: one with drained fruit, the other with berries tossed with sugar and potato starch.

After 10 minutes of attempting to drain the fruit, I realized the berries had to be crushed for the sugar to do its work. The fillings made with crushed berries, however, were juicy and jamlike, the bruised berries having disintegrated. The juices of the whole-berry pies were also thin — the blueberry juices in particular.

In my research, I had read about blueberries in Jeffrey Steingarten's *The Man Who Ate Everything* (Knopf, 1997). According to Steingarten, blueberry skins contain oxalic acid, which attacks nearly all starch thickeners. Peeling blueberries, he points out, "is an unheard-of task and would wreck their taste and shape. So we must expect irregular success in the thickening process." I confirmed the blueberry's unique problem with food scientist and cookbook author Shirley Corriher. According to her, however, the acid in the blueberry skins could only affect the uncooked starch. Adding the berries to cooked starch would seem to be the way to guarantee a consistently thickened pie.

The starch pastes that I had considered for peach pie made sense here. After much tinkering with water, starch, sugar, and berry quantities, I finally hit upon a ratio and technique that worked. I heated minimal water ($1/2$ cup) and enough potato starch ($1/4$ cup) and sugar ($3/4$ cup plus 2 tablespoons) to deliver a pie with soft, yet thick juices and just the right amount of sweetness.

The paste, however, was too thick to stir into the berries. By adding 1 cup of pureed blueberries to the cooked paste and stirring it into the whole berries, I solved that problem. Since the blueberries were more intense in flavor than peaches, and since the $1/2$ cup water in the blueberry pie resulted in frequent juice overflow, I decreased the fruit quantity from 6 to 5 cups.

The blackberry pie came together quite easily. Like blueberries, blackberries couldn't be sugared and drained, so I made a starch paste for this filling as well. Unlike blueberries, whose acidic skins wreaked havoc with the starch, the blackberry puree could be added with the starch and sugar from the start and did not require the ½ cup water.

Sour cherries are the variety of choice for cherry pie, but they're rare in fresh and frozen form. Using a hybrid method from both the peach and the berry pies, I made a great cherry pie with the canned variety. Since canned cherries are already floating in juice, there's no need to sugar them and let them stand. Unlike juicy peaches, however, the canned cherries were limp after they were drained. Instead of discarding the juice, I made a starch paste with some of it.

If the pastry and fruit are good, pies don't need much flavoring. Like the peach pie, cherry needed only a breath of almond extract. And after trying several different flavorings with the berry pies, I found a touch of grated lemon zest lightened their intensity.

Perfect Peach Pie

Makes one 9-inch pie

I usually have a pound or so of butter and a couple of shortening sticks in the freezer. Having those ingredients already chilled means I can start making a pie at a moment's notice.

Potato starch, sometimes referred to as potato starch flour, is available in the baking or the kosher section of the grocery store.

EASY PIE DOUGH

8	tablespoons (1 stick) unsalted butter, quartered lengthwise
$^{1}/_{4}$	cup vegetable shortening, frozen
8	tablespoons (4 ounces) cold cream cheese
$2^{1}/_{4}$	cups bleached all-purpose flour
2	tablespoons sugar
1	teaspoon salt

PEACH FILLING

6	cups peeled, sliced ripe peaches (about 6 large)
$^{3}/_{4}$	cup plus 2 tablespoons sugar
$3^{1}/_{2}$	tablespoons potato starch (see note above)
	Pinch salt
$^{1}/_{2}$	teaspoon almond extract
1	tablespoon unsalted butter, cut into small pieces

PASTRY WASH

1	egg white, lightly beaten
$1^{1}/_{2}$	tablespoons sugar

1   FOR PIE DOUGH: Cut butter, shortening, and cream cheese into $^{1}/_{2}$-inch pieces. Put butter in one bowl and shortening and cream cheese together in another bowl, and set in freezer. Have ready $^{1}/_{3}$ cup ice water.

2   Mix flour, sugar, and salt in a food processor to combine. Add butter; break up butter cubes with hands and coat with flour mixture. Pulse 4 times for 1 long second each time (say, "1 chimpanzee, 2 chimpanzees" to time each pulse). Break shortening and cream cheese into flour mixture; toss to coat. Pulse another 4 or 5 times, 1 long second each time, until fats are pea- and fine-gravel size. Dump mixture into a medium bowl and rub flour-fat mixture through fingertips to blend. Stir ice water

into mixture with a rubber spatula until dough clumps form. Press clumps together with palm of hand to form a cohesive ball. Press down on ball to gather remaining scraps, dipping fingertips in water and adding droplets to bottom of bowl if scraps refuse to adhere.

3. Divide dough into two-third and one-third portion sizes. Wrap each in plastic wrap, then press down to form each into a thick disk. Refrigerate until cold and firm, at least 1 hour. (Dough can be refrigerated for up to 2 days or double-wrapped in plastic and frozen up to 2 months.)

4. FOR FILLING: When ready to bake pie, place peaches in a colander; sprinkle with 2 tablespoons sugar and let stand until about 1/2 cup juice is released, about 30 minutes.

5. FOR PIE SHELL: Adjust oven rack to lowest position and place four 9-inch quarry tiles on rack to form an 18-inch square. (A pizza stone works as well.) Preheat oven to 400 degrees and let tiles heat for at least 30 minutes.

6. Set larger dough disk on a lightly floured work surface and roll into an approximately 14-inch circle. Fold dough in half and set a 9-inch Pyrex pie plate next to fold line. Quickly lift dough into pie plate and unfold. Lift edge of dough with one hand and press dough into pan with other hand so that dough fits in pan and is not stretched in any way. Trim excess pastry. Set pie shell in refrigerator while preparing filling.

7. FINISH FILLING: Transfer drained peaches to a medium bowl. In a small bowl, mix remaining 3/4 cup sugar with potato starch and salt. Add to drained peaches, along with almond extract, and toss to combine.

8. FOR ASSEMBLY AND BAKING OF PIE: As soon as filling is mixed, set remaining dough disk on a lightly floured work surface and roll to a 12-inch circle. Remove pie shell from refrigerator, add fruit filling, and dot with butter. Fold dough circle in half and set filled pie shell next to fold line. Quickly lift dough onto filling and unfold. Trim dough all around to 1/2 inch beyond pan lip. Roll overhanging dough under with fingertips so that it is flush with pan lip. Flute edge all around. Cut vent holes on top of pastry.

Set an 18-inch square of heavy-duty foil on tiles or pizza stone. Set pie on foil and bake until dough has set and just starts to color, about 20 minutes. Remove pie from oven, brush top with egg wash, and sprinkle with sugar. Continue to bake until golden brown, about 20 minutes longer. Bring foil around pie as shown. Continue to bake until filling bubbles, 15 to 20 minutes longer. Cool on a wire rack until barely warm, about 3 hours. Serve.

When the fluted edge of the piecrust has browned enough, bring the foil around the pie loosely to protect the edges.

Perfect Blueberry Pie

Makes one 9-inch pie

Because of the blueberries' impenetrable skins, they cannot be sugared and drained as can the peaches. In addition, blueberry skins contain oxalic acid, which attacks nearly all *uncooked* starch thickeners, often resulting in runny pie. To solve the problem, I cook the potato starch with sugar and as little water as possible to keep the baked pie from being runny. Once the paste is cooked, I thicken it with just enough pureed blueberries so that it can be mixed with the whole berries for the pie.

Easy Pie Dough (page 289)

BLUEBERRY FILLING

- 5 **cups blueberries (about 2½ pints), picked over, stemmed, and rinsed**
- ¾ **cup plus 2 tablespoons sugar**
  Pinch salt
- ¼ **cup potato starch (available in the baking or kosher section)**
- 1 **teaspoon finely grated lemon zest**
- 1 **tablespoon unsalted butter, cut into small pieces**

1 **FOR PIE DOUGH:** Proceed as directed in steps 1, 2, 3, 5, and 6 for Perfect Peach Pie (page 289).

2 **FOR FILLING:** Puree 1 cup blueberries in a food processor; set aside.

3 Whisking constantly, mix sugar, salt, potato starch, and ½ cup water to a very thick paste in a large saucepan over medium-low heat. As mixture thickens and starts to stick to pan bottom, whisk in blueberry puree and lemon zest and bring to a simmer. Place remaining 4 cups blueberries in a large bowl, scrape blueberry-starch mixture over them, and stir to combine.

4 **FOR ASSEMBLY AND BAKING OF PIE:** Continue as directed in steps 8 and 9 for Perfect Peach Pie.

Perfect Blackberry Pie

Makes one 9-inch pie

The filling for this pie is generous — soft, yet firm enough to slice cleanly.

Easy Pie Dough (page 289)

BLACKBERRY FILLING

5½ cups blackberries
¾ cup plus 2 tablespoons sugar
Pinch salt
¼ cup potato starch (available in the baking or kosher section)
1 teaspoon finely grated lemon zest
1 tablespoon unsalted butter, cut into small pieces

1 FOR PIE DOUGH: Proceed as directed in steps 1, 2, 3, 5, and 6 for Perfect Peach Pie (page 289).

2 FOR FILLING: Puree 1 cup blackberries in a food processor; set aside.

3 Stirring constantly with a rubber spatula, mix sugar, salt, potato starch, and blackberry puree in a saucepan over medium-low heat until it is the consistency of thick jam. Stir in lemon zest. Scrape thickener over remaining blackberries and stir to combine.

4 FOR ASSEMBLY AND BAKING OF PIE: Continue as directed in steps 8 and 9 for Perfect Peach Pie.

Perfect Canned-Cherry Pie

Makes one 9-inch pie

Two cans of cherries aren't enough to make a full pie. I use 3 drained cans, which yields just a little over 5 cups of cherries, about the same amount of fruit used to make the other pies.

Easy Pie Dough (page 289)

CHERRY FILLING

- 3 cans water-packed red, tart pitted cherries (16 ounces each), drained, 1 cup juice reserved
- 1 cup sugar
  Pinch salt
- 1/4 cup potato starch
- 1/2 teaspoon almond extract
- 1 tablespoon unsalted butter, cut into small pieces

1 FOR PIE DOUGH: Proceed as directed in steps 1, 2, 3, 5, and 6 for Perfect Peach Pie (page 289).

2 Stirring constantly with a rubber spatula, mix the 1 cup cherry juice, sugar, salt, and potato starch to a very thick paste in a large saucepan over medium-low heat. Place cherries in a medium bowl and scrape paste over them; stir to combine.

3 FOR ASSEMBLY AND BAKING OF PIE: Continue as directed in steps 8 and 9 for Perfect Peach Pie.

Light, Just Right Key Lime Pie

$\mathcal{C}$ooking was not permitted in my college dorm. I've often wondered if that was because the officials thought it was a fire hazard or because the dining hall supervisor feared the competition.

That didn't stop some of us from trying. With just a bowl and spoon, I could make a no-bake Key lime pie by mixing a can of sweetened condensed milk, frozen limeade, and a tub of Cool Whip, which I scraped into a graham cracker crust. Fortunately, the pie thickened without chilling, because we didn't have a refrigerator, either. I used to make these pies for my college beau; he proposed our final year. Love was at work, but I think my pies helped. I've improved my recipe a bit over the course of the nearly twenty-four years of our marriage, but this classic pie still demands very little oven and refrigerator time. There are many variations on a theme, but the typical Key lime pie recipe consists of just four ingredients. The method is equally simple: beat egg yolks with a can of condensed milk, then beat in lime juice and zest. The lime batter goes into a graham cracker crust, which is either baked in a moderate oven until the filling just starts to set, 10 to 15 minutes, or simply refrigerated until firm.

A good Key lime pie is pleasantly tart, not puckery, and nicely sweet, not treacly. It should be light without being like a mousse or soufflé.

I started with my traditional recipe:

4 egg yolks
1 can sweetened condensed milk
$^1/_2$ cup lime juice
$^1/_2$ teaspoon lime zest

I made two pies, baking one at 300 degrees for 15 minutes, as many recipes suggested. The other I simply refrigerated. The classic ingredients and proportions resulted in the heavy sweet-tart pies I remembered. The baked one was firm enough to slice, while the refrigerated one was a little loose.

Baking, it seemed, was key to a soft, yet firm texture. Egg safety, however, was a problem. Baked at such a low temperature and for such a short period of time, the pie barely reached 100 degrees and hardly seemed as safe as some of the recipes claimed.

So that I could compare several styles of Key lime pies, I decided to make twenty-one different fillings and taste them side by side. The pies in the first bake-off were all made to test the role of eggs. Though none of the fillings was perfect, I immediately saw ways to improve my recipe. Folding a beaten egg white into the filling subtly lightened the texture and cut the tart-sweet flavor, while 2 beaten whites turned the filling spongy and mousselike and diluted the flavor. Beating egg whites with a sugar syrup cooked to the softball stage was more trouble than it was worth, but beating sugar into the egg whites resulted in an extraordinarily smooth filling and was an improvement over just a plain whipped white. At this point, the extra sugar made the filling too sweet, but the technique had promise.

Beating the yolks until they were so thick they dripped from the beaters in ribbons resulted in an incredibly silky filling — another possible refinement. But beating an egg yolk with the condensed milk seemed to make the filling sweeter, if a bit lighter. Substituting 2 eggs for the 4 yolks also produced a lighter, smoother filling, but I preferred the one with the whipped egg white.

In another set of tests, I tried various cold mousses, pie fillings, puddings, curds, and lime-flavored whipped creams. None was an improvement on the simple classic. And none of the supposed timesavers — boxed vanilla pudding, Cool Whip, frozen limeade, lime Jell-O, cream cheese, sour cream, or whipped evaporated milk — tasted remotely close to my Key lime pie ideal. Many of these fillings contained folded-in whipped cream (or Cool Whip). After tasting them all, I decided that the cream belongs on top, not mixed in with the pie.

WHAT'S GOOD FOR LEMON MERINGUE IS GOOD FOR KEY LIME

So far, I'd learned that a whipped egg white would lighten the pie and that beating sugar into the egg white would smooth out the otherwise spongy filling. I also knew that beating the yolks to the ribbon stage gave the filling an extra-creamy texture. But just as I was about to incorporate these changes, I noticed that all the baked fillings containing egg whites had started to weep, giving off a syrupy liquid that saturated the crusts. Because the pies weren't baked very long, the egg whites weren't fully cooked, and as a result, they had broken down and liquefied.

Thanks to prior experience with lemon meringue pie, I already knew that adding a small amount of water-thickened cornstarch would stabilize the whites enough to keep them from weeping after baking. What worked for lemon meringue pie fixed the Key lime pie as well. I made a cornstarch paste by heating $^1/_3$ cup water and 1 tablespoon of cornstarch. (It was more than I needed for just 1 egg white, but making a smaller quantity was too difficult.) I beat half this mixture into my whipped meringue, then folded the now-stabilized egg white into the yolk (after beating it to the ribbon stage), condensed milk, and lime juice mixture, and baked it for 15 minutes. The resulting pie was light and refined without tasting foamy, and the cornstarch was absolutely undetectable. Best of all, there wasn't even a drop of liquid on the pie plate the following morning.

KEYS TO FLAVORS

With the meringue problem solved, I was finally able to focus on the pie's flavor, which at this point was noticeably sweet and light on lime. Reducing the sugar wasn't an option. The recipe called for a can of condensed milk, which contains sugar. Increasing the tartness, I suspected, might take care of the sweetness. I made my pie with 10 tablespoons of lime juice and a pinch of salt. Both worked. The extra lime juice perked up the pie, and both lime juice and salt toned down the sweetness.

Having made the pie with both Key limes and ordinary Persian limes, I think it matters which you choose. A Key lime is to a Persian lime what lemongrass is to lemons. Key limes are more aromatic and complexly flavored than ordinary limes. But if Key limes aren't available, pies made with Persian limes are still very good.

I would never have suspected the brand of condensed milk could make a difference, but surprisingly, it did. The differences in the two brands available to me — Eagle Brand and Carnation — were obvious as soon as I opened the cans. Eagle Brand was more caramel-colored than lily-white Carnation. The flavor differences fell along color lines. Eagle Brand tasted distinctly caramel-flavored, Carnation simply rich and sweet. The distinct color and flavor of the Eagle Brand milk dulled the color and competed with the lime, rather than complementing it. By contrast, the Carnation pie was a bright yellow, with a crisp, clean flavor.

IS IT SAFE YET?

Despite the filling's high acidity level, I knew the Egg Board wouldn't fully endorse a pie made with raw or partially cooked eggs. However, the next technique I tried made the pie safe and actually improved it. I decided to cook the filling on the stovetop once more. Rather than cook the eggs with the lime juice, I slowly heated them to a safe 160 degrees with part of the condensed milk. Since this stovetop version wasn't thick enough, I baked the pie until set, just like all the others.

Heating the egg yolks over low heat with part of the condensed milk added a step to the recipe, but tasters preferred the cooked-yolk filling's extra-silky texture to the pie made with eggs beaten to the ribbon stage.

After determining that 1¼ cups was the perfect amount of crumbs for a 9-inch pie plate, I set out to find the right ratio of butter and sugar for that quantity. Using graham crackers as the base, I started by making crusts with 4, 5, and 6 tablespoons of butter. The crust with 5 tablespoons held its shape during baking and crumbled less when sliced. With such a sweet filling, I had hoped to use as little sugar as possible. Two tablespoons was the minimum in the recipes I reviewed, but the crust made with that was a little crumbly. I reasoned that a larger amount of sugar melting in the oven, then solidifying during cooling, might help the crumbs to bind better. In fact, 3 tablespoons did the trick.

To see if any other crumb complemented lime pie better than graham crackers, I made crusts with vanilla wafers, shortbread, zwieback, gingersnaps, and imported wheat biscuits. Of all the crusts, only those made with graham cracker and zwieback perfectly matched the filling.

I like graham crackers, and I like zwieback, too. Their extra-crisp texture makes a beautifully crisp crust, and their barely sweet flavor, with hints of cinnamon, nutmeg, and mace, is the perfect base for the filling.

Light, Just Right Key Lime Pie

Makes one 9-inch pie

Key limes are more complexly flavored than the more common Persian limes, so use them if you can get them. You need only a small amount of the cornstarch paste to stabilize the egg white in the filling. I've made the smallest easily measurable quantity possible.

4   large egg yolks, plus 1 large egg white
1   can (14 ounces) sweetened condensed milk, preferably
     Carnation
1   tablespoon cornstarch
2   teaspoons sugar
1/2 teaspoon grated lime zest
10 tablespoons fresh lime juice (from 3–4 limes)
1/8 teaspoon salt
1   prebaked Graham Cracker or Zwieback Crust (recipe
     follows) or 1 store-bought graham cracker crust

1. Adjust oven rack to lower-middle position and heat oven to 300 degrees.

2. Whisking constantly, heat yolks and half of condensed milk in a small saucepan over low heat until mixture reaches 160 degrees. Turn off heat and stir in remaining condensed milk to keep eggs from curdling. Pour mixture into a medium bowl and set aside.

3. Whisking constantly, heat cornstarch and 1/3 cup water in a small saucepan over low heat until clear and thick, 2 to 3 minutes. Remove from heat. With a hand mixer, beat egg white on medium speed in a medium bowl until foamy. While gradually adding sugar, beat egg white until it's glossy and soft peaks form. Add half of thickened cornstarch to white and beat until just incorporated. Discard remaining thickened cornstarch.

4. Mix zest, lime juice, and salt, then beat into egg-milk mixture until well incorporated. Fold in egg white, then pour into prepared crust.

5. Bake until set but still jiggly at the center, 20 to 22 minutes. Cool to room temperature on a wire rack, then refrigerate until chilled, about 2 hours. Serve.

Graham Cracker or Zwieback Crust

Makes one 9-inch
pie shell

Graham cracker and zwieback make equally good crusts, but of different styles.

Don't look for zwieback in the cracker and cookie aisle. Instead, head to the baby food section. These wonderfully mild, crisp toasts not only are good for toddler snacks but also make a beautiful crust.

1¼ **cups graham cracker crumbs (11 whole) or zwieback crumbs (15 toasts)**
3 **tablespoons sugar**
5 **tablespoons unsalted butter, melted**

1   Adjust oven rack to lower-middle position and heat oven to 325 degrees.

2   Mix crumbs and sugar in a medium bowl. Add butter and stir with a fork until well incorporated. Dump crumbs into a 9-inch Pyrex pie plate and spread evenly over bottom. Use an 8-inch pie plate (or your fingers if you don't have one) to press crumbs up sides and, using each index finger, press crumbs around the top edge to even crust and secure loose crumbs.

3   Bake until fragrant, about 15 minutes. Let cool to room temperature while making pie.

Silky
Pumpkin Pie

Pumpkin pie is one of those consistently friendly, untemperamental desserts. Even if the crust is undercooked, even if the filling is a little grainy, even if the pie's too spicy or not spicy enough, people rarely complain. But I didn't want to serve pumpkin pie that guests ate without noticing. I wanted one that made them raise their brows, savor every bite, and, with clean plate in hand, ask for the recipe.

Perfection, however, meant simplicity. Although I might spend a Saturday afternoon seeding, baking, peeling, and stewing fresh pumpkin, I didn't want a pie that demanded it. The filling had to work with canned pumpkin puree and also had to taste distinctly of pumpkin. Too many recipes use pumpkin puree as a medium to showcase the spices. In my pie, the spices had to support, not overpower, the pumpkin. The filling also had to be light and silky smooth. Perfection meant the bottom crust had to taste baked. I had tasted one too many pumpkin pies whose filling was fully cooked but whose shell was raw.

FOR THE BEST TEXTURE, USE YOLKS

I used a common pumpkin pie filling as a starting point:

1	can pumpkin puree
1	cup sweetener
4	large eggs
1¹/₄	cups milk
1	teaspoon cinnamon
¹/₂	teaspoon ginger
¹/₂	teaspoon salt

Since I saw the most recipe variation with sweeteners — seven individual sweeteners, five pairs, and even two trios — I began my tests.

I tested fourteen sweeteners, alone and in combination with one another. The different sweeteners affected the filling's flavor, and they altered the color as well. Ranging from muted earthy peach to high-gloss caramel, the baked fillings looked like color variations on a paint-sample card. I liked the way light-colored sweeteners such as granulated and confectioners' sugars and light corn syrup helped the pumpkin retain its natural color, but they offered only hollow sweetness. On the other hand, dark sweeteners such as molasses, dark brown sugar, and dark corn syrup had too pronounced a flavor and turned the filling brown besides. Although I would eventually change my mind, light brown sugar was my early choice.

My research had shown that 3 eggs per filling was closer to the norm, but I had gone with 4. Since the filling was grainy from curdled eggs, I knew the quantity had to be reduced. I made two more fillings, one with 3 eggs, the other with 2. Since I knew that extra yolks prevent curdling and improve texture, I made two more fillings: one with 2 eggs and an extra yolk, the other with 2 eggs and 2 yolks.

As I suspected would be the case, 1 yolk helped, but the filling made with 2 yolks was the silkiest, smoothest, and least grainy of the lot.

SWEETENER AND DAIRY IN ONE CAN

The typical pumpkin-pie filling recipe calls for a cup or more of dairy liquid. For this round, I tested ten different milk and milk combinations. Progressing from rich to lean, I made fillings with heavy cream, sour cream, half-and-half, heavy cream–milk, sour cream–milk, condensed milk (I omitted the sugar in the recipe), whole milk enriched with a little butter, evaporated milk, whole milk, and low-fat milk.

After all the fillings had been tasted, it was clear that the dairy element in this pie was tricky. If the choice was too rich, the pumpkin flavor was muted. If it was too low in fat, however, the pie began to taste savory — like a sweet potato casserole. If it hadn't been for sweetened condensed milk, half-and-half would have been my choice. Without tasting excessive, the half-and-half filling was light, airy, and creamy, with a clear pumpkin flavor. Sweetened condensed milk, however, was a pleasant surprise. With built-in sweetener, this milk produced a filling that was a cut above any. Intense and sweet, but not high in fat, the condensed milk supported and enriched the pumpkin without masking its flavor. The filling was a little too dense, a problem that was easily remedied by adding some evaporated milk.

FROM COW TO CAN: EVAPORATED AND SWEETENED CONDENSED MILK

Since tasters found that pies made with evaporated milk and condensed milk were more intensely flavored and densely textured than those made with regular milk, I set out to discover how these milks were made and how they affect flavor and texture.

Tim Miller, quality assurance manager for Nestlé's Confection and Snack Division, explained that both products start with raw milk that is refrigerated in stainless steel silos. The milk's fat level is tested and adjusted — skimmed if too rich and enriched if too lean — to ensure consistent quality.

To break up and evenly distribute the fat globules and prevent the milk from separating, it is then homogenized. The homogenized milk is gradually heated, then pumped into a vacuum, where half its water is evaporated. Cooking milk in a vacuum means that it boils below 212 degrees, which helps preserve its flavor. After evaporation, the milk is fortified with vitamins and stabilized, then canned and pressure-cooked a final time.

Condensed milk is made from sweetened evaporated milk. Before being fortified and stabilized, the evaporated milk is transferred to a high-speed mixer, where a dry sweetener and a small amount of water are beaten into the milk. After further evaporation and a second homogenization, the condensed milk is cooled, at which time lactose (a natural milk sugar) is added to prevent the sugar from crystallizing.

The process of evaporation drives off what Miller calls "the bright dairy-flavor volatiles," which are prominent in regular milk and compete with the pumpkin and spices for attention. The sugar in the condensed milk helps it to bind better with the remaining liquid in the pie, resulting in a denser, less watery filling.

After tasting a dozen or so differently flavored fillings, I settled on three: ginger, cinnamon, and allspice. Ginger triumphed over cinnamon as the lead spice because it complemented rather than overshadowed the pumpkin flavor. Other spices were acceptable, but not essential. Nutmeg was okay. Cardamom and cloves I could take or leave. Booze-flavored fillings were turnoffs. Neither vanilla extract nor citrus zest was right.

Since I didn't want a gummy-bottomed crust, I started with a pre-baked pie shell. To avoid overcooking the already baked crust, I needed to warm the filling so that it would set quickly but remain silky smooth in the process. To accomplish that, I turned to a technique I had learned from Stephen Schmidt, author of *Master Recipes* (Clear Light Publishers, 1998). I briefly heated the pumpkin, salt, and spices on the stovetop, then added the condensed milk and heated it through. With the eggs in the blender and the motor running, I slowly added the hot pumpkin and pureed it. I immediately poured the warm filling into the pre-baked pie shell and baked it at 300 degrees until set.

The pie was perfect. The flavoring, sweetener, and dairy all worked together, with no fancy ingredients or flavorings needed.

Silky Pumpkin Pie

Serve this pie with lightly sweetened whipped cream made by beating or whisking 1 cup of chilled heavy cream with 2 tablespoons of sugar and ¹/₂ teaspoon vanilla extract to soft, billowy peaks. If you accidentally whip the cream too stiff, stir in a little more cream until you reach the desired consistency.

The butter and shortening should be thoroughly frozen, but the cream cheese need not be.

PIE DOUGH

- 1 cup plus 2 tablespoons bleached all-purpose flour
- ¹/₂ teaspoon salt
- 1 tablespoon sugar
- 4 tablespoons (¹/₂ stick) unsalted butter, cut into ¹/₂-inch pieces and frozen
- 4 tablespoons (2 ounces) chilled cream cheese, cut into ¹/₂-inch pieces
- 2 tablespoons vegetable shortening, cut into ¹/₂-inch pieces and frozen

PUMPKIN PIE FILLING

- 1 can (15 ounces) 100% pure pumpkin
- ¹/₂ teaspoon salt
- 1 teaspoon ground ginger
- ¹/₂ teaspoon cinnamon
- ¹/₄ teaspoon allspice
- 1 can (14 ounces) sweetened condensed milk
- 1 cup evaporated milk
- 2 large eggs, plus 2 large yolks

1 FOR PIE DOUGH: Have ready 3 tablespoons ice water. Mix flour, salt, and sugar in a food processor. Add butter; break up butter pieces with your fingers and coat with flour mixture. Pulse 4 times, 1 long second each time (say "1 chimpanzee, 2 chimpanzees" to time each pulse). Add cream cheese and shortening to flour mixture; toss to coat. Pulse another 4 or 5 times, 1 long second each time, until the fats are pea- and fine-gravel size. Dump mixture into a medium bowl. Add ice water and stir into mixture with a rubber spatula until dough clumps form. Press clumps together with palm of hand to form a cohesive ball. Press down on ball to gather remaining scraps, dipping

fingertips in water and adding droplets of water to bottom of bowl if scraps refuse to adhere.

2   Wrap ball in plastic, then press down to form a thick disk. Refrigerate for at least 1 hour. (Dough can be refrigerated for up to 2 days.)

3   Set dough on a lightly floured work surface and roll out into an approximately 14-inch circle. Fold dough in half and set 9-inch pie plate right next to folded dough. Quickly lift dough into pie plate and unfold. Lift edge of dough with one hand and press dough into pan with other hand so that dough is not stretched in any way. Trim dough all around to $\frac{1}{2}$ inch beyond pan lip. Roll overhanging dough under with fingertips so that it is flush with pan lip. Flute edge all around. Set pie shell in freezer for at least 1 hour. (Recipe can be doubled, and one half of dough wrapped in plastic and frozen for up to 1 month.)

4   Adjust oven rack to lowest position and heat oven to 400 degrees. Line pie shell with a sheet of heavy-duty foil and fill with weights. (I use a couple of cups of screws, nuts, and bolts, but dry beans and rice are fine, too.) Bake until fluting has lost its raw appearance and has started to turn golden, about 20 minutes. Remove foil, along with weights, and return pie to the oven until bottom of pie shell loses its raw appearance and starts to turn golden brown, about 5 minutes longer. Remove from oven; reduce oven temperature to 300 degrees.

5   FOR FILLING: While pie shell bakes, heat pumpkin, salt, ginger, cinnamon, and allspice in a medium saucepan, stirring, to blend flavors, about 5 minutes. Add condensed and evaporated milks; cook until heated through. Puree eggs and yolks in a blender. With blender running, add a spoonful of the pumpkin filling at first, then add the rest quickly as eggs heat up; puree to form a silky-textured filling.

6   Pour warm filling into warm pie shell. Bake until a thin-bladed knife inserted near center of filling comes out clean, 40 to 45 minutes. Let cool on a wire rack until warm, room temperature, or cold. Serve.

Pecan pie was the highlight of the table during the holiday celebrations of my childhood, and it's still my favorite pie. It's also one of the most difficult to get right.

The pecan pies of my childhood were simple. My aunts and mother followed the formula and instructions in the cookbook produced by the Home Economics Department at Auburn University. They rolled and fitted the dough into the pie plate and lined it with pecans. They heated the sugar and corn syrup, slowly beat them into the eggs, then added butter and vanilla. Once the mixture was cool, they poured it into the pie shell and baked it until it was set. Under its blanket of filling, the crust was undercooked; the filling often puffed in the oven, then cracked around the edge or curdled slightly, and the pecans often ended up as chewy as saltwater taffy. That was just how pecan pie was, we thought.

As an adult, however, I decided to try to improve on the pecan pie of my youth. Didn't my predecessors know that a soggy bottom crust would crisp up if it was pre-baked? Didn't they understand that cracking and curdling were the result of over-cooked eggs?

I was quickly humbled. It wasn't as easy as I thought to make a foolproof pie shell. During baking, my butter-rich pie shells often developed tiny cracks, pinholes, and bubbles, and the lava-like filling seeped through these openings, baking rock-hard onto the pie plate. Better, I thought, to eat pecan pie with a half-baked bottom crust than one whose crust couldn't be pried from the pan. Starting with an uncooked pie shell has its problems, too. Besides the problem of the soft, gummy pastry, a filled raw pie shell needs long, high heat for the crust to brown, by which time the filling is generally overcooked and curdled.

With these difficulties in mind, I set out to make a pecan pie that tasted of praline and caramel. More important, I wanted a filling that was soft, yet sturdy enough to cut, a crust that was rich and flavorful.

Knowing that I'd eventually have to solve the crust questions, I decided to hold off and start with the filling. I began working with the typical pecan pie formula, mixing together:

 1 cup sugar
 1 cup corn syrup
 3 eggs
 $^1/_4$ teaspoon salt
 2 teaspoons vanilla extract
 4 tablespoons melted butter
 1 cup chopped pecans

The pie may be called pecan, but it takes just one bite to understand that sweetener is the key ingredient. Most pecan pie formulas call for at least two kinds: one usually dry, the other liquid. Using light corn syrup as the constant, I tested fillings with granulated sugar, and one each with light brown and dark brown sugar.

Baked in a 300-degree oven until set, all three fillings curdled, but the filling made with dark brown sugar and corn syrup was the most stable and least weepy of the three. I also preferred its rich caramel flavor to the milder light brown sugar. By comparison, the granulated sugar filling bordered on bland.

In round two, I focused on liquid sweeteners, testing both dark brown sugar and granulated sugar, each in combination with the following:

Dark corn syrup
Equal parts light and dark corn syrup
Maple syrup
Lyle's Golden Syrup (a mild molasses-flavored syrup preferred by some pecan pie cooks)
Equal parts light and dark corn syrup and maple syrup
Light corn syrup flavored with honey

After baking and tasting all twelve fillings, I decided that although some were interesting, none appealed as much as the original simple dark brown sugar and light corn syrup combination.

Up to this point, I had been using 1 cup of each sweetener. The sweetening in other recipes ranged from $1^1/_2$ cups to $2^1/_3$ cups, with the ratios of each varying dramatically. I made a sampling of eight different pies to determine the proper ratio of the brown sugar and the corn syrup as well as the right quantity. In general, I found that the sweeter the filling, the softer the texture. Corn syrup provided a firm, jelly-like texture and sheen, but if it was allowed to dominate, the filling was bland.

Brown sugar offered great flavor, but if it was too prominent, the filling was soft and lusterless. Using a moderate amount of total sweetener and giving brown sugar (1 cup) a slight edge over corn syrup (³/₄ cup) resulted in the soft, praline-flavored, yet sliceable filling I was looking for.

EGGS AND SHELLS

With my new formula, I made fillings with six different egg quantities, ranging from 4 whole eggs to combinations of whole eggs and yolks. Three eggs and 2 yolks made a soft, yet supple pie.

Since I knew my crust would be baked, my filling could be — should be — hot. Added to the pie shells cold, the fillings took nearly an hour to set in a moderate oven — too long for crusts that would already be fully baked.

STUCK ON STARCH

A number of cookbook authors added starch — flour, cornstarch, or arrowroot — to their pies, presumably to keep the eggs from curdling. I hoped the starch might serve a second purpose as well. If thickened before baking, the filling might be less prone to seep through any cracks or holes in the crust. But if starch worked, which one, and where should it be added?

I tried a couple of different methods of incorporating the starch into my hot filling. In my first effort, I brought all the ingredients of the filling to a boil before pouring it into the crust. The baked filling had a deep center crater, as though something had hit it and exploded.

I also tried heating cornstarch and water and adding the sweeteners to the paste. When this mixture was hot, I stirred it into the eggs and baked it. The starch made the filling soft and pasty and muted the flavors.

Heating cornstarch with the sweeteners was the most promising of the methods. Although the filling curdled slightly around the edges, the texture was soft, yet firm, and the flavor was unaffected. Adding the cornstarch to the sweetener later in the game might work even better. So as not to overcook the corn syrup and brown sugar, I heated them in a metal bowl set over a pan of simmering water. Once the sweeteners were warm and the brown sugar had more or less dissolved, I whisked the mixture into the eggs and returned it to the bowl. I added the butter, then the cornstarch mixture, and warmed it. Prepared this way, the cornstarch prevented the eggs from curdling and helped cut the filling's intense sweetness.

Adding cream cheese to the butter and shortening makes the pastry more elastic and much easier to roll — no tears, no holes. It's friendly and forgiving — just what my pecan filling needed.

Sensational Pecan Pie

Makes one 9-inch pie

Use a serrated knife to cut the pie. It makes slicing through the crisp nuts and the soft filling much easier.

Pie Dough (page 304)

FILLING

- 1 **heaping cup chopped pecans**
- 1 **tablespoon cornstarch**
- 1 **cup dark brown sugar**
- 3/4 **cup light corn syrup**
- 3 **large eggs, plus 2 large yolks**
- 2 **teaspoons vanilla extract**
- 1/4 **teaspoon salt**
- 4 **tablespoons (1/2 stick) unsalted butter, melted**

1 **FOR PIE DOUGH:** Proceed as directed in steps 1–4 of Silky Pumpkin Pie (page 304), making sure that chunks of fat in step 1 are no larger than pea-size. Reduce oven temperature to 300 degrees once pie shell has baked.

2 **FOR FILLING:** Toast pecans in a pie plate in oven until fragrant, about 10 minutes. Pour nuts into pie shell and reduce oven temperature to 250 degrees.

3 Meanwhile, heat cornstarch and 1/3 cup water in a small saucepan over low heat, stirring frequently until thick; set aside. Heat brown sugar and corn syrup in a medium heatproof bowl over a pan of barely simmering water until warm and sugar has almost dissolved. Whisk eggs, yolks, vanilla, and salt in a medium bowl. Slowly whisk warm sugar mixture into eggs. Return mixture to heatproof bowl; whisk in butter, then whisk in warm cornstarch mixture. Heat, stirring frequently, until warm.

4 Adjust oven rack to middle position and set pie shell on oven rack. Pour warm filling into shell. Bake until pie just sets, 40 to 45 minutes. Cool to room temperature and serve.

A Chocolate Cake That's Got It All

Just as there are dog people and cat people, there are pie bakers and cake bakers. I'm in the pie camp.

Although I've made my share of cakes, I don't like doing it. They're testy. Then there's the frosting. I cringe every time I look at the ingredients list for a standard buttercream. Many recipes call for up to 3 sticks of butter for frosting one cake.

No wonder cake mixes are so popular. They're absolutely convenient and practically indestructible. Dump the dry ingredients in a bowl, stir in eggs and oil, pour everything in a pan, and bake. If your oven temperature is off or you bake the cake in a slightly different pan or on the wrong rack, it still comes out okay. These cakes are always moist, tender, and fine-crumbed, not always the case with the average homemade chocolate cake. And compared with the fat-laden classic buttercream, the average canned frosting has only about 1 1/2 teaspoons of fat per serving — and it's soft and creamy to boot.

But before putting cake mixes and canned frostings on a pedestal, I made six boxed chocolate cakes — two styles each from Betty Crocker, Pillsbury, and Duncan Hines — and tasted six frostings from the same companies. After sampling all the cakes and frostings, I report they aren't perfect. I detected an unmistakably soapy aroma and flavor in the cakes, probably the result of all the leavener. Both the frostings and the cakes tasted like a chocolate-like experience rather than an encounter with the real thing.

The chocolate cake I wanted would have all the ease and convenience of the boxed variety, plus the rich, intensely pure chocolate flavor of one made from scratch. The frosting would be soft, supple, and as low in fat as the canned stuff but with real, intense chocolate flavor.

Despite their varied recipe titles, all chocolate cakes are similar. After analyzing more than eighty recipes, I came up with the following one as a starting point:

2 cups bleached all-purpose flour

>   (But, I wondered, would unbleached all-purpose flour, cake flour, or some other combination work better?)

2 cups sugar

>   (But many chocolate cakes called for part or all light or dark brown sugar — even molasses.)

1 teaspoon baking soda

>   (Would I need more or less than this, or would baking powder do the trick?)

$^1/_2$ teaspoon salt

>   (No worries here. Salt always worked itself out over the course of testing.)

$^1/_2$ cup cocoa

>   (Would melted unsweetened or semisweet, alone or in combination with the cocoa, make the cake more intensely chocolate?)

1 cup boiling water

>   (How about milk, or buttermilk, or coffee? If so, should they be heated? What about part sour cream or yogurt?)

8 tablespoons fat

>   (Oil, butter, or a combination of the two? If butter was better, should it be melted?)

2 eggs

>   (More, or fewer? Should they be separated, and the whites whipped and folded in?)

1 teaspoon vanilla extract

>   (Like salt, it always worked itself out.)

Since my goal was to keep the cake simple, I wanted to avoid sifting and creaming, two steps that often kept me from making a homemade cake. So I started with the standard boxed-cake mixing method: whisking together the dry ingredients, then the wet, then beating them altogether. Cocoa was the one exception. Although it's a dry ingredient, I already knew that its flavor was heightened by being heated with liquid, so I mixed boiling water and cocoa to form a paste, to which I added the remaining liquid ingredients.

I started by baking chocolate cakes with different flours. I made cakes with unbleached and bleached all-purpose flour and cake flour, and another with equal parts bleached all-purpose flour and cake flour. Checking the boxed-cake-mix ingredients list, I noticed cornstarch in the formula. Intrigued, I made a final specimen with cake flour, substituting cornstarch for part of the flour. Just by touch, I recognized the flour in each cake. The unbleached all-purpose produced a firm, dense, muffin-like cake with virtually no spring. The cakes made with bleached all-purpose and the all-purpose flour–cake flour combination failed to impress. The chocolate flavor was clearer, but so was the unmistakable taste of baking soda. The cake flour produced a springy, tender cake. The process by which cake flour is chlorinated leaves it acidic, and that acid, in combination with the cocoa, neutralized the baking soda, leaving no unused leavener to ruin the cake's flavor.

But the cake flour–cornstarch combination was even better, the tenderest of the lot. I detected a slight starchy flavor, but by reducing the amount of cornstarch, I solved that problem. As the cakes sat, I observed that the one with cornstarch didn't dry out as quickly. The cornstarch seemed to be acting as a preservative — no wonder cake companies include it in their mixes.

As for sugar, many chocolate cake recipes call for at least some brown sugar, so I was surprised to find that granulated sugar produced the moistest, tenderest cake with the clearest chocolate flavor. The five other cakes I made with various sugars and sugar combinations — light brown, dark brown, a combination of each with granulated, as well as a mix of granulated with molasses — were generally drier.

THE MIX-UP

To determine both the kind of fat and the mixing method, I made cakes with creamed butter and with creamed shortening. I also made cakes with oil, melted butter, a combination of oil and melted butter, and mayonnaise, and I mixed them all by beating the wet ingredients into the dry ones. Six tests later, I was pleased. My chocolate cake was still simple. For richness and flavor, I had chosen melted butter over all the others. And because it was both simpler and superior, I picked the method of mixing the wet ingredients into the dry instead of creaming the butter with the sugar.

This simpler method was superior to creaming only when the ingredients were added in a particular order. When I stirred the melted butter into the cocoa-water mixture, then beat the wet into the dry ingredients, the cake was coarsely textured and slightly tough. But when I beat the melted butter into the flour mixture first, before adding the cocoa-water mixture, the difference was dramatic. This cake's texture was perfect: irresistibly tender and beautifully fine-crumbed. By coating the flour mixture with butterfat, I had prevented gluten development.

Mixing the sugar with the dry ingredients rather than creaming it with the butter meant that I didn't have to sift. The gritty sugar prevented the other dry ingredients from clumping, resulting in a well-blended, smooth mix. And since the cocoa was mixed with hot water, I didn't have to sift it, either.

Working with my revised formula of cake flour with cornstarch, granulated sugar, and melted butter, I made cakes with 1, 2, 3, 4, and 6 eggs. Because several of the chocolate cake recipes called for separating the eggs, whipping the whites, and folding them into the batter, I tried that as well. And finally, I made a cake with 4 whipped egg whites and no yolks.

Although I could tell little difference between the cake made with separated eggs and the one with whole eggs, the egg-whites-only cake stood out from the crowd. Without tasting like an angel food or chiffon cake, it was light, clean, rich, moist, and chocolatey.

To confirm that using only egg whites was the way to go, I performed another round of tests, trying the cake with fewer whites and with whites beaten together with a little sugar. The 4 whipped egg whites — no sugar added — withstood the challengers this time as well.

The cake could stand to be more tender, though, so I made egg-white cakes with differing quantities of melted butter. Sure enough, increasing the butter from 8 to 14 tablespoons resulted in a richer cake with wonderfully pure chocolate flavor.

ORDINARY COCOA TAKES THE CAKE

Of course, the kind and quality of chocolate in the cake had to make a difference. My regular grocery store carried one brand of unsweetened cocoa: Hershey's. Other brands, such as Droste (a Dutch-process, or less acid, cocoa) and Nestlé's, required a special trip. I wondered if fortifying the cake with melted unsweetened and semisweet chocolate, as some recipes suggested, would make a difference.

So I made another six cakes: one with each of the three major brands of unsweetened cocoa, one made with all melted unsweetened chocolate, and another two made with part cocoa — one enhanced with melted semisweet chocolate and another with unsweetened.

Although the cake made with Droste cocoa displayed the most clear, pleasant chocolate flavor, the cake made with Hershey's cocoa was very acceptable. I wasn't impressed with the fruity, commercial flavor of Nestlé's cocoa. The cakes made or enhanced with unsweetened or semisweet melted chocolate weren't an improvement on just plain cocoa. The cakes made with unsweetened chocolate, in particular, were dry.

I moved on to liquid. I had been using water to this point. I made another six cakes, this time with hot coffee, with hot milk, and with cold buttermilk. I made the final three with part hot water supplemented with yogurt in one cake, buttermilk in another, and sour cream in the third. The cakes made with sour cream and coffee caught my attention. The sour cream added richness and subtle tang, while the coffee rounded out and enhanced the chocolate flavor.

Up to this point, I had been using 1 teaspoon of baking soda. To see if that measure was right, I made four cakes: one with all baking powder, two with differing quantities of each, and one with 1½ teaspoons baking soda — ½ teaspoon more than I had been using.

After tasting all the cakes, I hadn't come up with any leavener that worked better than the 1 teaspoon of baking soda I had been using all along. The cake was rich and dark. It tasted subtly of sour cream and clearly of chocolate without tasting sour. It rose nicely without any hint of excess baking soda.

To intensify the chocolate flavor, I upped the cocoa from ½ to ⅔ cup.

THE FROSTING: SERIOUS CHOCOLATE

I wanted a soft, supple frosting that would swirl and peak like the stuff pictured on the can — but one with real flavor. From experience, I knew most classic chocolate buttercreams were so butter-logged that the chocolate flavor was barely detectable. I wanted to find a way to give the frosting body without relying so heavily on butter, but I also wanted serious chocolate. And I wanted to keep the frosting simple.

With these goals in mind, I eliminated all the recipes that called for 2 or more sticks of butter, as well as those requiring me to make sugar syrup, heat eggs, or perform hand-mixing over a double boiler. I also skipped over glazes and ganaches, or any frosting or icing that had to be heated up, then cooled down. Analyzing the ingredients on the label of the canned frostings, I noticed cornstarch, as well as a high water content. Thinking that manufacturers might be using a thickened cornstarch-water mixture to stand in for the butter, I made a few inedible cornstarch-thickened frostings.

Moving on, I came across a recipe from Lorraine Bodger's *Great American Cakes* (Warner Books, 1988). Titled "Double Chocolate Frosting," it contained only 8 tablespoons of butter compared with the usual 16 to 24. It used both cocoa powder and semisweet chocolate. It seemed to get its body from 2 eggs. One taste and I knew this frosting had promise, but not until I had solved a few problems. First and foremost were the raw eggs. Could this frosting be made with egg substitutes, which are pasteurized and safe? Without all the butter to balance the sugar, the frosting was quite sweet. And without all the butter to protect the sugar, the frosting quickly lost its sheen and started to crust.

I started by testing the frosting with Egg Beaters. Though it had slightly less body than the frosting made with leftover yolks from the cake, the Egg Beaters frosting was perfectly fine — and, more important, totally safe.

To solve the sweetness problem, I substituted an equal quantity of unsweetened chocolate for the semisweet. That not only decreased the sweetness but also increased the chocolate flavor. Dissolving a little instant coffee into the eggs also cut the sweetness. To make the frosting more supple and to ensure a long-term sheen, I added a little corn syrup, and that worked, too.

By making two tall layers and splitting them in half, I was able to make a four-layer cake. Spreading frosting over four layers rather than two ensured that I got frosting with every bite.

I had developed a rich, tender, moist, chocolate cake with a frosting that would peak and swirl with the best. And although I did have to melt a little butter and whip a few egg whites, this cake and frosting were almost as simple and foolproof as a boxed mix.

A Chocolate Cake That's Got It All

Makes one 8-inch
cake, serving 12

Since the cake is firm on the bottom and soft on top, it's important to invert it onto a plate, then invert it back onto the wire rack to cool. Otherwise, the soft top may end up sticking to the rack and tearing as it is removed.

2 cups sugar

1³/₄ cups cake flour

2 tablespoons cornstarch

1 teaspoon baking soda

³/₄ teaspoon salt

²/₃ cup unsweetened cocoa, preferably Dutch-process, such as Droste, but Hershey's is fine, too

1 teaspoon instant coffee

¹/₂ cup sour cream

1 teaspoon vanilla extract

4 large egg whites, at room temperature (you may want to save yolks to use in the frosting)

14 tablespoons (1³/₄ sticks) unsalted butter, melted, but not hot

Soft and Creamy Double Chocolate Frosting (page 318)

1 Adjust oven rack to lower-middle position and heat oven to 350 degrees. Generously grease two 8-inch cake pans and dust with flour.

2 Whisk sugar, flour, cornstarch, baking soda, and salt in a large bowl; set aside.

3 Place cocoa and coffee in a medium bowl. Whisk in ³/₄ cup boiling water to form a smooth paste. Stir in sour cream and vanilla; set aside.

4 With a hand mixer in a medium bowl, beat egg whites to soft peaks. Without cleaning beaters, mix melted butter into dry ingredients until mixture is smooth. Immediately add cocoa mixture, and beat until batter is smooth, 2 to 3 minutes. Carefully fold egg whites into batter until just incorporated.

Divide batter evenly between pans and bake until a skewer inserted into center comes out with wet crumbs, 30 to 35 minutes. Remove from oven and let cakes sit in pans to cool slightly, about 5 minutes. Following illustrations, invert each cake onto a plate, then onto a cooling rack, and split each cake to make 4 layers. Frost and serve.

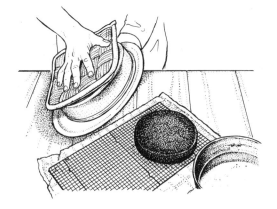

Invert each layer onto a plate.

Then invert each layer so that it sits top side up on a cooling rack.

Cut each layer around the perimeter with a serrated knife.

When the cake is almost completely split, saw across the middle of each layer to complete the cut.

Soft and Creamy Double Chocolate Frosting

Makes about 3 cups, or enough for 1 cake

If eating raw eggs is a risk you're willing to take, then feel free to use the yolks left over from the cake to make this frosting. Though frosting made with egg substitute is perfectly fine, the one made with egg yolks has more body and better texture.

¹/₂ cup egg substitute, such as Egg Beaters, or 4 egg yolks (left over from cake), with enough milk added to equal ¹/₂ cup, plus additional milk, if necessary
¹/₂ cup unsweetened cocoa
¹/₂ teaspoon instant coffee
1 teaspoon vanilla extract
¹/₄ teaspoon salt
8 tablespoons (1 stick) unsalted butter, at room temperature
4 ounces unsweetened chocolate, melted
3 cups confectioners' sugar (sifted if it contains hard lumps)
4 teaspoons light corn syrup

1 Mix egg substitute or yolks, cocoa, coffee, vanilla, and salt in a small bowl.

2 Beat butter in a medium bowl with an electric mixer until light and fluffy. Add melted chocolate and cocoa mixture; continue to beat until smooth. Add confectioners' sugar, 1 cup at a time, beating slowly at first, until sugar has been incorporated into mixture, then at medium speed until frosting is light and fluffy. Add corn syrup, and beat until frosting is smooth and glossy. If frosting is still stiff, add droplets of milk until it is spreadably soft. (Frosting can be refrigerated for up to 1 week and microwaved for a few seconds until just spreadable.)

Note: Page numbers in italics refer to illustrations.

Dressing
    Creamy Buttermilk, 212
    Creamy Vinaigrette, 207
    preparing, for Caesar Salad, 175–77
    preparing, for pasta salad, 198
    Soy-Sesame, 216
Drip Coffeemaker
    for brewing iced tea, 244
    Iced Tea Made in a, 248
Dumplings
    best fats for, 143
    best liquids for, 143
    best mixing method, 142–43
    Chicken and, with Aromatic Vegetables, 146–48
    Cornmeal, Chicken and, with Aromatic Vegetables, 148
    Herbed, Chicken and, with Aromatic Vegetables, 148
    shaping, *147*

E

Eggplant
    Broiled, 120
    and Pepper, Grilled, Pasta Salad with, 202
eggs
    in cake batter, 313
    in chocolate frosting, 314
    in cinnamon buns, 265
    in crab cakes, 104
    in Key lime pie, 296–98
    in meatballs, 53
    in oven-fried chicken, 30
    in pecan pie, 308
    in pumpkin pie, 302

F

Fajitas
    best beef for, 41–43

    best marinade for, 43–45
    with Charcoal-Grilled Skirt Steak and Peppers and Onions, 49–50
    cheat sheet for, 46
    Chicken, Charcoal-Grilled, 50
    Chicken, Pan-Seared, 48
    cooking vegetables for, 45
    with Pan-Seared Skirt Steak and Peppers and Onions, 47–48
Faraco, Jane and Jim, 223
Feta Cheese
    Greek-Style Pasta Salad, 203
    Mushroom Filling with Arugula and, 91
    Pasta Salad with Grilled Shrimp, Tomatoes, Olives, and, 205
fish. *See* Salmon; tuna
flour
    for biscuits, 254
    for chocolate cake, 311–12
    for chocolate chip cookies, 273–74
    for cinnamon buns, 264–65
    for dumplings, 143
    for peanut butter cookies, 280
    for waffles, 259
Fontina Cheese
    and Creamy Parmesan Sauce, Vegetable Lasagna with, 114–15
    taste-testing, 112
    for vegetable lasagna, 111
French Fries
    best frying method, 221
    best potatoes for, 220
    for the Home Cook, 222
    preparing potatoes for, 221
From Julia Child's Kitchen, 173
Frosting, Chocolate
    Double, Soft and Creamy, 318
    preparing, 314–15
fruit. *See also* fruit pies; *specific fruits*